ETIENNE PROVOST
Man of the Mountains

by

Jack B. Tykal

FIRST EDITION

To My Wife Helen

Who made this book possible

TABLE OF CONTENTS

Acknowledgements & Chronology v

Introduction by Dr. Fred Gowans xi

Preface xix

1 The Canadian Years, 1785-1814 1

2 The Early Fur Trade 9

3 St. Louis Beginning, 1815-1821 17

4 Return to Taos, 1822-1825 37

5 The American Fur Company, 1826-1829 67

6 The Trapper's Bride, 1829-1830 93

7 The Brigade Years I, 1831-1833 105

8 The Brigade Years II, 1834-1838 121

9 The Guide Years I, 1839-1840 155

10 The Guide Years II, 1841-1844 169

11 The Final Years, 1845-1850 187

Epilogue 199

Bibliography 203

Index 219

TABLE OF ILLUSTRATIONS

Front Cover - *Threatened Attack*   * Miller

xxvii Caravan en Route   Miller
     by permission from Boatman's Bankshares Inc.

xxviii Catching Up   Miller

16   *Joseph Philibert*
     by permission from Missouri Historical Society

57   *Indians Attacking Fur Boats*   Miller

92   *Trapping Beaver*   Miller

98   *John Wilson Knives*
     by permission from Museum of the Fur Trade
     Collections

129   *Green River, Oregon*   Miller

144   *Interior of Fort Laramie*   Miller

147   *Laramie Fort*   Miller

182   *d'Ortant*
     by permission from Felix Geffriaud

186   *Our Camp*   Miller

* Unless otherwise noted, all pictures are the work of
Alfred Jacob Miller and used by permission from
Walters Art Gallery, Baltimore

> *I had brought up with me from St. Louis only five men, who for my purposes were certainly worth ten. One of them was Etienne Provost, known as "L'homme des Montagnes"--the man of the mountains.*
>
> Joseph N. Nicollet
> in the report of his
> 1839 expedition.

ACKNOWLEDGEMENTS

No book of this nature is the work of one person. The efforts of many persons flow through the pen, or the keyboard, of the individual whose name appears on the cover of the book, and doubt it not that such a book cannot be written without the very real assistance of these most helpful individuals and organizations.

To begin with, the Missouri Historical Society deserves mention as the repository of probably the greatest aggregation of fur trade material relating to the American trade. The information contained in its archives was absolutely essential to any work I might produce, and the facilities were opened to me most willingly. The staff made every effort to assist me in finding material, and a particular note of thanks must go to Janice Fox for the special help she provided.

Still in St. Louis, Mrs. Coralee Paull deserves the highest accolade I can offer. As a professional researcher she was of inestimable help in running down bits and pieces of data for me in between those times I visited that city. Her participation in the research that went into this volume was invaluable.

On the west coast, The Huntington Library contains a wealth of information, and thanks are most gratefully given to Mrs. Virginia Rust who not only responded to my inquiry for information in a particular area, but also brought to my attention the hitherto unknown, to me, journal of young Lieutenant William Fairholme of the British Army.

There are others who could be mentioned, Fred Gowans who set the direction of this inquiry and Trudy McMurrin, who helped put this volume in its present state, and the myriad librarians, archivists and others in the many state historical societies, archive repositories and libraries I contacted or visited. My thanks to all.

And to my wife, to whom this book is dedicated. Her support in what amounted to a change in careers and circumstances enabled me to fulfill my hope to write of the fur trade, and return something to the sum of knowledge of it that I have for many years been enjoying in a passive sense as a reader of history.

CHRONOLGY
Etienne Provost, 1785-1850

1785	Etienne Provost born at Chambly, Quebec, Province of Lower Canada.
1809	Latest date by which Provost had left Chambly; almost certainly he left between 1800 and 1806.
1814-15	Enters fur trade in St. Louis. Missouri.
1814*	Joins Joseph Philibert's trading expedition to the southwest.

1814* Arrested by the Spanish and held for fifty-one days.

1815 Joins Auguste Chouteau and Julius de Mun company for trading in the south west.

1817 Arrested by the Spanish and held forty-eight days before being released.

1822 Columbia Fur Company formed with Kenneth McKenzie at its head to trade on upper Missouri and Mississippi rivers. William H. Ashley forms company to trap/trade in the mountains.

1822* Provost enters New Mexico trade following Mexican independence.

1823 Ashley party defeated by Arikara Indians; as a result he initiates overland route to the mountains.

1824 With partner (Francois) Leclerc, Provost leads company of trappers into today's Utah. Provost probably the first American to see the Great Salt Lake.
Attacked by Indians near present Provo, Utah, losing eight men.
Ashley leaves St. Louis with caravan for first mountain rendezvous.

1825 Meets Peter Skene Ogden on Weber River. Meets Ashley in eastern Utah and guides party to site of first mountain rendezvous.

1826 Returns to St. Louis in September.

1827 B. Pratte & Co. becomes Western Division of John Jacob Astor's American Fur Company (AFC).
Columbia Fur Company merges with American Fur Co. to become Upper Missouri Outfit (UMO) of the Western Division, with McKenzie remaining in charge.

1827*   Serves as an employee of the Chouteau
            interests for six months in spring and
            summer. Remains in St. Louis for re-
            mainder of the the year, probably
            engaged in tavern business.

1828   Becomes employee of American Fur
            Company and McKenzie sends him to
            encourage Crow Indians and independent
            trappers to trade at UMO posts on the
            Missouri.
            Attends rendezvous of 1828 and is in-
            volved in fight with the Blackfoot Indians.

1829   Marries in St. Louis.
            Forms partnership with AFC and returns
            to Upper Missouri.

1830   Partnership with AFC ends after minimal
            success.
            Ends active trapping role in the moun-
            tains.

1831   Leads supply caravan from Fort Te-
            cumseh to meet AFC brigade in moun-
            tains under William Vanderburgh.

1832   Serves as second in command under
            Lucien Fontenelle to supply AFC bri-
            gades, but misses rendezvous and meets
            Andrew Drips and Vanderburgh on
            Green River.

1833   Again with Fontenelle on supply caravan
            to Green River rendezvous.

1834   Leads first entirely overland AFC supply
            train to rendezvous on Ham's Fork
            (Granger, Wyoming).

1837   Third in command of supply caravan to
            rendezvous on Green River.
            Artist Alfred Jacob Miller paints only
            first- hand scenes of a rendezvous, in-
            cluding two in which Provost is identified.

1838	Sent to the upper Missouri to assess damage of 1837 smallpox epidemic that decimated the Indians.
1839	Serves as camp conductor for Joseph N. Nicollet mapping expedition, with John C. Fremont as Nicollet's second-in-command.
1840	Guides a party of British military officers on a buffalo hunt on plains of western Kansas.
1841	First emigrant train crosses the prairies to Oregon.
1843	Serves as guide for expedition of John James Audubon to Upper Missouri.
1844	Serves as guide for pleasure expedition of Armand Fouche, Comte d'Otrante, to Upper Missouri.
1846	Oregon question settled in favor of U.S. possession of present states of Oregon, Washington, and Idaho.
1849	Makes his last trip up the Missouri River.
1850	Dies in St. Louis on July 3 in his sixty-fifth year.

* Indicates activities which, based on the evidence, in the author's opinion took place, but which cannot be documented.

ABBREVIATIONS

A number of abbreviations have been utilized in the endnotes in order to facilitate reading and those are set forth below. These references are fully documented in the Bibliography.

Anderson Journals   Anderson: *The Rocky Mountain Journals of William Marshall Anderson.*

Ashley Diary   Ashley: "Diary of William H. Ashley."

Audubon Journal   Audubon: *Audubon and His Journals.*

Campbell Narrative   Fayel: "A Narrative of Col. Robert Campbell's Experiences in the Rocky Mountains Fur Trade from 1825 to 1835."

Fairholme Journal   Fairholme: "The Journal of Lieutenant William Fairholme, 1840."

Fremont Expeditions   Fremont: *The Expeditions of John Charles Fremont.*

Harris Journal   Harris: *Up the Missouri with Audubon: The Journal of Edward Harris.*

MANM   Mexican Archives of New Mexico

MHS   Missouri Historical Society

Nicollet   Nicollet: *Joseph N. Nicollet on the Plains and Prairies.*

NMHR   *New Mexico Historical Review*

SANM   Spanish Archives of New Mexico

Townsend's Narrative   Townsend: *Narrative of a Journey Across the Rocky Mountains to the Columbia River.*

INTRODUCTION
by Dr. Fred Gowans

The history of the Trans-Missippian Fur Trade has drawn the attention of numerous authors during the last century and undoubtedly will continue to be a topic of interest and research. The thrust made into the remote mountain streams of the western American landscape by French, Spanish, British and American trappers and traders in search of beaver has provided the historian with a variety of documents from which he might investigate this colorful era of the American West.

With the acquisition of the Louisiana Purchase from

France in 1803 and the return of Lewis and Clark from the headwaters of the Missouri River in 1806, the stage was set for the small river community of St. Louis to become a commercial giant in the American Fur Trade Industry and rival the Spanish and later Mexican communities of Santa Fe and Taos.

It should, however, be remembered that since the time of the City's founding in 1764, international rivalry had given rise to economic activity by both the French and Spanish within the St. Louis business community. Excellent narrative is to be found by Annie H. Abel, Aubrey Diller, A. P. Nassatir and Carl I. Wheat, representing research from various collections of French and Spanish documents. Their scholarly publications disclose the aggresive activities by both Spain and France to control the Indian Trade and Fur Industry of both the Mississippi and Missouri river countries during the period of 1764-1803.

During this same time period, the close of the 18th century, the Nootka Sound Controversy and Treaty put into motion the British Northwest Fur and Hudson's Bay companies' penetration of the Pacific Northwest. The journals of Alexander McKenzie, Alexander Henry and David Thompson express the high priority set by the British Government and private companies on the fur industry surrounding the upper Missouri River and the territory west of the "Great Divide."

In 1807 the citizens of St. Louis witnessed the departure of three major expeditions enroute to the upper Missouri, most important being the Manual Lisa Expedition which would establish Fort Raymond at the mouth of the Bighorn River and open trade relations with the Crow Indians. The city observed the succesful return of Lisa in 1808 and the formation of the St. Louis Missouri Fur Company during the winter of 1808-09. The community watched the Company's departure in the spring of 1809 for the Three Forks of the Missouri to rival the Blackfoot Indians for control of the fur trade on the River. However, in 1810, the arrival of John Colter in St. Louis with stories of death near the Three Forks at the hands of the Blackfoot forecasted the failure of the Americans to lure away from the British their Indian allies.

Authors such as Richard Oglesby, Donald Jackson, M.O. Skarsten, Burton Harris, Henry Brackenridge, John Bradbury, Hiram M. Chittenden, John C. Luttig and J. K. Rollinson, not only left for us the history of this period, but also an insight into the lives of such notables as Manuel Lisa, George Drouillard, John Colter, Pierre Chouteau, Reuben Lewis, John Weiser, Andrew Henry and Pierre Menard.

The overland Astorians commanded by Wilson Price Hunt were the topic of conversation around St. Louis in the spring of 1811 as the Expedition was departing for the mouth of the Columbia River to establish fur operations for John Jacob Astor and his newly-formed Pacific Fur Company. Through diaries, letters and notes of the Expedition members, the history of this epic journey has been preserved in the narrative of Washington Irving's *Astoria*.

Rumors spread quickly throughout the river community concerning the return of Andrew Henry in 1811 with news of failure on the upper Missouri and the removal of the St. Louis Missouri Fur Company from that region. Robert Stuart's return from Fort Astoria with optimistic reports of early success by the Pacific Fur Company was but a dream that was quickly destroyed by the British in the War of 1812. The business community of St. Louis was quickly realizing that the fur trade profits in the upper Missouri River country were indeed very elusive. So much so, in fact, that attempts were being transacted by various individuals, including Manuel Lisa, to make contact with Government officials of Santa Fe and Taos to open trade between the Spanish southwest and St. Louis. The Champlain-Williams Expedition of 1811-12 and the Chouteau-deMunn Expedition of 1815-17 represent but two of these early attempts. Unfortunately, both parties met with opposition from the Spanish authorities.

Due to the War of 1812, American fur trade activity on the upper Missouri dwindled under the British pressure. The majority of the fur trade activity between 1812-19, originating at St. Louis, was enroute to the lower Missouri tribes and Plains tribes west and southwest of St. Louis. However, in 1819, the United States Government's renewed desire to support the fur industry on the river and to assist private companies, such as the American Fur and the St. Louis Missouri Fur companies, to open a new era of trade relations with the Missouri tribes, launched the Yellowstone Expedition from St. Louis in the spring of 1819. The Expedition was to establish a military district on the upper Missouri and to oversee the agreements of the Treaty of Ghent of 1814, designating international boundaries. It was also to encourage the Indians of that region to establish peaceful relations with the United States Government, and if necessary to use force to maintain control. Even though the Expedition failed to reach its destination because of faulty steamships, the support generated by the Government towards private companies not only assisted in reopening the fur trade on the upper Missouri, but helped establish the American Fur Company as the dominant company on the River as the decade of the 1820's began.

Several important events took place in the 1820's that would have an impact on St. Louis and on the American fur trade industry. The British, realizing the economic and political significance of the Pacific Northwest, forced a merger of the Northwest Fur and Hudson's Bay companies in 1821 hoping to use the broad operational base of the H.B.C. to stop the advancement of the Americans into the northwest. Soon after the merger, Hudson's Bay official George Simpson issued orders to have the company's brigades "over trap" and make a "fur desert" out of the Snake River country, hoping to impede the Yankee trappers who represented the first real wave of American migration.

In Mexico and the Spanish southwest the revolution culminated in 1821 with the formation of the Republic of Mexico. Immediately, diplomatic representatives of the newly formed Mexican Government were suggesting closer economic ties with the United States. This international event triggered the beginning of the commerce that would develop between St. Louis and Santa Fe. The fur industry was but one of many commercial businesses represented in St. Louis that quickly took advantage of this opportunity and a very profitable trade developed over the Santa Fe Trail between the two commercial centers. Santa Fe and Taos became the hub of American fur trade activities in the southwest. American trappers and traders penetrated into the Gila River country of New Mexico and Arizona and north into the Colorado and Green rivers drainage systems of present day Colorado, Wyoming and Utah. Writers such as Robert G. Cleland, LeRoy R. Hafen, David J. Weber, David J. Wishart, Reuben G. Thwaites, E. L. Sabin, A. H. Favour, and Thomas James have written excellent histories of the beaver trade in the American southwest and introduced thousands of readers to the fur men of the southern Rockies such as Hugh Glenn, Jacob Fowler, William Becknell, Antoine Robidoux, Ceran St. Vrain, James O. Pattie, Ewing Young, Miguel Robidoux, Bill Williams and Kit Carson.

During this same period the United States Government's policies were changing in regards to the Indian trade. The practice of government control of Indian commerce was now designed to encourage the private sector to develop trade with the Indian nations through licensed companies. These decisions were timely in light of the international changes taking place on the American frontier.

It was into this setting that William H. Ashley, Lt. Governor of Missouri, along with Andrew Henry entered the fur trade. In the spring of 1822 and again in 1823 the Ashley-Henry Company left St. Louis with hopes of being competitive on the upper Missouri against the American Fur and St. Louis Missouri Fur companies, but due to unfortunate circumstances on the River the Company found itself at the brink of financial ruin in the late summer of 1823. At this point of frustration and economic disaster, the "Ashley Men," in early 1824, under the direction of Jedediah Smith and orders from Ashley and Henry, pushed across South Pass into the Green River country of present-day western Wyoming. The failure of the two preceding years was soon forgotten as the Americans found a bonanza of beaver west of the continental divide in present-day Utah, Idaho, Wyoming and Montana. Because of the abundance of beaver and the unique geographic conditions, the trading post of the upper Missouri river trade was replaced out of necessity by the annual rendezvous. The river system that had supported this earlier fur trade gave way to the supply caravan consisting of horses and mules laden with supplies from St. Louis.

The most significant change, however, was the emergence of the Mountain Man. This survivor spent 365 days a year in the mountains either preparing for the spring and fall hunt, trying the survive the elements at Winter Quarters or letting out all his frustrations at the Rendezvous. The success or failure of the companies depended upon him and his ability to excel in his profession trapping beaver. During the next fifteen years, the rendezvous system enabled this unique individual to explore and map every valley, stream and mountain pass in the north and central Rockies.

It was believed by many that a fortune was to be made in the Rocky Mountain beaver trade. Aggressive competition between fur companies in St. Louis soon developed. Nevertheless, the competition on the international level was even greater. There was bitter rivalry between the Americans and Mexican companies working out of Santa Fe and Taos. Yet there existed even more turbulent feeling between the Americans and the Hudson's Bay Company. This dislike for "foreign" competition in the Rocky Mountains on the part of the St, Louis companies continued through the entire fur trade era.

By 1834 the Rocky Mountain fur trade industry was dominated by the powerful American Fur Company which had entered the competition from both its trading posts on the upper Missouri and St. Louis and had forced other St. Louis-based companies to sell out under the pressure of cut-throat competition. The American Fur Company would dominate the rendezvous trade until its close in 1840. A number of commercial and political events and changing fashions in the European and American markets sealed the fate of the beaver fur industry. During the next thirty years, St. Louis' economy changed from a fur trade center to the gateway for the great western overland migration.

This unique period of time which spanned the beaver trade in the American Rockies is represented with an excellent collection of literature. A few represent the standard sought after by so many but achieved by so few. These include: Dale L. Morgan's *The West of William H. Ashley,* and *Jedediah Smith and the Opening of the West*; Charles L. Camp's *James Clyman*; David Lavender's *The Fist in the Wilderness*; Aubrey L. Haines' *Journal of a Trapper*; LeRoy R. Hafen's *Broken Hand*; David J. Weber's *Taos Trapper*; Elliot Coues'

Forty Years a Fur Trader on the Upper Missouri and Edwin E. Rich's *Hudson's Bay Company 1670-1870.*

It was into this panorama of events that Etienne Provost emerged. From his arrival in St. Louis as a young man until his death on July 3, 1850, he played a vital role in the fur trade economics of the city and certainly represented one of the community's most prestigious citizens during the first half of the nineteenth century. The events of his life represent a looking glass into the total history of the Rocky Mountain fur trade. It would have been very difficult to find a person closely associated with the beaver trade in the American west who did not only know Etienne, but considered him one of the outstanding individuals of that era. From Santa Fe and Taos to the remote valleys of the Rocky Mountains and the executive offices of the giant fur companies in St. Louis, his name was known and recognized as one who knew and understood every facet of the business. Whether it be trading with Ute Indians in the Great Basin, escaping the treachery of an ambush planned by Shoshone on a remote River which bore his name on early maps, attending the first rendezvous with William Ashley in 1825, guiding a fur trade caravan to or from the annual rendezvous, carrying messages, or accompanying new recruits for the American Fur Company up the River to a remote trading post, his services were recognized as invaluable. In his advanced years and after the close of the beaver trade, his reputation as one who knew the geography of the west and had the ability to survive in its environment, brought him many offers to lead scientific and exploratory expeditions into remote areas of the frontier.

Etienne Provost: Man of the Mountains, reveals the life and adventures of this giant among fur trade personalities and is a welcome addition to the understanding of this remarkable era of the American West.

PREFACE

Etienne Provost is a shadow, something of a will-o'-the-wisp in American history. Ask, and almost anyone familiar with the history of the American West will acknowledge hearing the name, but who was he—what did he do? "Oh, yes—isn't he the one Provo, Utah, is named after?" Yet in the early years of the nineteenth century Provost was recognized by all in the American fur trade as a power to be reckoned with.

The career of Etienne Provost as a fur trapper and trader spanned the golden age of the American fur trade. He was born in Canada in the waning years of the eighteenth century, entered the American fur trade in 1814 or 1815 when he was thirty years old, and remained in it until his death in 1850.

The period from 1806 to 1840 is the significant era of the American fur trade, beginning with the return of Lewis and Clark from their epic exploration and ending with the overlapping development of the silk hat to replace the beaver and the depletion of the beaver itself as a resource. However, neither its relatively brief length nor even its economic importance affected its heroic aura, for:

the spiritual residue of great events is just as important in history as the events themselves. Accurate descriptions of what actually occurred cannot exhaust the meaning of an epic. The tendency to portray the fur trade as a romantic pageant has produced a glorious literature that men will treasure for as long as heroism has a place in human esteem.[1]

Certainly the romance of that era is carried into our literature and activities today, as may be witnessed by novels such as Vardis Fisher's *The Mountain Man* and *The Big Sky* by A. B. Guthrie, both of which were adapted into successful movies, and the proliferation of mountain man organizations whose members dress in leather or period clothing and carry authentic-looking weapons and artifacts of the period. (The only seeming lack of authenticity is the almost uniform wearing of beards by these would-be trappers; the mountaineer of the fur trade was usually clean shaven.)

It has been difficult to develop a sense of Etienne Provost the man to replace the shadowy figure weaving in and out of the history of the American fur trade. He never learned to read or write, so we have nothing of his own to judge him by; his thoughts, opinions, likes or dislikes are all lost to us. Even the location of his grave remains elusive. His date of death is known, and the report of his death informs us he was buried in the St. Louis cathedral burial ground; however, no record has been located that tells where, or even if, he was moved when the New Catholic Cemetery where he was buried was closed and a few of those interred there were moved to Calvary Cemetery following its opening in 1853. Those graves in the New Catholic Cemetery not moved to Calvary were left, and over the years they have been covered by roadways and industrial buildings.

Though his final resting place is lost, Provost's appearance in life is known. There are no photographs of him, but the Baltimore artist Alfred Jacob Miller included and identified him in two of his paintings of the 1837 Rendezvous. In Miller's painting *Catching Up*, Provost is portrayed in profile as a portly figure calling for the horse guards to bring in the herd. Miller described him as, "Mo'sieur P. adipose & rotonde—'larding the lean earth as he walks along," comparing him to Shakespeare's Falstaff.[2]   In another work, *Threatened Attack*, Provost is depicted seated on his mule to the left of William Drummond Stewart as the caravan awaits a group of onrushing Indians. Again, Miller could not resist the opportunity to mention Provost's size. While praising Provost's ability as a leader and his plans for the defense of the column, Miller wrote, "Monsieur Proveau, subleader, with a corpus round as a porpoise."[3] In light of these two identified portraits, it is easy to surmise that Provost is the heavy-set figure mounted on the mule in the foreground of yet another Miller work, *Caravan en Route*. In the other pictures Provost is mounted on a mule or has one picketed by his tent and is shown wearing a distinctive hat. A similar hat is worn by the mountaineer mounted on a mule in the third picture.

Other verbal descriptions of Provost substantiate Miller's references to the well-fed mountaineer. Another writer who knew Provost and who was along as second-in-command of the 1837 caravan to the rendezvous was Sir William Drummond Stewart, a Scots nobleman, military hero, and gentleman adventurer. Beginning in 1833, he had made several excursions to the western mountains, and in 1837 he engaged Miller to paint the scenes of camp and caravan for him. In Stewart's *Edward Warren*, a romantic autobiographical novel, he tells of the 1833 Rendezvous where he first encountered Provost. While the story is romanticized, Stewart's descriptions of the many mountaineers with whom "Edward Warren" came in contact seem to be accurate. Stewart wrote of Warren arriving at "Fontinelle's" camp near Bonneville's fort in 1833.[4] Warren was directed to the tent of the leaders and observed that, "near the door stood a large, heavy man with a ruddy face, bearing more the appearance of a mate of a French merchantman than a scourer of the dusty plains." Later Warren attended a council of the caravan leaders at which was present "Old Provost the burly Bacchus I had before remarked."[5] Provost had a reputation as a drinker. We know too from his exploits that he was tough. The stories of his physical prowess and his ability to hold his own in any company stretch from the time he escaped from an Indian massacre in 1824 until a year or two before his death at age sixty-five.

Many uncertainties still surround Provost, among them the spelling of his name. Since Provost could not write, we have no record of his own preference. I have chosen to spell his name as it appears in the parish records of St. Joseph of Chambly in Quebec. His baptismal record reads "Etienne Provost," and most of the entries there concerning his family are consistent with that spelling. That, however, is no guarantee, for in a notarial record of the village of Chambly the family name was spelled three different ways in the same document: Prevot, Provot and Provost. Others who wrote about him spelled the name phonetically, which has resulted in an even wider variety of choices. The records of the American Fur Company carried his name as both Provos and Proveau, the latter spelling appearing most frequently.

Of course, another spelling of the name is Provo, as in the city in Utah. Most references state that the city was named after the man, but I have found nothing to substantiate that assumption. The river on which the Mormons founded their settlement in 1849 was called the Provo, and from the available records it appears that the Mormon church named the settlement after the river. I have found no record of any intent to name the new settlement after the man, nor have I found any indication that the church hierarchy knew that Provost was still alive in 1849 when the party of thirty families under Elder John S. Higbee left Great Salt Lake City to "make a settlement on the Provo River."[6] Nor have I found any indication that Provost was aware, in that year before his death, that the settlement existed. In September of 1849 Thomas Bullock, accompanying Brigham Young on a visit to the new settlement, noted that they crossed the Provo River, and he described it as being a fine stream, some five rods wide and sixteen to twenty inches deep. The next month the church declared at its semi-annual conference that, "a city (Ogden) be laid off in Captain Brown's neighborhood and one (Provo) in the Utah Valley."[7] This is the first recorded use of the name for the settlement. In January of 1850 the General Assembly of the State of Deseret approved "An Ordinance Providing For The Location Of Counties And Precincts Therein Named, &c" which provided in Section 11 that "All that portion of country called Utah Valley, shall be called Utah County; the County seat of which shall be located at Provo City."

The Provo River on which the settlement was founded was not the original stream of that name. George C.

Yount recalled that in 1829 he was with a party under
Ceran St. Vrain when "they reached a stream at that
time called 'Provos Fork,' but which the Mormons now
call the Jordan.'— it empties into the Eutas Lake— the
Mormons call this lake by another name." [8] The river on
which the Mormons built their town had initially been
called the Timpanogos by the trappers and Indians[9]
and the Jordan River of today was then known as
Provos or Proveaus Fork. By 1845 Provost's name had
been shifted to the Timpanogos flowing into Utah Lake
from the Wasatch Mountains to the east. In that year
Kit Carson with John C. Fremont came westward and
from the Kamas prairie "crossed to Provost Fork. We
traveled down the Provost to Little Utah Lake and
followed its outlet almost to Great Salt Lake."[10]

If the city was not consciously named for Etienne
Provost, the river certainly was, even if initially it was
a different river. Why it was so named shall be related
later; however, it is interesting to note other reported
sources for the name of the river. In his *History of Utah*
Orson Whitney repeated a story that the river was so
named because a horse owned by Colonel Charles
Fremont had the misfortune to die on that river.
Fremont was said to have prized the horse highly, and
having purchased it from a Frenchman named
"Proveau," named the river after him. It seems more
likely that had such an event actually occurred, Fremont would have named the river after the horse.
Fremont's own words suggest as much. In his report of
his expedition of 1842 he wrote, "My horse was a
trained hunter, famous in the west under the name of
Proveau."[11]

In his *Far West Notebooks*, F. W. Cragin related a
tale told him in 1901 by one Caleb B. Rhodes, that in
the winter of 1844 a party of mountaineers wintered on
the river near the shore of Utah Lake. They had an
ample supply of whiskey, and while celebrating Christ-

mas one of their party, a Frenchman called "old Provost," fell into the Yule fire and was burned to death. In honor of this macabre celebration the river was named after the deceased.

To have a river, and subsequently a canyon and a city, named after one's self is heady stuff, and one might think that fame in such a circumstance would be everlasting. Not so in the case of Etienne Provost. Harvey L. Carter, in the monumental *Mountain Men and the Fur Trade* volumes edited by LeRoy Hafen, wrote "The Ashley men such as Jedediah Smith, William Sublette, Thomas Fitzpatrick and Jim Bridger have become familiar figures while their more successful rivals, William Vanderburgh, Lucien Fontenelle, Etienne Provost and Andrew Drips are much less well, and much less favorably known."[12]

William H. Ashley was a St. Louis politician and lieutenant governor of the newly admitted state of Missouri when in 1822 he organized a company of trappers, in partnership with Andrew Henry, and revolutionized the fur trade. The "Ashley men" were the explorers, the ones willing to take big risks for big profits by continually pushing into new country. The "more successful," if lesser known, traders and trappers were employees of the American Fur Company, John Jacob Astor's giant outfit that did not encourage individual entrepreneurage.

The operations of the company were always conducted with caution and sound judgement. Its career was marked by few brilliant strokes of policy, but rather by a conservative and continuous advance so fortified and supported that each step was permanent progress. It permitted other and more adventurous concerns to break the ground in new and dangerous territory rather than run the risk of invading those untried fields.[13]

To this, John E. Sunder added in his *The Fur Trade on the Upper Missouri, 1840-1865*, "They [Astor and his senior St. Louis partner, Pierre Chouteau, Jr.] remembered that the Upper Missouri was the cornerstone of their western fur empire." Whatever else the company did, it always remembered its power base in the posts on the Missouri River and acted to protect that structure. This philosophy hardly provided the opportunity or the atmosphere to bring fame to those employed by the company.

During his lifetime Provost was well known and highly regarded in the trade, but that respect was based on his performance before becoming a Company man. Provost had preceded William H. Ashley into the mountains, operating from a base in Taos, and had established his reputation by the mid-1820's. After 1830 he was no longer an active trapper, but became known within the company as one who could be counted on to carry out a task. Throughout his later career with the American Fur Company, if there was a difficult job to be done it was frequently given to him.

Many accounts of his life are peppered with errors. For years Provost was thought to have been a member of the original expedition of William H. Ashley, having responded to an advertisement which first appeared in the *Missouri Gazette* for February 13, 1822:

To Enterprising Young Men. The subscriber wishes to engage ONE HUNDRED MEN, to ascend the river Missouri to its source, there to be employed for one, two or three years - For particulars, enquire of Major Andrew Henry, near the lead mines, in the County of Washington, (who will ascend with, and command the party) or to the subscriber at St. Louis. - Wm. H. Ashley.[14]

Many of the names now famous in the fur trade did start with Ashley in this venture; however, Provost's

Caravan en Route

Catching Up

was not among them.

Dale Morgan, in the sketch of Provost in his book *Provo: Pioneer Mormon City*, attributes the origin of the errors to Hiram Martin Chittenden and his book *American Fur Trade of the Far West*, first published in 1902. Chittenden found that Provost had been in the Great Basin at the same time as Ashley and erroneously concluded that he, therefore, was an Ashley employee. Further, Chittenden had access to a letter written in 1860 by William Marshall Anderson, who had gone out to the 1834 rendezvous as a member of William L. Sublette's train and there had met Provost. In this letter Anderson made reference to Provost's discovery of the Great Salt Lake, and Chittenden presumed that if Provost was the discoverer of the lake, then he must have arrived on its shores by crossing South Pass. Thus, Chittenden placed Provost at the head of the party Andrew Henry sent to the southwest in 1823 from the mouth of the Bighorn River. Harrison C. Dale, for lack of better evidence, accepted Chittenden's work, as did most writers of that era, and while qualifying his statements about Provost's activities, also assumed he had been with the Ashley expedition in Utah.[15] At the time Chittenden credited Provost with leading the party across South Pass and into Utah he had just returned from New Mexico.

Because Provost left no journals or other accounts of his own, the material herein has come from references to him by others: from the accounting ledgers of the American Fur Company, from journals of other mountaineers who made mention of him, and from the journals and letterbooks of the trading posts. In some instances material is included for its informative value because Provost was there at the same, or nearly the same, time and thus experienced the same sights and conditions. In these instances I have told the story of Provost with the same thought expressed by William

Marshall Anderson in a letter written to Robert Campbell in 1871, at a time when both men were more than thirty years removed from their experiences in the mountains: "You and I have looked upon the same bold and beautiful scenery, the same noble and manly faces, with expressions too dear to die."[16]

Provost had shared that same time and place, and parts of his story must be told by relating those of his compatriots.

NOTES

1. Phillips, *The Fur Trade*, 2:574.
2. Ross, *The West of Alfred Jacob Miller*, Plate 197.
3. *Ibid.*, Plate 76.
4. Bonneville built a trading post along the Green River near present-day Daniels, Wyoming, in 1832, and it was the focal point of the 1833 rendezvous.
5. *Edward Warren*, 241, 260.
6. Jensen, *Encyclopedic History*, 683.
7. *Journal History*, entry for October 7, 1849.
8. *George C. Yount and His Chronicles of the West*, 70. Yount was recollecting his experiences more than twenty years later.
9. Ferris, *Life in the Rocky Mountains*, 250n.
10. Quaife, ed., *Kit Carson's Autobiography*, 88.
11. Fremont, *Report of the Exploring Expedition ... in the Year 1842*, 20.
12. Hafen, IX: 143.
13. Chittenden, *A History of the American Fur Trade of the Far West*, 375.
14. Morgan, *The West of William H. Ashley*, opposite p. 1, and letter of Dale Morgan to Charles Kelly, March 11, 1943, Utah State Historical Society Collections.
15. Morgan, *Provo: Pioneer Mormon City*, 25-6.
16. *Anderson Journals*, 3.

CHAPTER ONE
The Canadian Years, 1785-1814

December of 1785 was cold, bitterly cold, in Chambly, Quebec, in the Province of Lower Canada. The water was frozen in the basin of the Richelieu River around which the small settlement was laid out. Fort Chambly with its imposing stone bastions marked the southern edge of the basin where the river came tumbling and rushing from an eleven-mile journey over the rapids. Clustered about the fort and the parish church of that Catholic community, the Paroisse de St. Joseph de Chambly, were the homes of the settlement's residents. Officers of the fort had been seen ice-skating on the river a month ago, so early had the winter arrived.[1]

It was into a home of this settlement, that of the farmer Albert Provost, that Etienne Provost was born on December 21, 1785.[2] Albert and Marie Anne Mainard had been married on the twenty-fifth of January of that year and Etienne was the first son born of this, his father's third marriage.[3]

Etienne's grandfather, Gabriel, had established the family at Chambly, a small settlement twenty miles south of Montreal, sometime before 1751. Gabriel was born in Varennes, but at the time of his marriage to Marie Anne Bourassa in 1746 he was living in La Prairie, eight miles above Montreal on the St. Lawrence River. Their first child, Albert, Etienne's father, was born in La Prairie on September 18, 1749.[4]

Within the next two years Gabriel had left La Prairie and was farming in Chambly, for his second son, Joseph, was born there in January of 1751.[5] In that same year he entered into agreement with other farmers of the Chambly area on an issue of water rights. It was there, on January 29, 1770, that the twenty-year-old Albert married Marie Louise Paquet. Eight children and twelve years later Marie Louise died, a month after the birth of her last child. Four of their children lived to maturity: Isabelle (Elizabeth), Joseph, Charles and Pierre.

It was but a year following the death of Marie Louise that Albert married Magdeline Le Beau and soon became a widower again with her death in August of 1784. Albert took his third wife, Marie Anne Mainard, in January 1785, and Etienne was born in December.[6] He was followed by Toussaint, Julien, Antoine, Raphael and Francois. Both Raphael and Francois died within a month of their birth.[7]

Albert was a successful and prosperous farmer of Chambly. The experiences of the young Etienne grow-

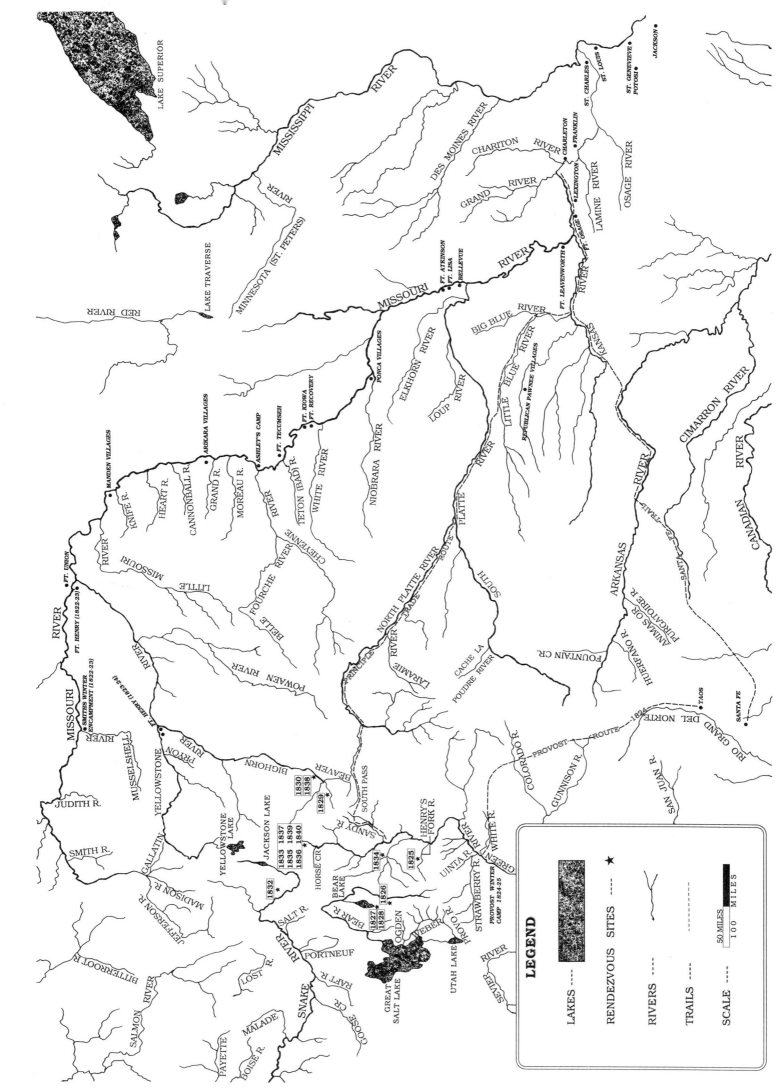

ing up in a small river community certainly included hard work on the farm and hunting and fishing in the woods and waters around Chambly, and his later character was certainly influenced by his early years on what was still the frontier. Living in the shadow of the fort undoubtedly had its effect on the lives of all residents of the village, but by Etienne's time the fort no longer played an important protective role in the community. He had to be aware of his community's role in the illicit fur trade between the residents of Lower Canada and the English traders at Albany and Boston to the south.

In the early days of Lower Canada the fort had played a very important role. No famous battles were fought at its gates, as at Quebec or Louisbourg, but those fought there were no less important. In July of 1665 Jacques de Chambly, a captain in the Regiment of Carignan, was ordered to the falls on the Richelieu to build a fort as protection for the town of Montreal twenty miles away on the St. Lawrence River. There Captain Chambly built a palisaded wooden structure that for many years served as the military key to Montreal.[8] The small outpost was intended to hold the Iroquois when they attacked Lower Canada by way of the natural water route of Lake Champlain and the Richelieu, while warning was sent to Montreal.

Through popular usage the fort became known as Fort Chambly after the captain was granted the Seigneury of Chambly in 1672, and so it has been known ever since. At the time it was built, there were no white settlers along the Richelieu, though they were not long in coming; the commercial advantage of the location was quickly noted. Situated as it was at the foot of the rapids and at a point where the river widened to form a large natural basin, the location formed a natural landing for traders using the river route between Lake Champlain and the St. Lawrence River.

Thus within five years of its building the fort was doubling as a trading post.

From its origin until well into the eighteenth century the settlement remained small and the life difficult.[9] The people were poor and lived mainly by hunting, fishing, and fur trading; Chambly was known as an important smuggling passage for furs moving to the English traders to the south.[10] By 1714 the illicit fur trade constituted from one half to two thirds of the total beaver pelts trapped in Canada, and for good reason. One beaver pelt traded south at Orange (Albany) or Boston brought up to four times the value of that same pelt traded in Montreal.[11] Little wonder, then, that the same river route that brought the Iroquois down on the Lower Canada settlements in the seventeenth century now witnessed a tide going the other way.

In the mid-years of the eighteenth century Fort Chambly surrendered its position as the principal fort defending Montreal to newer forts built upriver along the Richelieu. By 1750 the fort was relegated to the role of supply warehouse and troop staging area for those newer forts.

With the establishment of British Canada, Fort Chambly was occupied by the British until 1775, when it was taken by the American forces under Ethan Allen at the beginning of the American Revolution. A year later the British re-occupied the damaged remnants of the fort burned by the retreating Americans. It was rebuilt in 1777 and used to hold American prisoners from 1780 to 1784, the year before Etienne's birth.

The good citizens of Chambly retained both their French culture and language, so it was not surprising that they were not entirely supportive of the British during the American Revolution. Both the British and the "Bostonnais" sought their support, and their actions certainly favored the colonies in the fight against Britain. Ethan Allen had only thirty men with him when he came to Chambly in September of 1775. The residents willingly served as guides and performed guard duty for him on the way to Montreal. One hundred Chamblians were with him in the conquest of that city, and they later assisted Allen in his capture of Fort Chambly.[12]

The frontier origin of Chambly, its involvement in fur smuggling, and the attitudes of its people toward the new nation to the south served as a broad base of influence in the early years and education of Etienne Provost, so it is not surprising that he would be found, still on the frontier, at age thirty in St. Louis and would spend the rest of his life there in the fur trade. However, no record has been located of his involvement in the Canadian fur trade. He found in St. Louis a large population of fellow French Canadian emigres, who were the backbone of the American fur trade. Most of the French merchants of St. Louis were of Canadian origin as well and retained many close ties to Canada.

In 1796, when Etienne was in his eleventh year, his father died at age forty-six. Albert Provost had been a successful farmer in Chambly and left a sizeable estate. The inventory ran to fifteen pages and itemized both personal property valued in excess of £5,500 and several pieces of real property to which no monetary value was attached. At his death Albert left nine heirs: the four living children of his first marriage, the four living children of his third marriage, and his widow, who was named guardian of her own children and assumed control of that portion of the estate passing to Etienne and his brothers.[13]

The family continued to reside in Chambly, for records of land transfers, weddings, and other facets of life in the community mention the family name. But no record of Etienne exists to indicate when he left Chambly, or why. He seems to have been gone by 1806, when he was twenty-one years of age. He probably would not have left before 1800, when he was fifteen, a minimum age for employment.[14] In September of 1806 his brother Toussaint, two years his junior, was married. Etienne's name does not appear as witness in either the parish record of the marriage or the notarial record of the marriage contract. Certainly had he been then living in Chambly he would have represented the family in the marriage contract as the eldest son and attended his brother's wedding.

If it is uncertain whether he left between 1800 and 1806, there is no doubt that he had left Chambly before 1809. On December 18, 1819, Etienne's brother Toussaint acknowledged having received the sum of thirty-nine pounds from his mother as a one-seventh share of the property belonging to Etienne. Their mother agreed to guarantee the return of this money to Etienne should it ever be determined that he was not dead. He had at that time been absent for over ten years.[15]

Whether Etienne left Chambly prior to 1806 or a year or two later, he effectively dropped out of sight until 1817, when his presence in St. Louis is verified by a statement documenting his incarceration in a Spanish prison in Santa Fe.

NOTES

1. Auclair, *Chambly*, 19. Description of the fort from the author's personal observations in 1983.

2. Register, Paroisse de St. Joseph de Chambly, which reads, (translation) "The 21st December, 1785, the undersigned Cure of Chambly has baptised Etienne, born the same day of the legitimate marriage of Albert Provost and Marie Anne Mainard." In the parish register the name is spelled "Provost," and that is the spelling used throughout. Various documents spell the name in a variety of ways: Prevost, Prevot, Provot, Preoveau and Provau.

3. *Dictionnaire National des Canadiens Francais, 1608-1760,* vol. II. Etienne Provost's family in Canada can be traced to Pierre and Charlotte Vie Prevost "de Montreuil-sous Bois." Their son, Martin Prevost, Etienne's great-great-great grandfather, was born in 1611, and on November 3, 1644, Martin married an Indian, or part-Indian, Marie Olivier Sylvestre Manithabehick. Martin married again (Marie D'Abancour, November 8, 1665), but the line that included Etienne almost a century and a half later had its origins in his first marriage.

4. Parish register, La Nativite de la Prairie de la Magdeline Catholic Church, La Prairie, Quebec. In the register the name is spelled "Provau" in both the record of Gabriel's marriage and the baptism of Albert.

5. Tanguay, *Dictionnaire Genealogique des Families Canadiennes,* 442, and Notarial Records, Archives Judiciare de Montreal, No. 51, June 25, 1751.

6. Like "Provost," the spelling of "Mainard" varies with references to Marie Anne. It appears as Mainard in the parish register; elsewhere it has been spelled variously Maynard, Mennard and Menard.

7. Register, Paroisse de St. Joseph de Chambly.

8. Auclair, *Chambly,* 20-21; and Nadon, "Fort Chambly Interpretation Papers," npn.

9. In the census of 1681 there were seventy-eight people, not counting the military complement: thirty-two adults and forty-six children in eleven families, and ten unmarried adults. The settlement occupied and farmed 133 arpents of land.

10. Jurkovich, "Fort Chambly Interpretation Papers," npn.

11. Nadon, "Fort Chambly Interpretation Papers," npn.

12. Duffet, "Fort Chambly Interpretation Papers," npn.

13. The Notarial Records of Francois LeGuay (son)

for March, 26, 1796 (Notarial Records of Chambly, 1793-1807, no. 278), contains a detailed inventory of personal property. Listed were items as trivial as "three old earthenware pots," valued at less than half a pound. He left one fusil, with powder horn and bullet pouch valued at twelve francs. Among the items directly related to the farm were several carts, carryalls and sledges, a plow and several log chains. Livestock consisted of four pair of oxen, identified as to age; ten cows; two stud bulls, and thirteen others identified only as bulls. Of horses he had six, and mares two; twenty-six ewes, with their lambs, and one ram. Also listed were eleven sows of varying ages, a flock of thirty chickens, and apparently eleven sheep kept elsewhere. He had the appropriate cow and hog sheds, as listed, and one thousand bales of hay with which to feed his livestock.

14. Hudson's Bay Company Archives, Record of Employments 1799 to 1815.

15. Rene Boileau, "Notarial Records of Chambly, 1803-1842."

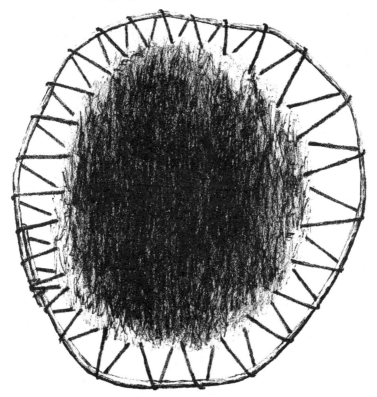

CHAPTER TWO
The Early Fur Trade

To better understand Provost's role in the fur trade a brief overview of those major events which transpired prior to 1814 will assist in placing his participation in perspective.

As has been mentioned, the "Golden Age" of the American fur trade was the period from 1806 to 1840. Of those years, the most active phase was from 1820 to the mid-1830's. The trade involved principally beaver pelts; however, by 1840 the beaver hat was long out of style, the beaver in the mountains were by then too few to make trapping economically viable, and the emigrant trains were about to scar the plains with their wagon ruts as a mark of the westward expansion destined to consolidate a nation from coast to coast.

The American fur trade had its origins long before the Mountain Man era, although it was not of particular significance and, of course, the trade in buffalo robes continued until the near extinction of the buffalo in the late 1800's. And throughout there was the trade in the more common hides, such as deer and bear skins, that filled the immediate needs of the citizens in their day-to-day living. In those early years the commercial activity was conducted by trading with the Indians rather than actually trapping the furs. In 1786 the first efforts of the new nation to regulate the trade were taken when the government required that the trader be a citizen in good standing and be licensed.[1]

In the two decades following the Revolution, however, most of the traders in American territory were not American but British operating out of Canada. The British concentrated on the fur trade whereas the American interest in the years immediately following the Revolution was predominantly land speculation and settlement. Daniel Boone was more the role model than the roving trader and the goal was to settle the land for farming by driving the Indian away, by force if necessary. The new American government policy supported and encouraged removal of the Indian and settlement of the land rather than trade, for occupancy of the Indian lands would establish right of possession in any future dispute with England.[2]

Most of the limited American trade was usually carried on by independent traders while the British utilized large trading companies operating under government charter and support. The Hudson's Bay Company, founded in 1670, had the trade monopoly in the Hudson's Bay Basin known as Rupert's Land. Other major British companies were the North West

Company, founded in 1784, the General Company of Lake Superior and the South, which was more frequently called the General Store, and the Miami Company, formed at Detroit. These companies, and others, operated in lands claimed by the United States lying south of the Great Lakes from the Appalachian Mountains to the Mississippi River.

To the west, on the western bank of the Mississippi River, and not yet a part of the United States, was the settlement of St. Louis, founded in 1764 as a trading post. Although Spanish in its government, most of the citizens were of French Canadian origin. Names such as Labadie, Pepin, Sarpy, Robidoux, Cerre and Gratiot all had Canadian backgrounds and it was, therefore, not surprising that the St. Louis trade at the close of the American Revolution was almost entirely with Canada.

Despite the economic ties between Canada and St. Louis, the Spanish government was as vexed as the Americans over the British incursion into its territory. The territory that was to become known as the Louisiana Purchase was Spanish in the late 1700s, and that government wished to maintain its dominance over the entire area. It was, therefore, with irritation that the Spanish watched the North West Company send its traders to the Upper Missouri River region, mostly around the Mandan villages at the Great Bend of the Missouri.[3] The company later also had its traders as far west as the Yellowstone River in Montana.

In an effort to drive the British from the Upper Missouri River, the Spanish government subsidized the Commercial Trading Company in 1794; however, politics and infighting for control soon supplanted trading activities and the St. Louis merchants who had been supporting the venture withdrew. The company died as an effective economic venture.

In 1796 the U.S. Congress established trading houses "at such posts and places on the western frontiers, or in the Indian country as (shall be judged) most convenient for the purpose of carrying on a liberal trade" with the Indians. Each trading house, or "Factory" as they came to be known, was in charge of an agent with the necessary clerks under him. They were in the employ of the government and not allowed to trade for their own accounts.[4]

The Factory system became a permanent fixture of Indian trade, and it was not until it met strong opposition that it was finally abolished in 1822. At the same time the Congress established the Factory system to control the trade, it authorized independent traders to operate within the Indian lands through licensing, thus creating competition for its own system on the one hand and placing the independent trader under a competitive disadvantage on the other. For twenty-six years the systems operated side by side, with the traders slowly gaining the upper hand by virtue of their flexibility and ability to go where the trade demanded.

The Louisiana Purchase in 1803 swiftly established St. Louis as the center of the new American fur trade. The town, even while under the Spanish and French flags, had long been ideally suited to serve as the center of the western fur trade, but for many years this potential had been virtually ignored in favor of the river traffic. By 1803 the St. Louis merchants had extended the fur trade up the Missouri River only as far as the Council Bluffs, just above Omaha, Nebraska, and on the Mississippi northward to the Des Moines River. The vast country north of those points was left to the Canadian traders of the North West Company.

The success of the British incursion into American territory encouraged an increase in American activity. In 1803 President Jefferson submitted a plan to Congress for an expedition of exploration to the Pacific. Jefferson's phrasing specified "for literary purposes," but his supporting arguments showed that the fur trade in the western lands was of paramount interest.[5] Congress approved the President's proposal and Jefferson named Meriwether Lewis to lead his 1804 company of explorers. Lewis chose William Clark to be his co-captain for the venture. Their two-year journey across an unexplored land and safe return to St. Louis engendered a new enthusiasm for the fur trade on the upper Missouri River and in the Rocky Mountain region.

As the company of explorers paddled downriver on its return to St. Louis in 1806, it encountered traders heading upriver, forerunners of the many to follow. Manuel Lisa was among the earliest, leading an expedition upriver to establish posts where the Indians had no previous contact with Americans.

On Lisa's return from his first expedition he circulated glowing accounts to the St. Louis merchants of the trade potential of the Upper Missouri region, and he had no difficulty organizing the St. Louis Missouri Fur Company in 1809 for the purpose of trading on the headwaters of the Missouri. As partners Lisa had Benjamin Wilkinson, Auguste and Pierre Chouteau, William Clark, Reuben Lewis (a brother of Meriwether Lewis) and Andrew Henry.[6]

Sitting in the relative comfort of New York, a thousand miles from the frontier town of St. Louis, John Jacob Astor viewed the sudden burgeoning of the fur trade with considerable interest. Astor wished to control the entire American fur trade. As the nineteenth century began he had already established an extensive trade in the Great Lakes region but had been unsuccessful in an effort at getting a foot in the door of the St. Louis trade.[7]

In June of 1810, Astor formed the Pacific Fur Company for the purpose of establishing a trading post at the mouth of the Columbia River. The post was to be supported by both a string of posts along the Missouri

River and ships coming to the west coast. He accomplished his initial intent when he successfully established his post, called Astoria, at the mouth of the Columbia River, but his plan ultimately failed with the outbreak of war in 1812.

The implacable hostility of the Blackfoot Indians was an insurmountable problem in the early years of the mountain trade and was a major factor in the abandonment of the Rocky Mountain region by 1811. And the trade restrictions imposed before the War of 1812 both reduced beaver prices by half and established trade barriers with Canada which made the obtaining of trade goods very difficult. Further, since the St. Louis trade still moved primarily to Montreal, there was a new danger of having the furs seized by the American government and Auguste Chouteau was reluctant to risk violations of the law to continue the trade.[8]

With the outbreak of the War of 1812, Astor's Pacific venture collapsed both from fear and collusion between the British and some of the partners, the result of which was that Astoria was sold to the North West Company. The loss of the post ended the only American attempt to establish a trading venture in the northwest. It was a considerable loss to the United States politically, since it was understood by both governments that ultimate title to the northwest would be determined by possession.[9]

The war and trade problems forced a retrenchment, and by 1815 the St. Louis fur trade extended little farther than it had in 1804; however, the end of the war brought a renewed demand for furs, and the St. Louis traders began to expand again, both westward and to the southwest. It was into this setting that Etienne Provost stepped sometime prior to 1815.

NOTES

1. Phillips, *The Fur Trade*, 2: 68.
2. *Ibid.*, 12.
3. *Ibid.*, 231. The Great Bend is near Bismark, North Dakota.
4. *Ibid.*, 74.
5. *Ibid.*, 253.
6. Phillips, *The Fur Trade*, 2: 262. Lisa and Wilkinson were to manage the trade. A number of the partners, such as Chouteau, had joined Lisa simply because there was at that time no opportunity to compete with him. The articles of agreement were, therefore, far more protective and restrictive than developmental. All of the partners but Clark were required to either accompany the expedition, or appoint a deputy to represent them, since a partner in St. Louis would not trust those in the field, and *vice-versa*.
7. Astor had undertaken to collect debts which Auguste Chouteau and Charles Gratiot owed to a Montreal firm. Rather than press for payment, Astor suggested that the two St. Louis merchants consign their furs to him in New York rather than ship to Montreal, at a savings to both. Gratiot was willing to accept the offer; however, Chouteau did not even deign to respond to Astor's proposal, possibly seeing Astor's intent. Without Chouteau, Astor felt his plan stood no chance of success and did not pursue it further.
8. Phillips, *The Fur Trade*, 2: 68.
9. Stuart, *On the Oregon Trail*, 10-11.

Joseph Philibert

Beaver Trap

CHAPTER THREE
St. Louis Beginnings, 1815-1821

The St. Louis to which Etienne Provost had come by 1815 had its beginnings fifty-two years earlier when, standing on the east bank of the Mississippi River in the fall of 1763, at a point a few miles below its junction with the Missouri River, Pierre Laclede Liguest and his stepson and clerk, fourteen-year-old Auguste Chouteau, selected the site for their trading post.[1] Although the fall weather in that part of the country is usually mild and pleasant, it was too late in the season to begin construction of the new post. That had to wait until March of the next year when Laclede Liguest placed the young

Chouteau in charge of a party of thirty men to establish
the trading post of St. Louis on the site they had
chosen.[2] Among the thirty original settlers was Jean
Sale dit La Joie, a trader who figures in Provost's life.[3]

The original grant from the King of France called for
the founding of a trading post, not a military fort, and
Laclede Liguest and Chouteau met with a degree of
success from the start that they could have hardly
imagined in their planning.[4] Trading was so successful
that the residents of the post neglected such basic necessities as farming, and within three years of its
settlement St. Louis was known as far away as Montreal as "pain court," short of bread.

Money was also always in short supply and for years
furs were the principal medium of exchange. Deerskins, bearskins, buffalo robes, and the pelts of beaver,
lynx, fox and marten were accepted as currency.[5] Over
the years, however, other forms of currency found
vogue: in 1809 Bernard Pratte announced that he
would accept either cash or pork in payment for the
merchandise he sold; another merchant offered to take
in payment, in addition to furs and hides, whiskey,
country-made sugar or beeswax.[6]

By 1810 almost two thousand people crowded the
town, and the riverfront was still the center of the
thriving St. Louis commerce, despite Manuel Lisa's
success on the Upper Missouri and the resultant
growing interest in the fur trade.[7] The "hectoring, ex-
travagant, bragging boatmen of the Mississippi" and
the "gay, grimacing, singing, good-humored Canadian
voyageurs" were seen in ever-increasing numbers.[8]
Elsewhere within the town, Indians and occasionally a
hunter in leather outfit roamed the streets.

Washington Irving perhaps best described the St.
Louis of about the time of Etienne Provost's arrival, in
his *Astoria*:

St. Louis was, at that time, a frontier settlement and the last fitting-out place for the Indian trade of the Southwest. It possessed a motley population, composed of the Creole descendants of the original French colonists; the keen traders from the Atlantic States; the backwoodsmen of Kentucky and Tennessee; the Indians and half-breeds of the prairies; together with a singular aquatic race that had grown up from the navigation of the rivers - the "boatmen of the Mississippi."[9]

Irving's "boatmen" were keelboatmen who muscled their boats up the Mississippi and Missouri rivers by pole and cordelle.

The exact year in which Etienne Provost arrived to join this eclectic settlement is not known, but it is likely that, like so many others, he came to St. Louis because it was still a French community and he had relatives there. Most of the fur company engages were of French-Canadian origin, and as Thomas Scharf noted in his history of St. Louis, in 1804 at least two thirds of the population were cousins. In 1826 Provost attended the wedding of his cousin, Jean Baptiste Provost, son of another Jean Baptiste Provost.[10] Thus it seems quite likely that there had been cousins on his father's side of the family in St. Louis when he arrived some years earlier.

On his mother's side Etienne also had relatives in St. Louis. His mother's uncle, Louis Menard, was there in 1802 when his wife, Anne Salle dit Cayolle, died.[11] Provost also had a distant in-law relationship with the family of Joseph Robidoux, which had come to St. Louis from Canada. Louis Antoine Provost, half-brother to Etienne's grandfather, married Barbe Amable Robidoux in 1761 and Marie Francoise Robidou married Louis Menard (a second Louis and great-great uncle to Etienne) in 1725. It's not surprising, therefore, that St. Louis attracted Etienne Provost. The town was a magnet for the French-Canadian voyageurs and abounded with them.

In 1815 Provost signed on with the expedition of Auguste P. Chouteau and Jules deMun destined for the southwest to trade along the Arkansas and Platte rivers. They were bound for an area bordering on Spanish lands, but there is no indication that they intended any incursion into Spanish territory on their trading venture.

The Spanish authorities did not welcome American traders. Highly suspicious of American intent, the Spanish jealously guarded their domains. They were not fur traders or trappers and knew little of that business. What minimal trading they did on the northern frontier was for the useful skins needed in their everyday lives, deerskins and buffalo hides. They took no interest in the exotic uses of the beaver, lynx, or marten pelts in the fashion industry of Europe. The northern provinces of Mexico were intended primarily as buffer zones to protect greater Spanish interests to the south, and thus they received much direction and little support from the Spanish central authorities. The border with the United States was zealously protected.

American interest in the area was growing, however, and the threat of Spanish arrest did not deter those more intrepid frontier spirits who cared little for government, whether theirs or someone else's. As early as 1810, the Spanish authorities had a report of five foreign beaver hunters among the Indians in the Spanish lands. They were not located or identified by the investigating force, having fled, according to the Indians, when they learned of the approach of the Spanish.[12]

In 1812 four Frenchmen of Manuel Lisa's company appeared in Taos, creating considerable excitement and concern.[13] These four were members of a larger party, including Ezekiel Williams, which had been sent south by Lisa in 1811 from his post on the Missouri River.[14] They were under the command of Jean Baptiste Champlain and Jean Baptiste Lefargue. Because of Indian problems the men found they could not return to Lisa on the Missouri, so they split into two groups, with four men opting to seek refuge in the Spanish settlements.[15] Instead of refuge they were given residence in a Spanish jail.

That same year, Robert McKnight tested the Spanish resolve by organizing a trading expedition from St. Louis to Santa Fe. He lost, and he and his men were arrested and confined, and their trade goods confiscated and sold. They were not to be freed until Mexico gained its independence from Spain in 1821.[16]

These and other indignities were well known in St. Louis when on April 3, 1814, Joseph Philibert led his party out with a license to trade on the Arkansas River.[17] Philibert was a merchant of French-Canadian origin born about 1775.[18] He had come to St. Louis in 1801 and would remain there as a successful businessman for the rest of his life.

No roster exists of the men with Philibert, but we know from Ezekiel Williams that the total number was "18 Frenchmen called Phillebers company" which he and his companions joined in May of 1814.[19] Some of the party may be identified in the tales of Pierre Lesperance, a trapper whose greater forte was storytelling. A "widely known" New Mexican legend placed Lesperance in a group of fifteen or so Frenchmen who trapped the mountains from the Platte to the Spanish settlements and were arrested and brought into Taos. Lesperance's tales identified many individuals with whom he shared his adventures, including Joseph Bissonette dit Bijou.[20] The legend certainly fits the circumstances surrounding Philibert's activities and the eventual arrest of his party, and although several of those named in Lesperance's tales do not fit the time frame of

Philibert's company, many others do and could well have been with him, and later Chouteau and deMun.

One member of Philibert's group identified by Ezekiel Williams was Michael (Francois) La Clair. The question is, was Etienne Provost a member of the party? Both he and Joseph Bissonett were later members of the Chouteau-deMun expedition. A careful examination of the available evidence suggests that Provost started his career in the fur trade with Philibert in 1814.

The Philibert and Williams parties traveled together at least as far as the Arapaho nation, where Williams had come to recover the furs he had cached there in 1812. There Williams hired Michael La Clair away from Philibert to assist in bringing the furs back to St. Louis. Williams later had difficulties with La Clair, or LeClerc, and in a public advertisement disavowed the note of payment for services made to "Francois L'Clair." In the articles of engagement with Williams LeClerc's name is given as "Fraceway Licklier."[21] No matter the spelling, LeClerc appears to be the same one who later joined with Provost in a partnership to trap out of New Mexico.

After leaving Williams and LeClerc, Philibert continued to the southwest.[22] By early September he was probably in Spanish territory at a camp "about four leagues north of the place where Captain Pike was taken by the Spaniards."[23] Once camp had been established, he sent two men out to search for likely trapping sites. These two had the misfortune to run into a group of forty Spaniards who were catching wild horses, and they were captured and taken to Santa Fe. Once the Commandante had questioned the two, according to Philibert's account, 250 men were sent to bring him, the remaining members of his party, and all traps, furs and merchandise to Santa Fe.[24]

Although Philibert and his men were not thrown in jail and were, in fact, given free run of Santa Fe, it was fifty days before they were released by the Spanish authorities and told to return to American territory. Philibert's goods were confiscated to pay the expenses of their capture and subsistence. The weather prevented their immediate return, however, for it became so bad that the group was permitted to sit out the winter in the mountain village of San Fernando de Taos, about eighty miles northeast of Santa Fe.[25] There they remained until February of 1815, when they were finally able to make their way to American territory. Philibert promptly returned to St. Louis with half his men to restock and return to the Arkansas. They arrived in St. Louis in July 1815, bringing word of not only their incarceration, but also of other Americans then held by the Spanish. Among them were the four Frenchmen of Lisa's company—Lafargue, Vesina, Grenie and Roi. Others identified by Philibert were members of the Robert McKnight party of 1812.[26] As with Philibert, these men had not been imprisoned but were given the freedom of the town in which they were held.[27]

On leaving for St. Louis, Philibert had instructed those men remaining in the field to rendezvous with him on Huerfano Creek in the fall.[28] Where they roamed in the interim cannot be ascertained, but an entry in the Spanish Governor's diary for May 1, 1815, noted that six of the seventeen Frenchmen who had been ordered from Santa Fe to "Luisiana" in February had returned to Taos and had again been ordered to depart for American territory.[29] By the sixth of June the Frenchmen were again on their way out of Spanish lands; however, on the eighteenth of June two of the six had for a third time returned to Taos, having fled from some Jicarilla Apaches. They were once more ordered out of Spanish territory.

What those nine men did between June and December has never been learned. Presumably Philibert had left instructions to do whatever trapping and trading was possible in his absence, for his expedition to date had accomplished nothing. Whatever else they might have done, they persisted in trying Spanish patience.

On Christmas Day, 1815, they once more returned to Taos.[30] Philibert had not returned as expected so their future was at best uncertain and, most pertinent, they had run out of supplies. They undoubtedly recalled the friendly treatment accorded them in Taos the previous winter. In any event there were warm quarters and food in Taos, both of which were lacking on the Huerfano, so they determined to seek the shelter of that far more hospitable location.

Their arrival prompted further correspondence between the Governor at Santa Fe and the Commandante General at Durango. In February 1816, Commandante General Bernardo Bonavia wrote to the Governor that foreigners coming from Upper Louisiana should be viewed with distrust. They should be required to return to their own country by the same route over which they had entered Spanish land. Bonavia specifically instructed that this should be done with the nine Frenchmen who had recently arrived in Taos and were the subject of the Governor's inquiry.[31]

In September of 1815, while Philibert was still in St. Louis and his men in the mountains, Auguste P. Chouteau and Jules deMun had enlisted a crew of men and outfitted a trading expedition to the Arkansas River which departed St. Louis on the tenth.[32] They had a trading license issued by Governor William Clark authorizing them to go to the headwaters of the Arkansas and trade with the Arapaho and other Indians found there.[33] Joseph Philibert chose to accompany them. He had resupplied himself and been granted a new license to trade on the Platte and Arkansas rivers.[34] En route to the Arkansas Philibert sold his entire interest in the venture to Chouteau and deMun, to include all his furs, goods, horses, and the remaining time of his men.[35]

Thus Chouteau and deMun acquired a sizeable number of additional men, both those awaiting Philibert on the Huerfano and those accompanying him on this return trip. Etienne Provost was one of these men; to which group did he belong? Three options present themselves for consideration: he was going out with Chouteau as a new recruit in 1815; he had been a member of the party Philibert had brought back in the spring, and now signed on with Chouteau; or he might have been one of the nine left to rendezvous with Philibert on the Huerfano. Whichever was the case, he participated in the experiences of the Chouteau-de-Mun party.

The expedition arrived at Huerfano Creek, site of the planned rendezvous with Philibert's remaining men, in early December, but no men were at the camp. A search failed to locate the missing men but did turn up some Indians who informed them that the men had run out of supplies and, not knowing when, or if, Philibert would return, had retired to Taos for the winter. Chouteau and deMun made their winter camp there, and in January of 1816 deMun took eight men with him to go in search of their men in Taos. He found them and noted that they had been warmly received in the village and shown the greatest hospitality. They had been allowed to pass the winter there,[36] although that permission was more likely a local decision for, as has been noted, the Commandante General certainly held no such friendly view.

DeMun decided it would be politic to make his presence in New Mexico known to the Spanish authorities, so he left his men in Taos and proceeded to Santa Fe to see the Governor. Initially he intended to merely explain his presence; however, after noting the abundance of beaver in the streams along his way, he determined to seek permission to trap those streams.[37] The Governor, Don Alberto Maynez, could not grant de-

Mun's request on his own authority, but he did offer to
write to the Commandante General asking for the
necessary authorization to permit deMun's return with
his men.[38] It was just prior to deMun's arrival that the
Governor had written the Commandante General
concerning the nine Frenchmen who were then in Taos.
The Commandante General's response of February,
1816, was circulated to a number of the northern
settlements. The strong phrasing of that letter could
well account for the rough treatment later accorded
Chouteau and deMun.

DeMun returned to the camp on the Huerfano with
the Taos contingent. It was understood that he would
return to Santa Fe for the answer to his request for
permission to trap the Spanish streams. In the mean-
time, the party now found itself with many more men
than anticipated and too few supplies. The leaders
decided that Chouteau and the men would remain in
the mountains to continue trading while deMun would
return to St. Louis to resupply the expedition. He left at
the end of February, taking with him Philibert, who no
longer had an interest in the trade, and a man named
Cohen.[39]

They arrived in St. Louis forty-six days later, by
deMun's account, and he immediately began to pro-
cure supplies and recruit additional men for the party.
He also received a new license to trade from Governor
William Clark and, on the June 15 started again for the
mountains, where he was to meet Chouteau on the
Kansas River.

While on his way to meet deMun, Chouteau had a
run-in with the Pawnees and lost one of his men in a
battle at what was afterward called Chouteau's Island
in the Arkansas.

Once the two parties were reunited at the Kansas
River, they shipped their furs back to St. Louis in the
care of some of their men and, forty-five strong, they

once again started for their hunting ground. En route they encountered Spanish traders who warned them of hostile Indians in the area where they were intending to hunt. The news prompted a change in plans. Chouteau and most of the party were to wait near "La Sangre de Christe" pass, while deMun went to Sante Fe to learn what had been decided with respect to his trapping request. He and two of his men rode with the Spanish traders toward Taos; however, at a small village on the Rio Colorado, deMun was halted and forbidden to proceed farther. He wrote a letter to the Governor at Santa Fe, and then turned back to find Chouteau in the mountains and await the Governor's reply. When it finally arrived, the Governor had written only that they would not be permitted to remain on Spanish land and that they must leave.[40]

With little choice left to them in the matter, Chouteau and deMun took their men back across the mountains and spent the winter of 1816-17 on the eastern slope. DeMun believed that to establish their winter camp on the eastern slope of the mountains would present no problem to the Spaniards. He noted that traders from the Spanish villages came almost weekly to their camp with supplies and horses and that a regular commerce existed, implying that the Spanish authorities were well aware of their location.[41]

In the spring of 1817, deMun once more went to Taos to learn the answer to his request, and he was utterly shocked by the accusation that his party had constructed a strong fort on Spanish lands and manned it with twenty thousand men, cannon and munitions. DeMun most vociferously protested against these charges, and subsequent Spanish investigation proved the allegations to be false. By this time, however, the delays encountered in disproving the allegations caused them to abandon their original plan of trading with the Crow Indians on the Platte River far to the north. They

attempted instead to enter the mountains to the north
of the Arkansas River; however, heavy snow blocked
the way and forced a return to their starting point.[42] It
was here on the Greenhorn River, south of Pikes Peak,
that the party was taken into custody by the Spanish
on May 24 and escorted to Santa Fe under guard.[43]

In the record of Spanish military actions for the
period is the report of an action in May of 1817 in which
Teniente Coronel (Lieutenant Colonel) Don Pedro Maria
de Manse captured and imprisoned twenty-one French
foreigners. Another record of military actions by the
Spanish reported that in 1817 there was a campaign
led against some French foreigners in which there was
a show of arms.[44] If these are reports of the apprehen-
sion of Chouteau, deMun, and their party, as they
certainly seem to be, apparently the Colonel did not
identify himself to deMun, for in his letter to William
Clark deMun stated that the arresting party of Spaniards was commanded by Sergeant Mariano Vernal.[45]
However, a large detachment would certainly be commanded by someone of greater rank than a sergeant,
and in the deposition given upon deMun's return to St.
Louis the Spanish force was numbered at two hundred
or more. That same deposition identifies the individual
bearing the arrest order as the "commanding officer,"
so deMun is quite possibly in error in his letter.

After forty-eight days, during which time both deMun
and Chouteau had been in irons at least part of the
time, the company was permitted to return to the
United States. Their property, however, was confiscated and they were allowed to take with them only one
horse apiece, and the worst ones at that.[46] Their return
to St. Louis was reported in the *Missouri Gazette* for
Saturday, September 13, 1817, with appropriate cal-
umnies heaped upon the Spanish authorities. The
paper reported that they had been deprived of their
property by the Spanish and compelled ignominiously

to kiss, upon their knees, the stupid and oppressive mandate of the Governor. The "mandate" was the Governor's order permitting their departure but confiscating their goods to pay the cost of their incarceration. It was there in St. Louis that a deposition was written and signed by eleven members of the party, including Etienne Provost:

United States, Territory of Missouri,
County of St. Louis, sct.
The undersigned having been first duly sworn on the Holy Evangelists, severally depose and say: that in the beginning of September, 1815 that they were engaged by Auguste P. Chouteau and company, at St. Louis in the territory of Missouri for a trading expedition, with the Indians of the head waters of the rivers Arkansas and Platte. The party conducted by the said Auguste P. Chouteau, proceeded to their grounds on the head waters of the Arkansas, and continued the trade until the spring of 1817; at which time, our encampment was visited by a guard of Spaniards, two hundred or more in number; the commanding officer of which guard, was the bearer of an order from the Governor of New Mexico, to conduct our whole party to Santa Fe. This order was executed. Auguste P. Chouteau, together with the whole party, consisting of twenty one persons, accompanied the troop or guard, and on our arrival at Santa Fe, was reviewed by the Governor, and immediately put into close confinement. At the time of the arrest of our persons, within the limits of the United States, Mr. Chouteau, conscious no doubt, that he had violated none of the Spanish regulations, took with him a part of his property, to defray expenses; none of which he was permitted to retain, to exchange, or to make any use of. Not only that, but also the whole stock of the company cached or concealed in the ground, near our camp east of the mountains, and on the head waters of the Arkan-

sas, was seized by the Spaniards under special order from the Governor and taken to Santa Fe. We remained in prison (some of us in irons) forty-eight days, during which time we were dieted in a very coarse and meagre manner, with boiled corn or beans, without salt.

When we speak of the review and confinement of the party, we mean the men generally, for Mr. Chouteau and the conductors of our trade, preceded us, and arrived first at Santa Fe. We know not the particulars of their reception or of their treatment, except that when they were liberated (after forty-eight days) that their property was not restored to them.

Long previous to our arrest, Mr. Chouteau had equipped several parties for different parts of the upper country, all, as we constantly understood, within the acknowledged limits of the United States. Of the fate of these detached parties, we know nothing. Our arrest and detention in the Spanish province, interrupted that correspondence on which their success must in a great degree have depended. As well as we recollect, Mr. Chouteaus's party, on leaving St. Louis, amounted to forty-six.

JEAN BATISTI BRIZAR, his x mark
BAPTISTI FICIO, his x mark.
CHARLES BOURGUIGNON, his x mark.
JOSEPH CISDELLE, his x mark.
ETUNNE PROVOTT, his x mark.
FRANCOIS MAUANT, his x mark.
PIERRE LEGRIS, his x mark.
FRANCOIS PAKET, his x mark.
FRANCOIS DERPORT, his x mark.
ANTOINO BIZET, his x mark.
JOSEPH BISSONET, his x mark.[47]

This testimony is the first information after his

baptismal record that places Provost at a given point at a specific time.

The deposition, which was certainly phrased in a manner calculated to best serve the interests of Messrs. Chouteau and deMun, was written in September 1817 to support the claim filed by the partners of the expedition with the United States government against the Spanish government seeking recompense for their losses. Since none of those signing the deposition could write, as witnessed by each signature being by mark, the deposition of necessity had to have been written by someone else, and from its tenor, it was obviously prepared by one very sympathetic to Chouteau and deMun, if not by one of the principals themselves.[48]

Twenty-four years later, on December 20, 1841, Etienne Provost gave another deposition regarding his arrest by the Spanish. This was in furtherance of the still-unsettled claim of Chouteau and deMun for their losses suffered in 1817. This later deposition sheds no additional light on the incident but it is the only record in which Provost's own views are reflected, even though written in the third person. He "takes no pleasure in reverting to the horror and suffering of that expedition. He, with the others, was taken prisoner they were literally stripped of every thing and suffered almost beyond endurance."[49]

The names of all those with Chouteau, deMun and Philibert may never be known with certainty. Beyond the eleven signers of the 1817 deposition, those known to be with Chouteau and deMun were Toussaint Charboneau (of Lewis and Clark fame), Michael Carriere, Cohen, Lewis, and one Barony (or Baronet).[50]

Provost was certainly with Chouteau and deMun after deMun's return from his trip to Taos, because the entire company was then together for the first time. But when and with whom did he first come to the Arkansas? The answer to that may never be known, but there are certainly valid arguments that he was with Philibert's "18 Frenchmen" in 1814. Most historians have accepted that Provost was with the Chouteau-deMun expedition from the beginning; however, if one examines all the circumstances of Provost's later involvement in the fur trade emanating from Taos, then the likelihood of his earlier involvement with Philibert is quite logical.

Provost and Joseph Bissonett were with Chouteau and deMun when they were arrested by the Spanish. Their names both appear on the 1817 deposition, which attests that all the signers had been employed by Chouteau in St. Louis in early September of 1815. But if Pierre Lesperance was in Philibert's company and Bissonett was with Lesperance, then Bissonett was also with Philibert, and the question of just when he actually signed on with Chouteau and deMun is unanswerable. Provost is arguably in the same situation.

Several possibilities exist: the first and most obvious is that Provost did, indeed, sign with Chouteau in September of 1815 as the deposition states and that trip was his initiation to the southwest. A second is that both Provost and Bissonett were with Philibert in 1814 and were among those who returned with him to St. Louis in 1815, either to be signed on by Chouteau in September or to become attached to Chouteau and deMun through Philibert's subsequent sale of his interests to the partners on the trail. A third possibility is that Provost was with the men left in the field by Philibert to rendezvous with him on the Huerfano.

To establish some basis for any postulation other than Provost's signing on straight-away with Chouteau in September of 1815, it is necessary to leap forward many years. In 1843 the naturalist and artist John James Audubon sought Provost as the guide for his expedition to the Upper Missouri. In his letters Audubon noted that his party might have the services of "an old

Voyager who has been in the trade for 29 years....This Mr. Provost...."[51] Subtracting twenty-nine years from 1843 takes the date back to 1814 as the year Provost first entered the fur trade. It must also be remembered that Michael (Francois) LeClerc was with Philibert in 1814. Some years later Provost was in partnership with one LeClerc, first name unknown. Francois LeClerc has been considered the most likely candidate of a number of LeClercs in the fur trade at that time.[52] What better opportunity to meet a future partner than outbound from St. Louis as members of the same expedition?

Finally, after Mexican independence was established in 1821, the Americans moved rapidly into New Mexico to trade and trap. And welcome they were. Among them were Provost and his partner, LeClerc. Having been with Philibert would have given him a far more extensive knowledge of New Mexico, and particularly of Taos, than could have been gained from forty-eight days in a Santa Fe jail. He would have spent at least one winter in Taos and perhaps a second if he was one of the nine left to await Philibert's return. Not only were they received most hospitably during those winters, but they also had the opportunity to establish contacts and relationships that would serve in the future.

NOTES

1. Foley and Rice, *The First Chouteaus*, 3.
2. Auguste Chouteau, *Narrative Fragment*, 3.
3. Thomas, *History of St. Louis County*, 19.
4. Quigley, *St. Louis*, npn.
5. Phillips, *The Fur Trade*, 2: 246.
6. Drumm, ed., *Glimpses of the Past*, Vol. 8, 1941.
7. Flint, *Recollections of the Last Ten Years in the Valley of the Mississippi*, 303, n1. On December 9,

1815, Sheriff John W. Thompson conducted a census that counted almost 2,000 inhabitants.

8. Irving, *Astoria*, 134.

9. *Ibid.*, 133.

10. Marriage record from Parish Register, St. Mary and Joseph Church, St. Louis, Mo., Carondelet Baptisms. I have been unable to identify Jean Baptiste Provost, the father, as there are so many with the same name both in St. Louis and Canada. He was not, however, the same Provost who accompanied Lisa on his 1812 expedition. From the Parish Register it appears that both he and his wife, Marie Vernet or Vermet, were both born in Prairie of the Magdeleine, Quebec, Canada.

11. Collett, *Index to St. Louis Cathedral and Carondelet Burials*. Interestingly, Anne was a much older sister of Marie Rose Salle dit Lajoie who became Etienne's wife in 1829.

12. SANM, II, Twitchell #2308, March 27, 1810.

13. *Ibid.*, Twitchell #2484, April 11, 1813.

14. Phillips, *The Fur Trade*, 2: 506.

15. Letter of Ezekiel Williams to the *Missouri Gazette*, August 7, 1816, published September 14, 1816. Following Williams' account strictly would place this event in 1813, not 1812; however, in recounting his adventure of that period he was more accurate as to detail than chronology.

16. Phillips, *The Fur Trade*, 2: 506.

17. *St. Louis Gazette*, July 29, 1815.

18. *Daily Missouri Democrat*, February 6, 1866, and Philibert family papers. His age was given as ninety-three in his 1866 obituary, and as ninety-one on his tombstone.

19. Ezekiel Williams' letter.

20. Janet Lecompte, "Antoine and Abraham Ledoux," 3: 174, 175 and "Pierre Lesperance," 6: 241, 242, in Hafen, ed., *Mountain Men and the Fur Trade*.

Among those mentioned by Lesperance were Bijou, Levanway (Joseph Livernois), Ledoux, Nolan, Duchesne, LaLande, Pierre Leroux, Antoine Leroux, Charles Beaubien, Manuel Alvarez, and Grenier.

21. Voelker, "Ezekiel Williams," 26.

22. Ezekiel Williams' letter.

23. Weber, *The Taos Trappers*, 45.

24. *St. Louis Gazette*, July 29, 1815.

25. There was no actual village of Taos. The village was San Fernando in the Taos Valley; however, it was popularly called Taos by the Americans.

26. Monroe, *Message from the President* (April 15, 1818), and "William Waldo-Recollections of a Septuagenarian," in Drumm, ed., *Glimpses of the Past*, 7: 78. Some of McKnight's party have been identified as James Baird (Beard), Samuel Chambers, Benjamin Shrive, Alfred Allen, Michael McDonough, William Mines, Peter Baum, Thomas Cook and Charles Miers.

27. *St. Louis Gazette*, July 29, 1815.

28. Near Pueblo, Colorado.

29. SANM II, Twitchell #2585, Governor's Diary of events between April and December, 1815.

30. *Ibid.*

31. *Ibid.*, Twitchell #2646, February 13, 1816.

32. "Journal of Jules deMun," September 10-November 30, in Jules deMun Family Papers.

33. Monroe, *Message from the President*, April 15, 1818; letter from Jules deMun to Governor William Clark.

34. Carter, *Territorial Papers of the United States*, 15: 85.

35. Monroe, *Message from the President*.

36. *Ibid.*

37. *Ibid.*

38. This letter is indexed in the SANM II, Twitchell #2639, Index of Correspondence, no. 1.135, January 1816, but the letter itself could not be found.

39. "Journal of Jules deMun," Feb. 27-April 8, 1816, 1.

40. Monroe, *Message from the President.*

41. *Ibid.*

42. *Ibid.*, also Weber, *The Taos Trappers*, 47.

43. Hafen, "Joseph Bisonnet dit Bijou," 9: 30, in Hafen, ed., *Mountain Men and the Fur Trade*, and Bell, *Journal of the S.H. Long Expedition*, 178.

44. SANM II, Twitchell #2953 and 2778, Service Records.

45. Monroe, *Message from the President.*

46. *Ibid.*

47. *Ibid.*

48. Dale Morgan described the deposition as a "bootless document."

49. Etienne Provost, Deposition of December 20, 1841. The National Archives.

50. Monroe, *Message from the President*, and "Journal of Jules deMun," in Jules deMun Family Papers.

51. Audubon, *Audubon in the West*, 46-47.

52. Morgan, in his *Jedediah Smith*, states (401 n18) that "Francois (LeClerc) who was born at St. Joseph, Michigan, November 17, 1795, has been regarded as most probably the partner of Provost."

CHAPTER FOUR
Return to Taos, 1822-1825

At dawn on a beautiful morning in early May a steamboat from New Orleans approached the raw town of St. Louis sprawling along the levee of the river. Its boilers had consumed firewood voraciously and the steamboat had completed its journey only by "making free with the fence rails of Judge Bent for fuel" as it passed his home below the town. From the river the town presented a cheerful appearance and the two largest houses in evidence were the stone homes of Auguste and Pierre Chouteau with wide verandas on three sides and gardens enclosed by stone walls. Along the river itself there were no buildings; the nearest stood atop the natural levee. There were a half dozen barges and Mackinaw boats moored along the river-bank.[1]

Aboard that May morning was Henry Shaw, whose observations on his arrival as a new resident provide a detailed description of the town. Shaw noted that the habits of the residents were orderly and moral and that their pastimes and amusements consisted of smoking pipes, playing cards, drinking coffee, and dancing parties in the winter. He also commented that only the young spoke English and that the "old fashioned" people of both sexes wore moccasins.

Timothy Flint arrived in St. Louis in 1816 and had his own views of the city's appearance in his *Recollections*:

St. Louis, as you approach it, shows, like all the other French towns in this region, to much the greatest advantage at a distance. The French mode of building, and the white coat of lime applied to the mud or rough stone walls, give them a beauty at a distance, which gives place to their native meanness when you inspect them from a nearer point of view. The town shows to very great advantage when seen from the opposite shore, in the American bottom. The site is naturally a most beautiful one, rising gradually from the shore to the summit of the bluff like an amphitheatre (p. 81-82).

It was to this St. Louis that Etienne Provost returned in 1817 and maintained his home here for the rest of his life, watching the growth of the city as the Gateway to the West.

In 1820 the census reported that the town had a population of 4,598. According to the *Missouri Gazette* for December 6, 1820, that number included 685 laborers, 470 mechanics, 92 persons engaged in commerce, 49 grocers and tavernkeepers (a grocer was a saloonkeeper in the parlance of the times), 106 clerks and agents in various businesses, 23 attorneys and counsellors at law, 15 practicing physicians and 317 foreigners.

Water for the town came principally from the Mississippi River and was described as "most wholesome and convenient." Sleds pulled by ponies hauled the barrels of water up to the town, where the mud was settled out of it in large earthen jars. The cost of a barrel was either a picayune (6 1/4 cents) or an esculin, or bit, (12 1/2 cents). No reason was given for the price differential, but it may have been for settled versus unsettled water.[2]

Following Provost's return to St. Louis after the failure of Chouteau and deMun in the southwest, there is no evidence to suggest what he did for the next few years. During those years the fur trade was still seeking stability and organization. The War of 1812 and the hostility of the Blackfoot Indians had driven the traders off the Upper Missouri, and the Spanish were an ominous presence in the southwest. Manuel Lisa's St. Louis Missouri Fur Co. had concentrated its efforts on the lower river in the vicinity of the Council Bluffs during the war. Following the war, there were no organized efforts of note other than Lisa's. He had promptly moved back to the upper river, aided this time by a Congress which had passed legislation prohibiting British fur companies from trading on American lands. He was further protected in his venture by the Convention of 1818, which had established the border between the United States and Canada as the 49th Parallel from the Lake of the Woods country to the Continental Divide.

Lisa's renewed success on the upper river, coupled with postwar prosperity and an increased demand for furs, prompted him to reorganize the company once more in 1819, establishing a four-year partnership led by himself. In 1820 Lisa died and leadership of the company fell to Joshua Pilcher, one of the partners of the reorganization.[3]

As an awareness of the wealth to be obtained through the fur trade in the western mountains grew in the settled lands, the newspapers of the day were quite outspoken in calling for the development of a company powerful enough to carry the trade to the "white capped mountains" and to the headwaters of the Missouri.[4] The *St. Louis Enquirer* went further, proposing a company that would reach well beyond the Rockies to the Columbia River in the Oregon territory, which the Convention of 1818 had placed under joint occupancy of the United States and Britain for ten years.[5]

The St. Louis merchants began to see the profit potential of the fur trade, and soon the mercantile firm of "Berthold and Chouteau, Merchants" was reorganized by the partners as "Berthold, Chouteau and Company, Fur Merchants." In 1823, Bernard Pratte, Sr., and John P. Cabanne became associated with the company, which was thereafter called B. Pratte & Co.[6] This company, through many changes over the years, dominated the St. Louis fur trade for many years and employed Etienne Provost for most of his time in the trade.

The renewed activity was initially directed toward the Upper Missouri and the mountain trade. The harsh treatment accorded the Chouteau-deMun party in 1817 and the awareness that other Americans still languished under Spanish arrest served for several years to cool the enthusiasm of the traders and trappers for expanding into the southwest. Before long, however, circumstances changed, and the opportunity arose to open up the New Mexican trade, heralding a resurgence of interest all along the American frontier. Etienne Provost was in the forefront of this movement to the southwest.

Attitudes toward foreigners and trading changed when Mexico achieved its independence from Spain in 1821. The Spanish had maintained a policy of isolation and insulation from the Americans along the northern frontier, with New Mexico serving as a buffer between the United States and the Spanish central government in Mexico. Foreign trade was discouraged and the foreign trader who attempted to break this isolation frequently suffered severe penalties.

Trapping in New Mexico in the early 1820's was conducted almost exclusively by Americans and French, but the record of names of American trappers of that era is scant, and with good reason. For those who wished to comply with the Mexican regulations, and thus submit themselves to the requisite taxes and duties on export of the furs, the licenses were issued in the name of a Mexican citizen and the American trapper's name appeared nowhere in the records. Others operated out of Taos and Santa Fe without license or authority. Quite simply, they were smugglers transporting their pelts to the United States by a variety of devious routes. They ranged over nearly half the American west, from California's central valley into Utah and Colorado on both sides of the Rockies, into Wyoming, and all along the Grand (Colorado), Green and Rio Grande rivers.[7]

Trapping was made difficult, but trading was encouraged; and William Becknell is credited with being the first trader from St. Louis to Santa Fe in 1821, and regarded as the founder of the Santa Fe Trail. He was warmly welcomed in New Mexico and made a considerable profit on the rapid sale of his goods. In that same year, others made the journey to Santa Fe: John McKnight (brother of the imprisoned Robert) and Thomas James, who set up a headquarters there.[8]

In 1822 William Becknell made a second trip to

Santa Fe; James Baird of McKnight's 1812 party had a company on the trail, as did Benjamin Cooper and the Robidoux brothers, probably with Etienne Provost as a member of their caravan. Another trader, Hugh Glenn, had as his chronicler Jacob Fowler, whose journal is of particular interest because it is the first record of passage over the trail along the Arkansas from Fort Smith, Arkansas, to present day Pueblo, Colorado, and of the Taos trail from Santa Fe to Pueblo. It also presents valuable insights into the character of Taos and its citizens in the early days of Mexican independence. But beyond the historical value there is a joy to be found just in reading Fowler's journal. His spelling and construction are highly original, his punctuation limited to dashes. Of his spelling, "Its entire originality, its effusive spontaneity, its infinite variety, will charm the reader while it puzzles him, and make the modern manufacturer of Dialect despair."[9]

On one occasion, while the company was camped on Huerfano Creek and temporarily under Fowler's command, the men were invited to an Indian camp. Fowler wrote, "we Ware In vited this day to Eat With one of the arrapoho Cheefs He Seet before us a dish of fat meat of Which We Eat plentifully We ware then asked if We new what kinds of meat We Ware Eating We told We did not He then Said it Wa[s] a dog telling us it [was] a great feest With the Indeans - and that He Invited us for that purpose."[10]

Fowler described the poverty of San Fernando de Taos and its residents as he saw it: "We heare found the people extremly poor. and Bread Stuff Coud not be head amongest them as the Said the grass hopers Head Eat up all their grain for the last two years and that the Head to Pack in all their grain about one Hunderd miles-for their own use-We found them Eaqually scarce of meet-We must Soon leave this Reeched place-"[11]

To illustrate the moral attitudes of the good citizens

of Taos, Fowler told the tale of his Negro servant, Paul, who had been invited with two others to the home of an absent Spanish captain by the captain's wife and two daughters. Fowler was not present but was informed by the other two of what happened:

it Is a Custom With the Spanierds When Interdused to Imbrace With a Close Huge - this Ceremoney So Imbareshed Pall and maid Him So Shaimed-the trap door threw Which the desended Into the Room being Shut down [for the Went In at the top of the House] there was no Poseble Way for Him to make His Escape-now the Haveing but one Beed in the House and that so Large as to be Cappeble of Holding the three Copple of poson-there Ware all to lodge to geather and the mother of the daughters being oldest had of Corse the ferst Chois of Bows. and took pall for Hir Chap takeing Hold of Him and drawing Him to the beed Side Sot Him down with Hir arms Round his Sholders. and gave Him a Kis from [?] Sliped Hir Hand down Into His Britches-but it Wold take amuch abeler Hand than mine to discribe palls feelings being naturly a little Relegous modest and Bashfull.[12]

According to Fowler's Paul made a successful escape as soon as opportunity permitted.

Fowler paints a descriptive picture of Taos in the early years of American activity there, and his observations and comments have been borne out by others writing of those years. Provost arrived in that Taos in the early 1820s.

Entering the Santa Fe trade during this time were the Robidoux brothers of St. Louis, with whose family Provost was to be associated for the next few years. Joseph was the eldest of six brothers and operated primarily in Missouri as the managing force within the family: Antoine and Louis were his field agents and first

brought the family caravans to Santa Fe in 1822.[13] The
family activity in the mountains may date even earlier,
for Antoine once said he had first gone to the Rocky
Mountains in 1820.[14] There is an undocumented story
that Provost and LeClerc were backed by Joseph Robidoux in their 1824 venture, and if such was the case,
then their association probably began before Robidoux
invested money in their venture. It seems reasonable to
assume that Provost was with the Robidoux brothers in
Santa Fe in 1822.

While the Santa Fe trade was capturing the imagination and support of eager traders, changes were
occurring in the trade on the Upper Missouri River that
were to have a profound effect on Provost. In 1821,
realizing that continued competition between the
Hudson's Bay Company and the Montreal-based British North West Company would bring greater harm
than good to either, the two Canadian fur giants
merged, thus placing the entire Canadian fur trade
under one monopoly. As a result, a number of former
Nor'west men found themselves unemployed. Some of
them now banded together to form a new company to
operate south of the Canadian border. Kenneth McK-
enzie, Joseph Renville, William Laidlaw, Honore Picotte, James Kipp, Daniel Lamont— all Canadians and
ex-Nor'westers— and two Americans, William Tilton
and S. S. Dudley, began to operate on the Upper
Missouri and Mississippi rivers. The new company was
generally known as the Columbia Fur Company, but
for official purposes took the name of Tilton and
Company.[15] The United States was no different in some
respects from Mexico in requiring that trading licenses
be granted only to American citizens. This accounts for
the use of Tilton's name. Little is known of Tilton
himself. The trader at the post of the Columbia Fur
Company at the Mandan village was named Tilton, and
was presumably the same man.[16]

With McKenzie at its head, the Columbia Fur Company established Fort Tecumseh at the mouth of the Teton River as its main post on the Missouri River and met with considerable success from the start. McKenzie was most capable and directed the fledgling company well in its competition with the St. Louis trading operations.

While the Columbians were busy establishing themselves on the upper river, Samuel Abbott came to St. Louis, representing John Jacob Astor, to establish the American Fur Company's (AFC) Western Department. Initially the St. Louis firm of Stone, Bostwick & Co. signed an agreement with the AFC to represent Astor's interests in the west; however, Astor was dissatisfied with that firm's performance and the contract with Bostwick was not renewed in 1826. Bernard Pratte & Co. then entered into an agreement with the company which lasted into the 1830s.[17] Shortly after this agreement was concluded, Provost began his long association with the AFC.

Provost was not involved in one very significant development in the burgeoning fur trade, the formation in 1822 of the William H. Ashley and Andrew Henry trading venture to the Upper Missouri. It was significant not only because Ashley's enterprise marked the real beginning of the fur trade in the mountains, but also because among his early recruits were names that became synonymous with the fur trade and the mountaineers. Among them were Jim Bridger, Thomas Fitzpatrick, Jedediah Smith, and Milton Sublette. Milton's older brother William joined the Ashley party later, in 1823.[18] Into the early twentieth century, historians persisted in placing Provost in the Ashley company of 1822. There is no evidence, however, to place him with Ashley; there is, in fact, no evidence of his presence anywhere on the Upper Missouri that year.

In the spring of 1823 Ashley launched another

expedition up the Missouri River, one destined to revise the course of the American fur trade. En route to the Upper Missouri by keelboat to join Henry and the men who had wintered with him in the mountains, Ashley's party had a run-in with the Arikara Indians. He lost a number of men and was forced to reevaluate his situation. Recognizing the impossibility of continuing upriver by boat, Ashley sent part of his men overland to the mountains under Jedediah Smith and thus initiated a route not dependent upon the Missouri River. From this innovation grew the rendezvous system that was so important in the fur trade until the late 1830s.

While Ashley was readying his 1823 expedition for the upper river, Provost and LeClerc were in Santa Fe. They had returned to St. Louis by mid-summer. The account ledgers of Chouteau and Sarpy contain an entry under "Cash: For Balance of Wages of the Following." Among the listed names is that of "Provost" who received $9.00 on July 8, 1823, indicating both his presence in St. Louis on that date and his employment in some capacity by the Chouteau interests.[19] The payment of wages does not necessarily establish where the work was performed. A letter from the U.S. Agent for Indian Affairs at Ft. Atkinson, Benjamin O'Fallon, implies that Provost was in Santa Fe in early 1823. O'Fallon wrote the Governor of Santa Fe on August 1, 1823, saying that he had been informed by "Majors Laclaire and Provost" that the authorities in New Mexico were seeking to make peace with the Indian nations that were constantly raiding the Mexican settlements and trade caravans. The essence of the message O'Fallon received through Provost and LeClerc was that the Mexican authorities sought the good services of the American government in facilitating this peace.[20]

In his classic work on the history of the American

fur trade, Hiram Martin Chittenden stated that Provost was an Ashley man and was sent by Andrew Henry in charge of a party that crossed South Pass in 1823.[21] This claim, repeated by many historians, cannot have been the case since Provost was in New Mexico in early 1823 and by July was in St. Louis, as noted by both the Chouteau account ledger entry of July 8 and O'Fallon's letter of August 1.

Accepted belief has Provost and LeClerc returning to the mountains by the fall of 1823 and launching a trapping expedition from Taos.[22] Although such might very well have been the case, since it is not known where Provost spent the winter of 1823-24, the belief is based on a false premise. It stems from a letter of Ceran St. Vrain in Taos to Bernard Pratte, Jr., in St. Louis. The text is dated April 27, 1824. However, on the envelope the date is written as "Touse 29th, 1825"; and a notation on the envelope reads, "Ceran St. Vrain, 27 April recu 10 Juin,1825."[23] St. Vrain wrote he was awaiting Provost's return from his hunt. Without noting the discrepancy of dates between the letter and the envelope, it could well appear that Provost and LeClerc were in the mountains in the winter of 1823-24.[24]

The attraction of the beaver in New Mexico's streams drew many trappers to New Mexico in the 1820s. Josiah Gregg estimated that in 1822-23 some 120 Americans took the trail to Santa Fe, many of whom were trappers.[25] By 1824 the beaver had been so depleted in the area surrounding Santa Fe that it became necessary to go farther afield in search of worthwhile streams. The trappers expanded into the Colorado and Green river basins, where they soon came into contact with Ashley's men working southward along the Green, and Hudson's Bay Company men from the Oregon Territory. By the end of 1824 there were at least six large parties operating out of Taos: Those of William Wolfskill, Thomas (later Peg-leg) Smith, William

Huddart, Antoine Robidoux, William Becknell, and Etienne Provost.[26]

Provost and his partner, LeClerc, were among those moving into the Great Basin in 1824, possibly with backing by Joseph Robidoux.[27] Several groups leaving New Mexico for the trapping grounds banded together, leaving Taos about the first of August in 1824. They traveled westward thirty days, covering about 700 miles; then they parted, each group going its separate way.[28]

Provost and LeClerc were probably not among this band; it is more likely they went north out of Taos along the Spanish Trail into the Great Basin.[29] Almost fifty years before, in 1776, the Spanish Franciscans Dominguez and Escalante, seeking a route from New Mexico to the California missions, had come north from Santa Fe, up the Dolores River into Colorado, across the Uncompahgre Plateau, and descended to the Green River, which they named the San Buenaventura, near present-day Jensen, Utah.[30] This trail offered a far more logical and direct route into the area of northeastern Utah where Provost and LeClerc headquartered. They also could have followed other northerly trails blazed by earlier Spanish traders along the same general course. They had a sizeable number of men with them, and it is possible that Antoine Robidoux accompanied them along their route to the Uintas, separating from them after arrival.[31]

Once they had reached the Green River area, Provost and LeClerc established their winter camp at the junction of the Green and White rivers. From their base camp, Provost and his men worked their way westward along the base of the Uinta Mountains and into the valley of the Great Salt Lake. There were two routes by which he could have come to the valley, both following the Duchesne River to the Strawberry River and up the Strawberry to its headwaters. From there he either crossed the rim and came down to the present Heber Valley, where he could cross the south end of the valley and pick up the Provo River, following it down to Utah Lake, or from the source of the Strawberry, he could cross the Wasatch to Center Creek Canyon and the Kamas Prairie to pick up the Weber River, and down the Weber to the Great Salt Lake. The latter route would have brought him directly to the shores of the Great Salt Lake, whereas the former would have brought him to Utah Lake, from whence he would have followed its outlet to the Great Salt Lake.

Provost had a good claim as the discoverer of that body of water, probably arriving on its shores a few weeks, if not a few months, before Jim Bridger. It may be more accurate to say he was most likely the discoverer of the lake from the American side of the fur trade, for it is quite possible that Donald McKenzie of the British North West Company saw the lake while trapping the Snake and Bear rivers in the years 1818 to 1822.[32]

In October 1824, along the narrow river winding northward from Utah Lake to the Great Salt Lake, Provost encountered a band of Snake (Shoshone) Indians and survived the ensuing fight that gave his name to the stream connecting the two lakes. The story is best told by Warren Angus Ferris in his narrative of his years in the mountains. Ferris was not in the mountains in 1824, but around the winter campfires he listened to the many tales of Provost's fight and included one in his journal:

There is one evil genius among them, called the "Bad Gocha," (mauvais gauche - bad left-handed one) who fell in with a party of trappers led by a well known mountaineer, Mr. E. Proveau, on a stream flowing into the Big Lake that now bears his name, several years since. He invited the whites to smoke the calumet of peace with

*them, but insisted that it was contrary to his medicine to
have any metallic near while smoking. Proveau, knowing the superstitious whims of the Indians, did not
hesitate to set aside his arms, and allow his men to
follow his example; they then formed a circle by sitting
indiscriminately in a ring and commenced the ceremony;
during which, at a prearranged signal, the Indians fell
upon them, and commenced their work of slaughter with
their knives, which they had concealed under their
robes and blankets. Proveau, a very athletic man, with
difficulty extricated himself from them, and with three or
four others, alike fortunate, succeeded in making his
escape; the remainder of the party of fifteen were all
massacred.*[33]

On the map of his travels Ferris identified "Proveau's
Fork" as the river named the Jordan by the Mormon
settlers. In his "Chronicles," George C. Yount wrote
that in 1829 when he was with St. Vrain they "reached
a stream at that time called 'Provo's Fork,' but which
the Mormons now call the 'Jordan'— It empties into the
Eutaus Lake— the Mormons call this lake by another
name." That is today the Great Salt Lake and Yount's
narrative identifies the area with Provost by name in
1829, just five years after his fight.[34]

The number of men with Provost and the number
killed varies with the teller; however, the most consistent number, and the one with perhaps the best
documentation, is eight men killed. William Gordon in
his 1831 report gave the figure as eight, as did Peter
Skene Ogden in the journal of his 1824-25 Snake River
expedition.[35] Ogden had the opportunity to learn first-
hand of Provost's fight, as did William H. Ashley, since
both men spent time with Provost within a few months
of the battle. In the draft copy of his letter of December
1825 to General Henry Atkinson, Ashley wrote, "a war
party of the Shoshone in Octr. 1824 met a party of ten

of our Citizens who had Crossed the Country from Taus and killed Eight of them."[36] When Provost and Ashley met in the early summer of 1825 and traveled together to the first rendezvous, the tale of the attack on his party was undoubtedly related in full detail to Ashley, including the number lost. Ashley's account of ten men with two survivors is at odds with Ferris's account; however, Ferris was relating a campfire tale learned some years later. Whatever accuracy it may lack, his story of the massacre is the only written record of that campfire tale passing among the mountaineers.

Peter Skene Ogden offers a probable reason for the attack on Provost. In a letter to his superiors of July 10, 1825, Ogden explained that the Hudson's Bay Company party of the previous year under Alexander Ross had stolen horses and furs from a band of Shoshone (Snake) Indians and in the ensuing skirmish killed one Indian. Provost and his party fell in with this same band of Indians shortly afterward and suffered their revenge.[37]

Following their escape from the Shoshone, Provost retreated to the established camp on the Green River where he holed up for the winter. The disastrous fall hunt had not only cost the lives of many of his men but also had been unsuccessful as a trapping venture.[38]

Antoine Robidoux was on the Green River during the fall of 1824, and at the same time, Ashley was setting out from St. Louis en route to the first rendezvous to be held in the mountains. In September a new license to trade with the Indians was issued to Ashley, and on October 20 he was at Fort Atkinson.[39] Ashley's path would cross Provost's, possibly for the first time, in the spring of 1825.

Ashley's expedition from Ft. Atkinson to the Green River was a long and difficult trip, with much suffering; they reached the Green River in April of 1825.[40] Upon arrival, Ashley divided his party into four groups, one

each under himself, Thomas Fitzpatrick, James Clyman, and Zacharias Ham. The other three were to lead
their brigades to trap the country while Ashley took his
brigade to explore the course of the Green. Before
heading downriver, Ashley gave instructions to his
brigade leaders about how he would mark the place
they were to meet prior to July tenth for the rendezvous.

Also in the mountains during that winter of 1824-
25 were William Becknell and Antoine Robidoux. Becknell had made a very late start from St. Louis, and he
and nine others in his party left Santa Cruz in early
November heading north into the Great Basin of the
Colorado.[41]   Once in the mountains he met several
groups of Indians, including, he later learned, those
who had attacked Provost the previous October. In the
five months before he returned to the Spanish settlements, Becknell did little but suffer every misery that
could be inflicted upon a man in the mountains in mid-
winter except robbery.

Sometime that winter Antoine Robidoux came across
Provost's party in its camp on the Green. What transpired there is not known, but when Robidoux came
into Taos in February of 1825, he was accompanied by
about twenty-five men of Provost's company.[42] Why
these men returned to Taos is a matter of conjecture.
Presumably they came for supplies to carry back to
Provost in the mountains. However, there is only one
piece of evidence indicating that any of the company
returned to the Green. Provost and LeClerc may have
ended their partnership that winter, for LeClerc was
probably with the group returning to Taos and he may
not have returned to the Green River.[43] However, Ceran
St. Vrain wrote a letter from Taos in April of 1825 in
which he said he was expecting Provost and LeClerc to
return to that town. If LeClerc had come in with
Robidoux in February and not returned to his partner,
it is inconceivable that St. Vrain was not aware of it.

In the spring of 1825 Provost again set his feet westward with about a dozen men and trapped along the streams of the Uinta Basin. As before, he worked up the Strawberry River to its head and crossed over into Center Creek Canyon and Kamas Prairie. There he picked up the Weber River, following it through present Weber Canyon toward the valley of the Great Salt Lake.

While Provost was working his way west and north, Peter Skene Ogden was moving southward with his Snake River expedition. Annually the Company sent a party to the Snake River country to trap and trade. Ogden was an experienced trader and a former Nor'wester who had remained after the merger of 1821 and had been appointed to succeed Alexander Ross as the leader of the 1825 expedition. He had been accompanied to the Snake by the party of Jedediah Smith, who had been into the Oregon Territory the previous year and was now returning to meet Ashley on the Green River.[44]

Just as Ogden was breaking camp on the morning of Sunday, May 22, 1825, one of his trappers came into camp with two former Hudson's Bay men who had deserted from Flathead Post three years earlier. From them he learned of a party of about thirty nearby, "fitted out by the Spainerds & Traders on the Missouri." To his surprise and consternation, he also learned he was then but fifteen days' journey from Taos.[45] On that morning Ogden was camped near present Huntsville, Utah, on a river he named the New River because it appeared to him that no white men had yet set foot in that valley. (The area today is the Ogden Valley and the river is the Ogden River.) On that same day Ogden moved his party over hilly country about ten miles, coming to what he again called the New River, where he made camp. Ogden apparently called the river by the same name because the two streams join prior to reaching the Great Salt Lake. Today that second river is the Weber River and the camp Ogden set up was just west of present Mountain Green, Utah, where in 1983 there still remained a large grove of cottonwoods in a wide meadow that invited a camp.

Early the next morning, "a party of 15 men Canadians and Spainards headed by one Provost & Francois one of our deserters arrived."[46] William Kittson, a clerk of the Hudson's Bay Company and Ogden's lieutenant on his 1824-25 expedition, wrote that in Provost's party were three Canadians, a Russian, and an old Spaniard.[47] It was Kittson who named the campsite "Deserter Point," in recognition of events resulting from the visit to their camp by some of Ashley's men later that day.

The tranquility of the camp was broken by the arrival of the brash, aggressive Johnson Gardner with twenty-five other Ashley men and fourteen of Ogden's trappers. Unfortunately, as a result of the tumult caused by Gardner's undoubtedly dramatic entrance, Ogden made no further mention of Provost or of anything that transpired during their meeting. Gardner, who had arrived flying a flag, insisted that Ogden's party was on American soil and therefore all of Ogden's men were under no further obligation to the Hudson's Bay Company. He offered to buy beaver pelts at $3.50 a pound and to sell goods cheaply to the Hudson's Bay trappers. Gardner was a member of the party headed by John H. Weber, an Ashley lieutenant. Weber was not in the group confronting Ogden, nor was Jed Smith or Bill Sublette, who were most likely at the main Weber camp by this time.[48]

Gardner's pronouncements on the afternoon of his arrival were loud and insulting, but it was not until the next morning that he made the more serious challenge. He raised the question of territorial sovereignty again, to which Ogden replied that the sovereignty of Oregon had not yet been determined. Gardner proclaimed that

Ogden was infringing upon American territory and demanded that he withdraw immediately. Ogden was equally adamant that he would not withdraw without instructions from his company. What had long been a "cold war" over occupancy of the Oregon Territory very nearly became a shooting war because of Gardner's belligerence toward the British party.[49] But the greatest problem Ogden faced was the threat to the integrity and safety of his camp. Gardner insisted that since the company was on American soil there were no demands that Ogden could make upon his men and he encouraged them to desert the Hudson's Bay Company. Several of Ogden's Iroquois Indian and French trappers did desert to the Gardner camp, taking their furs with them. Ogden had harsh words with both Gardner and one of his own men, John Grey, a half-Iroquois, half-American Hudson's Bay employee who incited his Iroquois cohorts to desert with all their possessions. Ogden and Kittson promptly seized the property of men still absent from camp and the horses that had been loaned to the Iroquois. A momentary confrontation occurred; then Gardner backed down after seeing Ogden's determination, settling for a final barrage of insults heaped on Ogden.

During the night Ogden received word that his camp was to be attacked in the morning. When morning came and Gardner saw that Ogden was prepared for him, no fighting broke out. Ogden retreated to Flathead Post, not for fear of a fight with the Americans, but because of the loss of men and furs going to the American camp and his fear of additional desertions if he remained.[50]

If one considers the true soveriegn boundaries and the location of the ground on which the confrontation occurred, the bystander Etienne Provost was the only one of the three leaders legitimately operating in his own territory. At that spot on the Weber River, they

were all below the 42nd Parallel and in Mexican territory. If Provost was operating with a license from the
Mexican government, and there is no evidence to
indicate that he was, he was in his own trapping area
and the others were trespassers. By the Adams-Onis
Treaty of 1819 the United States and Spain had settled
the boundary between the Louisiana Purchase and
Spanish territory at the 42nd Parallel, the present
southern boundary of Idaho.

As the British were not a party to the Adams-Onis
Treaty, they felt no constraint about operating below
the 42nd Parallel. In that sense, Ogden had more right
to be where he was on the Weber River than did
Gardner or any of Ashley's men. Beyond the Continental Divide, in that vast land known as the Oregon
Territory, joint occupancy by England and the United
States had been the agreed rule since 1818.[51] The
Russian claims to coastal territory below 54 degrees,
40 minutes had been dually ceded to the United States
in 1824 and to the British in 1825; thus both nations
felt they had equal claim to the lands of the northwest.
However, the American territorial claim was bounded
on the south by the terms of the Adams-Onis Treaty,
whereas the British interest was not.

Ogden was quite sensibly occupied with his own
troubles and made no further mention of his visitors
from Taos. We may presume that Provost took his men
up the Weber, trapping as they went, and back toward
the Green River by the same route over which they had
come. Perhaps he had an arrangement with his partner
and was expecting to find the men who had gone to Taos
awaiting him on the Green with supplies.

Instead he found William H. Ashley. Ashley's exploration of the Green River had become something of a
disaster, and he had come close to losing his life when
his boat encountered rough water. Ashley related in his
diary how, when he perceived his boat was in difficulty,

Indians Attacking Fur Boats

he gave instructions that succeeded in bringing it through the roughest part intact but filled with water.[52]

Shortly thereafter Ashley laid over to hunt meat, having met two members of Provost's party on the Green River who informed him that the country downriver was almost devoid of game. In their meeting with Ashley, the Provost men told him they were part of a group of twenty or thirty who had come into the area from Taos.[53] The record of this meeting is Ashley's first mention of Provost's party. The day after the meeting, Ashley cached the greater part of his goods and continued downriver, on the twenty-first passing the mouth of the White River, "the wintering place of Mess. Provo &c," as he noted. There he found a note for Provost's hunters directing them to drop downriver six miles where they would find "Mr. La clare" with supplies. Ashley continued downriver but failed to find LeClerc or any members of Provost's party. While there is no additional evidence, this note suggests that LeClerc did return from Taos to the camp on the Green with the supplies. Ashley made another cache here and sought Indians from whom he could obtain horses for overland travel. He was able to trade for only five horses, two from a band of Indians and three more from a group of "6 Frenchmen" encountered on his way.

With only the five horses, Ashley began to ascend the "Euwinty" River, according to his diary, on June 1, 1825.[54] On June 7, in the vicinity of Red Creek, near present-day Fruitland, Utah, he "met Mr. Provo and party consisting of 12 men."[55] Provost told him the location of Weber's winter quarters.[56] He also undoubtedly told Ashley then of his meeting with Ogden, of the incident with Gardner, and of his fight with the Indians the previous fall.

Provost would have learned of Ashley's presence in the mountains and of the rendezvous plans from members of Gardner's party two weeks previously. In his diary, Ashley wrote that Provost had "heard of my being in the Country that he had gone over to green river in search of me" (entry of June 7). If he was aware that Ashley was exploring the Green River, he might have realized that Ashley would have to leave the river and travel overland to reach his designated rendezvous. With this in mind, and with his already extensive knowledge of the country, he might have planned to help Ashley and at the same time find both a purchaser for his furs and a supplier for his party. Aside from the note found by Ashley, no further mention of LeClerc has been located. There is no evidence that he, or any others of the company, returned to the Green, as apparently agreed. The note that Ashley found indicated that members of Provost's party awaited him on the Green, yet Ashley's diary contains no indication that Provost even mentioned them. Perhaps Provost did not expect LeClerc or anyone on the Green, the note notwithstanding; that with the departure in February of the twenty-five men who accompanied Antoine Robidoux to Taos the partnership with Leclerc was ended. But if so, why was St. Vrain expecting both men in Taos?

Ashley persuaded Provost to go to the Green River to recover his cached goods, then set up his own camp on the river and waited seven days until Provost returned on the afternoon of June 14. What trade arrangements might have been discussed Ashley did not reveal in his journal, but he did engage Provost to guide his brigade to the rendezvous site, and on the next day the combined parties set out westward, following the route Provost had already traversed at least twice within the past year. On June 16 they camped near the headwaters of the Strawberry, and on the following day they crossed over the Wasatch and followed Center Creek Canyon to the Kamas Prairie and the Weber River.[57] Provost was retracing his route of less than a month earlier. He left Ashley on the upper Weber River briefly, continuing alone down the river to trade for a day or two with the "Euteaw" Indians. Perhaps that had been his destination when he encountered Ogden. Ashley did not note the day Provost left the party to engage in his trading venture, but it was probably June 20.

Ashley, meanwhile, was searching for Johnson Gardner and no wonder, for Provost had no doubt informed Ashley that in the aftermath of the incident with Ogden, twenty-three of Ogden's men had deserted, taking with them 700 beaver pelts.[58] Ashley learned that Gardner had already passed eastward beyond his camp on the Weber, so he rested his horses for a day and then set out after Gardner's party on June 23. Provost had returned to camp on the night of June 21, and the entire company was now headed eastward toward the rendezvous site. They journeyed up Chalk Creek to the Bear River, then down the Bear until they could turn east again to the Big Muddy. They followed down that river in a southerly direction to the point where it made a bend to the east. Here they turned southwest to Henry's Fork of the Green.[59] At this point they were about sixty air miles from the rendezvous site designated by Ashley. They traveled down Henry's Fork, probably arriving at the rendezvous on June 30.[60] Ashley's diary ended on June 27, so his travel time and arrival at rendezvous must be estimated. The rendezvous was on Henry's Fork, about twenty miles from its confluence with the Green River, with an ample supply of both forage for the horses and water for all.[61]

Ashley opened the rendezvous on July 1. A total of 120 men were there, comprising all of his men and other mountaineers who had heard of the gathering. That July day in 1825 signaled the opening of an era, the beginning of the rendezvous system that allowed the trappers to sell their catch and still remain in the mountains all year. Hereafter they came to the great annual gathering for several weeks of release from the never-ending watchfulness of life in the mountains. A chance to visit and drink with old friends, to learn who had, and who had not, "gone under." It was the time to sell their year's catch of pelts and to resupply for the coming year before tying on the west's biggest bender. Although all future rendezvous were legendary binges, this first one was actually quite decorous as there was no alcohol at the gathering.[62] The demand assured that such an oversight would not occur again, but the July rendezvous of 1825 was a fearful dry.

This rendezvous was also unique for its brevity: the actual trading lasted only one day. Ashley was paying his own men $3.00 per pound for pelts; however, he bought Provost's beaver at only $2.50 a pound. No reason was given for the lower price paid Provost, although most likely the pelts were of inferior quality. Provost and his men spent part of their earnings on coffee, sugar, ribbon, cloth, fishhooks, and other sundry items.[63]

On the next day Ashley gathered up his accumulated furs and started homeward with fifty men, half of whom were to accompany him only as far as the Big Horn River. There he could make bull boats and float his catch downriver. The escort would then return with the horses and spend the winter trapping in the mountains. On arriving at the mouth of the Yellowstone he encountered General Henry Atkinson and Major Benjamin O'Fallon with their military escort. They were on a mission up the Missouri to conclude treaties with the various Indian tribes living along the Missouri. General Atkinson offered Ashley the benefit of an escort downriver, which offer Ashley graciously accepted. (There has been some speculation that Ashley had planned this encounter from the beginning.)

Back on Henry's Fork the mountaineers would not

have been overly eager to break up this first mountain social, for it was far too early to begin the fall hunt, and certainly the opportunity for such a convivial gathering would not come again before at least the winter camp. Then many of them would gather to spend the coldest winter months in as comfortable a spot as could be found. A favorite wintering ground was in the Willow Valley as it was then called, renamed Cache Valley within a year or two and still known by that name today. There was no need for Provost to return to Taos, since he had traded with Ashley for his needs, and he well might have remained to enjoy the sociability on Henry's Fork.

Later, with winter upon them, the trappers did go first to Willow Valley; however, the weather turned so bitterly cold, the snow was so deep, and the winds so severe that it became necessary to move to a more comfortable location. In mid-December the entire winter camp moved down to the Salt Lake Valley.[64] Provost is not mentioned in the accounts of this winter experience, and limited evidence indicates that he returned to the area of Utah Lake where he set up his own winter quarters and a trading post.

NOTES

1. *Gateway Heritage*, Summer, 1984, vol. 5, no. 1:3 and "Henry Shaw's reminiscenses of St. Louis," Henry Shaw papers, Missouri Botanical Garden Archives. Shaw arrived in St. Louis on May 4, 1819.

2. Shaw, "Henry Shaw's reminiscenses of St. Louis."

3. Sunder, *Joshua Pilcher*, 29-30.

4. Dale Morgan typescript from *Niles Register*, 12: 348 (July 26, 1817), Morgan Collection, Utah State Historical Society.

5. *Niles Register*, 15: 182 (November 7, 1818). The Anglo-American Convention of 1818 failed to settle the

question of the Canadian-American boundary beyond the Continental Divide. It decreed joint occupancy of the lands west of the Divide for a period of ten years, following which the matter would be again discussed.

6. Scharf, *St. Louis City and County*, 1: 183, and, Pratte, "The Reminiscences of General Bernard Pratte, Jr.", from *The Missouri Republican*, in the *Missouri Historical Society Quarterly* (October, 1949).

7. Yount, *Chronicles of the West*, 2.

8. Weber, *The Taos Trappers*, 54.

9. *The Journal of Jacob Fowler*, xvi.

10. *Ibid.*, 68.

11. *Ibid.*, 105.

12. *Ibid.*, 107-8.

13. Robidoux, *Memorial to the Robidoux Brothers*.

14. Letter of Dale L. Morgan to Charles Kelly (May 24, 1948) in which Morgan quotes from the journal of Joseph L. Heywood, reporting an 1856 conversation between Heywood and "Antwine Rubido."

15. Mattison, "Fort Union," 8 and Gray, John S., "Honore Picotte, Fur Trader." *South Dakota History*, 6:2, 188. Gray states that in 1822 McKenzie, Laidlaw and Lamont became naturalized citizens. Tilton and Dudley obtained the trading license for the new company from William Clark, the Indian Superintendent at St. Louis.

16. Morgan, *Jedediah Smith*, 103.

17. Chittenden, *American Fur Trade of the Far West*, 1: 320-22,

18. Sunder, *Bill Sublette, Mountain Man*, 35.

19. Chouteau and Sharpy Ledger C, Folio 42, Chouteau Collection.

20. Covington, "Correspondence between Mexican Officials." It would be most interesting to know when, and for what reason, the military titles were given to Provost and LeClerc.

21. Chittenden, *American Fur Trade of the Far West*,

1: 271.

22. Morgan, *Jedediah Smith*, 147; and Hafen, *Old Spanish Trail*, 197.

23. Chouteau-Papin Collection, MHS.

24. Morgan later noted the correction in his *The West of William H. Ashley.*

25. Weber, *The Taos Trappers*, 58.

26. Wishart, *The Fur Trade of the American West*, 127-8; and, Weber, *The Taos Trappers*, 79.

27. *Anderson Journals*, 343.

28. Testimony of Augustus A. Storrs, Senate Document 7, 18th Congress, 2nd Session, 1825.

29. Weber, *The Taos Trappers*, 75.

30. Eddy, *et al.*, *Archeological Mitigation*, 24; and Cline Collection.

31. Weber, *The Taos Trappers*, 75.

32. Ross, *The Fur Hunters of the Far West*, 135, 152-53.

33. Ferris, *Life in the Rocky Mountains*, 308-9.

34. Jensen, in his *History of Provo, Utah*, 29, wrote that later the sight of Provost's fight was known as "Provost's Hole or Hollow," although no other documentation of this has been found.

35. Message from the President, Senate Executive Document 90, 29; and, Ogden, *Ogden's Snake Country Journals 1824-25 and 1825-26*, 50.

36. Morgan, "A New Ashley Document," 87.

37. Hafen, "Etienne Provost," in Hafen, ed., *Mountain Men and the Fur Trade*, 6: 374.

38. Ogden, *Ogden's Snake Country Journals 1824-25 and 1825-26*, 49.

39. Morgan, *The West of William H. Ashley*, 98.

40. Morgan, *Jedediah Smith*, 158-61.

41. Becknell, "Journals."

42. Eddy, *et al.*, *The Archeological Mitigation Program*, 29.

43. Weber, *The Taos Trappers*, 76; and, Morgan, *The*

West of William H. Ashley, 279, n151. In September of 1825 one Francois LeClerc was in St. Louis where, with his brother Antoine, he was engaged in settleing his father's estate.

44. Miller, "Peter Skene Ogden's Journal of His Expedition to Utah, 1825,: 173.

45. *Ibid,* 179.

46. Ogden, *Peter Skene Ogden's Snake Country Journals 1824-25 and 1825-26,* 51.

47. Kittson's Diary in *Ogden's Snake Country Journals 1824-26,* 233.

48. Morgan, *Jedediah Smith,* 148.

49. Miller, "Peter Skene Ogden's Journal of His Expedition to Utah, 1825," 181-2.

50. Carl Russell, "Rendezvous Period," 8. John McLoughlin wrote to Governor George Simpson on March 20, 1846, regarding the Ogden incident of twenty-one years earlier: "When you and I came in 1824 you recollect that we sent Mr. Ogden (to the Snake River) with the result that his men left him and joined the Americans. We could not ascertain how the business was managed or the cause of the misconduct of the Snake men, but we believed as was told us it proceeded from their bad disposition. I ordered the books to be brought to Ft. George and saw it proceeded from the bad system in which the business was carried on and charging exorbitant prices for the supplies to the men."

51. Sunder, *Joshua Pilcher,* 32.

52. Ashley "Diary" entry for May 14, 1825: Once through the worst and in an eddy, "two of the most active men then leaped into the water took the cables and towed her to land just as from all appearance she was about making her exit and me with her for I cannot swim & my only hope was that the boat would not sink."

This occurred in "the Suck," as it was called by Jim Beckwourth. Much of what Beckwourth said of events is true; it is his claim to be the hero of all these magnificent exploits that shatters reality. In this instance, Beckwourth claimed to be the one who, heedless of his own safety, dove into the raging torrent to heroically save his expedition leader from certain death. The truth is that at the time he was at least 150 miles away and on the other side of the mountains with James Clyman's brigade of trappers.

53. Ashley, "Diary," entry for May 17, 1825.

54. The Duchesne River, which flows into the Green from the west. In his diary Ashley has two "June 1" entries and none for May 31. From the context it would appear that he actually started up the Duchesne on May 31.

55. Ashley, "Diary."

56. In *The West of William H. Ashley*, 284, n182, Morgan identified this as the Cub River.

57. Ashley "Diary," entry for June 19, 1825.

58. Morgan, *The West of William H. Ashley*, 286 n. 195.

59. Gowans, *Rocky Mountain Rendezvous*, 10.

60. Morgan, *The West of William H. Ashley*, 288 n. 205.

61. Gowans, *Rocky Mountain Rendezvous*, 12.

62. Morgan, *Jedediah Smith*, 171, and transcribed remarks of Dr. Fred R. Gowans to the Utah Westerners on the site of the Green River Rendezvous in July, 1984.

63. Morgan, *The West of William H. Ashley*, 119.

64. Sunder, *Bill Sublette, Mountain Man*, 62.

CHAPTER FIVE
The American Fur Company, 1826-1829

After the rendezvous the mountaineers readied for the fall hunt. Ashley's men returned to the territory most familiar to them north of the towering range of the Uinta Mountains stretching east to west just below the present Utah-Wyoming border, and they came to their wintering ground in the Willow Valley as the streams froze and the beaver trapping ended until the spring thaw.

Provost returned to the land most familiar to him as well, south of the mighty Uintas in the Uinta Basin and along the shores of the two lakes at the western edge of the Wasatch Range. There he either built, or returned to, two trading posts near the lakes. One was on the Timpanogos River[1] near its mouth on Utah Lake, and the other on the Jordan River between the two lakes, probably closer to the site of Salt Lake City[2]. Provost built these posts either in 1824 before his run-in with the Shoshone or after the rendezvous of 1825. He had no time for such an undertaking between winter quarters of 1824-25 and the rendezvous of 1825, since he was fully occupied in the mountains, meeting first Ogden and then Ashley, and guiding Ashley to the rendezvous.

Where he wandered in the year following the rendezvous has never been determined, but he had no reason to return to his old winter camp on the Green River. He had his remaining men with him, and his partnership with LeClerc seems to have been dissolved, so there was nothing to prevent his remaining in the vicinity of the lakes to operate his trading posts. These were not permanent structures like the river forts of the American Fur Company; they were temporary structures used solely to carry on trade and abandoned when the trader moved on. The Shoshones camped along the shores of the lakes long before the white men ever ventured into their domains, and Provost would have welcomed the opportunity to trade with them.

Provost's posts in the valleys may account for the never-documented stories of "Ashley's Fort" on the shore of Utah Lake.[3] Ashley himself never saw either of the valley lakes and no evidence has ever been uncovered that Ashley caused such a post to be built.

While Provost was operating in the Uinta Basin and along the lakes in 1825, his name was invoked in both Taos and St. Louis; he was beginning to enjoy a reputation in the fur trade. He had been expected in New Mexico during the winter of 1825. Perhaps he was aware that the market in Santa Fe was in the doldrums, for he never appeared there. Every village was filled with unsold, and nearly unsalable, merchandise.[4] By 1824 the area had been saturated by the trade coming over the Santa Fe Trail from St. Louis, as Provost could have known before he headed into the Great Basin country. Or perhaps he had no desire to be taxed on his furs, as he certainly would have been had he turned up in Taos with furs for the St. Louis market.

Ceran St. Vrain was waiting for Provost in Santa Fe. St. Vrain and Francois Guerin had left St. Louis for Santa Fe as partners in a trading venture in November of 1824 and arrived in March of 1825. B. Pratte & Company owned a one-third interest in St. Vrain's venture, having supplied the partners in hopes of cornering the Santa Fe fur trade, but after arrival their partnership dissolved and Guerin returned to St. Louis with a letter from St. Vrain to B. Pratte explaining only that "Guerin and myself have dissolved partnership for reasons too teajus to mention" and that Guerin would advise Pratte of all the details.[5]

St. Vrain's letter has caused some confusion because of a discrepancy between the dating of the letter and its envelope. The letter is dated "April 27, 1824"; however, the outer wrapper, or envelope, bears the date "Touse 29th 1825." A notation by a clerk in Pratte's office reads "Ceran St. Vrain 27 April recu 10 Juin 1825." Clearly the letter was written in 1825. St. Vrain reflected upon the lack of commercial opportunity in that year:

It is now thirty seven days since we have arrived and we have sold but verry fue goods and goods is at a verry redused price at present. I am in hopes that when the hunters comes in from there hunt that I will sell out to Provoe and LeClere. If I do not succeed to sel out to them and other hunters, my intention is to buy up goods and articles that (illegible) the market of Sonora to purchase

*mules but I shall FIRST doe all I can to make arrange-
ments with Provoe and LeClere to furnish them with
goods.*

Jean P. Cabanne also mentioned Provost in a letter
to Pierre Chouteau, Jr., in November of 1824. The letter
reiterated Cabanne's frequently voiced conviction that
the company must move into the mountains to continue to be successful in the fur trade. His letter,
written from his post at the Council Bluffs, noted the
recent passage of William H. Ashley's company. However, Cabanne misread Ashley's intent and was convinced that he was headed for Taos intending to seek
exclusive rights to trap in Mexican territory. Cabanne
therefore proposed a similar move, "if events require,"
and stated his own intent to obtain sufficient merchandise and a cadre of hunters and engages "in case of an
arrangement with Provost, Leclerc or Bierd."[6]

Mention of Provost and LeClerc by both St. Vrain
and Cabanne confirms that the two men were well
known in St. Louis. No further identification or expla-
nation was necessary for either Pratte or Chouteau.
That recognition implies more extensive experience
than only the trapping expedition of 1824; it lends
support to the argument that Provost was involved in
the Santa Fe trade at least as early as 1822.

Ashley returned from the first rendezvous with
8,829 pounds of beaver fur, fully committed to the idea
of a summer rendezvous in the mountains.[7] With the
next year already in mind, twenty-six days after reaching St. Louis in early October Ashley sent Jedediah
Smith back to the mountains with $20,000 in goods.
Smith was a partner of Ashley by then, Andrew Henry
having left the partnership in 1824, after the disastrous year of 1823. With Smith were Robert Campbell,
who was entering the trade this year, Louis Vasquez,
Jim Beckwourth, and Hiram Scott.[8] With Ashley's de-

velopment of the rendezvous system, Taos declined in importance for the traders in the mountains of Utah and Wyoming. Though it was a closer supply point than St. Louis, it could not compete with a caravan bringing the supplies to the hunters.

As the weather moderated in the spring of 1826 and Jed Smith was working his way westward along the Platte River, Provost once more set his traps along the streams of the Uinta Basin. North of the Uinta Range lay the more open Green River Basin, its myriad streams trapped by the Ashley forces. The 1826 summer rendezvous had been set for the south part of the Cache Valley, about five miles from the confluence of the Logan River and Blacksmith's Fork, near present Hyrum, Utah.[9]

Although circumstances suggest that Provost probably was not at the 1826 rendezvous, his presence is a matter of some legitimate speculation. Jim Beckwourth places him there; but Beckwourth was not one to let accuracy get in the way of a good story, and a close examination of his narrative discloses that he has combined events of the rendezvous of 1826, 1827, and 1828 in one lengthy narrative. The heroic tale in which he included Provost actually occurred at the 1828 rendezvous on Bear Lake, where Provost was promoting the interests of his new employer, the American Fur Company. Nothing, Beckwourth's story aside, indicates his presence in 1826. Ashley was there, as were about one hundred trappers, probably no more than half of them Ashley men.

The major event of the 1826 rendezvous was the sale of the partnership of Ashley and Smith to a newly formed partnership of Jed Smith, William Sublette and David Jackson, to be known as Smith, Jackson and Sublette.

This partnership, and its lineal descendants, would be the primary opposition to the American Fur Com-

pany for the next nine years. The actual sale did not
take place at the rendezvous but shortly after at a
meeting between the principals held on the Bear River.[10]
Ashley felt no attachment to the mountains. He had
entered the fur trade and endured the many hardships
imposed upon him for only one reason, to achieve
financial independence which would permit him to
pursue his real interests: "the State of Missouri, its
gentilities of the drawing room and the fox hunt, its
urbane savageries of politics and business."[11]

Accounts of these early years of the fur trade
contained several misconceptions about Provost which
have gained general acceptance. Among them was the
story promulgated by Chittenden that Provost and
Ashley had a falling out at the rendezvous of 1826,
possibly because Provost had not been included in the
new business arrangement, and he thereafter bore an
unrelenting grudge against Ashley. According to Chittenden, Provost hastened to St. Louis to make an offer
to the Chouteau interests for a joint venture to supply
the rendezvous of 1827 in a deliberate effort to under-
cut Ashley. Ashley, however, made a similar overture
on his return to St. Louis and his proposal was the one
accepted. Ashley thereby eliminated Provost as competition and thus forced his acceptance of employment
with the Pratte, Chouteau interests, where he remained as an employee for the rest of his life.[12] Chittenden's erroneous conclusions were picked up by other
historians of the early twentieth century and com-
pounded by repetition. Since it is does not appear that
Provost was even at the 1826 rendezvous, it would have
been impossible for them to have had that falling out.

Ashley did seek a trade agreement with B. Pratte
and Company on his return to St. Louis. The evidence
does not indicate that Provost sought a similar agreement. When Ashley returned to St. Louis in the fall of
1826, he hoped his financial success would relieve him

of the need to ever again make the trip to the mountains. He was now in a position to make a purely financial investment in the mountain trade, thereby sharing the risks and the profits of the supply caravan without further risk to his own hide. It was with this in mind that he approached B. Pratte and Co. in October of 1826, offering a one-half interest in the supply caravan to the 1827 rendezvous. The negotiations continued for some months, and Ashley expressed his exasperation in his correspondence with Chouteau and Pratte. Perhaps he was unaware of the new developments within B. Pratte and Co. Perhaps Pratte and Chouteau were delaying their response to Ashley until the new agreements affecting their company were firmed up.

B. Pratte and Co. was about to take a pivotal role in the future of the western fur trade, a role which would greatly affect Provost's career as well. In December of 1826 the company agreed to serve as the sole western agent for the American Fur Company, and was thereafter known as the Western Department of the American Fur Company. The agreement between these two companies had its origins the previous year with the marriage of Ramsay Crooks, Astor's chief lieutenant, to Bernard Pratte's daughter Emilie.[13] Thus Astor became a supplier for one of his two greatest rivals in the fur trade, the other being the Columbia Fur Company operating on the upper Missouri.

While Ashley, Pratte, and Chouteau were still seeking an accord, a search began to find a leader for the next expedition. Ashley had suggested Auguste Chouteau, of the Chouteau-deMun venture, as the caravan's leader. Chouteau declined the offer. Instead, in a letter from his post on the Ver de Gris, Chouteau suggested "Ligueste" and "Millicoure" if the principals would have them.[14] Chouteau added that, "Ligueste speaks to me of Quenon Provot, of having him as

engage or to give him an interest."[15] Perhaps Chouteau
meant "Etienne" rather than "Quenon," yet one would
think that having shared two years on the trail and a
Spanish prison with him, Chouteau would have known
the name. Or perhaps it was Ligueste who had the
name wrong and Chouteau did not realize the error. In
any case, Chouteau's recommendations were not accepted.

One of the most intriguing comments about Provost
in his lifetime was made by Bartholomew Berthold, a
partner of B. Pratte and Co., in a letter to Jean P.
Cabanne during this time. In response to Cabanne's
inquiry seeking his opinion of the proposed venture
with Ashley, Berthold wrote:

*I cannot hazard an opinion of the project with Ashley,
yet it seems to me we would be well advised to assure
ourselves of Provot, who is the soul of the hunters of the
mountains-he will do us harm, and if only to prevent his
reunion with the Robidoux, it seems necessary to me to
make sure of him.*[16]

The reference to "the Robidoux" is plural, indicating
Berthold was thinking not merely of Joseph, but of all
the brothers. This remarkable statement certainly indicates the high regard in which Provost was held
among the fur trade leaders, and it gives additional
credence to the idea that Provost was very active in the
Santa Fe trade from its inception. Certainly he was a
power to be reckoned with if, by joining the competition, he could do harm to the strongest fur company
then on the western frontier.

Ashley and B. Pratte and Co. came to an agreement,
and the caravan headed out in the spring of 1827 under
the leadership of James Bruffee and Hiram Scott.[17]
Scott's tragic death on the return to St. Louis lent his
name to Scotts Bluff on the North Platte River. Scott

became severely ill on the return trip, and was left by the main party in the care of others until he either recovered or died. The party rejoined the main group, reporting Scott's death; however, the next year a skeleton was found well away from where Scott had allegedly died, giving sway to the belief that he had been abandoned while still alive, and had tried to crawl to some destination before death overtook him.

Provost seems to have been in St. Louis in 1827, thus missing the rendezvous held that year at the south end of Bear Lake in present-day Utah.[18] A small cannon in Ashley's caravan gained distinction as the first wheeled vehicle to cross South Pass. The cannon was fired to honor Jedediah Smith on his arrival from his first venture into California, and surely it was fired many other times in exuberant celebration and to impress the Indians present.

The mountaineer at rendezvous was a unique sight, recorded so ably in Alfred Jacob Miller's portrayals of the Indians, mountaineers, and scenes of the camp and rendezvous. In a similar vein, George Frederick Ruxton, in his *Life in the Far West*, presents a verbal portrait of the mountaineer: "The elder of the company [Killbuck] was a tall gaunt man with a face browned by twenty years' exposure to the climate of the mountains; his long black hair hung almost to his shoulders, but his cheeks and chin were cleanly shaved, after the fashion of the mountain men."

Another excellent description of the mountaineer may be found in Washington Irving's *Bonneville*:

The wandering whites who mingle for any length of time with the savages have invariably a proneness to adopt savage habitudes; but none more so than the free trappers. It is a matter of vanity and ambition with them to discard everything that may bear the stamp of civilized life, and to adopt the manners, habits, dress,

*gesture and even the walk of the Indian. You cannot pay
a free trapper a greater compliment than to persuade
him you have mistaken him for an Indian brave;and, in
truth, the counterfeit is complete. His hair, suffered to
attain to a great length, is carefully combed out, and
either left to fall carelessly over his shoulders, or plaited
neatly and tied up in otter skins, or parti-colored ribbons.
A hunting shirt of ruffled calico of bright dyes, or of
ornamented leather, falls to his knee; below which,
curiously fashioned leggins, ornamented with strings,
fringes, and a profusion of hawks' bells, reach to a costly
pair of moccasins of the finest Indian fabric, richly
embroidered with beads. A blanket of scarlet, or some
other bright color, hangs from his shoulders, and is girt
round his waist with a red sash, in which he bestows
pistols, knife and the stem of his Indian pipe; preparations for either peace or war. His gun is lavishly deco-
rated with brass tacks and vermillion, and provided
with a fringed cover, occasionally of buckskin, ornamented here and there with a feather.*(p. 110-11)

The success of the 1827 supply venture encouraged
Pierre Chouteau, Jr., to continue the trade in the
mountains despite a decade-long distaste originating
with his brother's disastrous venture of 1817. In 1827,
Chouteau also had the vehicle by which to enter the
competition for the mountain trade: the Columbia Fur
Company. Its merger with the AFC led to the development of a new arrangement in the fur trade and a new
employment for Provost. By 1828 McKenzie had extended his company's activities to the Great Lakes in
the east and to well above the Mandan villages at the big
bend on the Upper Missouri in the west, near present-
day Bismarck, North Dakota. Fort Tecumseh, near
present-day Pierre, South Dakota, was the company's
first as well as its most important post. The company
was a thorn in the side of the American Fur Company

and it was apparent that soon either an all-out battle for supremacy would take place or some compromise must be arranged. Both sides recognized that while one company might emerge on top, neither side would win in a fur war, so negotiations began between the two competitors. In July of 1827, the companies agreed to a merger; it was the consolidation of two successful operations rather than a takeover. The old Columbia Fur Company was henceforth to be known as the Upper Missouri Outfit of the American Fur Company and Kenneth McKenzie was to remain at its head. The Columbians gave up all rights to the Great Lakes and Upper Mississippi River areas but retained the Upper Missouri country as before. The partners of the old company became proprietors of the new and conducted its affairs almost as independently as before.

The merger became effective at the beginning of 1828 and the establishment of the Upper Missouri Outfit was to greatly affect Provost's life. Pierre Chouteau, Jr., aware of Ashley's success in the mountains, wished to send a similar caravan under Kenneth McKenzie in 1828. The company, while interested in the mountains, preferred a slower course without unnecessary risk and therefore overrode Chouteau. Instead, a trading post was established at the mouth of the Yellowstone which would afford both a safe and a convenient base for any future effort into the mountains. McKenzie was chosen to direct this task.[19]

Thus, Fort Floyd (renamed Fort Union in 1830) was built in 1828 on the north bank of the Missouri River, about six miles above its junction with the Yellowstone rivers. The fort commanded a high gravelly bank of the Missouri, and behind the post the prairie stretched to McKenzie's Butte. Within the rectangular, 220-foot by 240-foot cottonwood palisade there were a two-story agent's house, employees' quarters, powder magazine, artisan shops, storehouses, and stables. Two double-storied stone bastions defended the southwest and northwest corners of the 20-foot-high palisade, and a double gate stood at the entrance. There was a cannon at the base of the flagpole in the center of the post yard.[20] By 1842 Fort Union had replaced Fort Tecumseh as the company's largest, most heavily manned and elaborately furnished and supplied post on the Upper Missouri.

In September of 1826, Etienne Provost returned to St. Louis, and on the twenty-second of that month he sold B. Pratte and Co. 402 pounds of beaver for the grand sum of $1,608.[21] Four hundred pounds of beaver fur comprised four "packs" of about one hundred pounds each. Each pack consisted of approximately 60 pelts, so Provost had about 240 pelts to show for his trapping effort, not counting those pelts traded to Ashley the previous year.

Provost also sold the company nine horses for $162, giving him a total credit of $1,770 on the company books. He immediately began to supply himself for town living; in September and October he withdrew a total of $941.80 in cash[22] and bought predictable items for a man just returned from two years in the wilderness: shoes, hose, and material for shirts and trousers. A ledger entry for September 30 lists "1 pair shoes to his cosin." He also purchased "3 galls whiskey to his cosin" on October 2.[23]

The whiskey was for a festive occasion. On October 2, he attended the wedding of his cousin, Jean Baptiste Provost, signing the parish register by his mark as a witness to the event.[24] Jean Baptiste was forty-two years old at the time of his marriage, and his bride, Agnes Delor Constant, was thirty-one and entering her second marriage. Also undoubtedly present at the wedding was the family of Lambert Salle dit Lajoie, whose wife Magdeleine was a half-sister to the bride and the mother of Etienne's future wife.

Provost's return to St. Louis leaves a question about his Taos venture: who provided the financial backing for his expedition into the mountains of Utah? As we have seen, the backing of the Robidoux brothers is one of the foremost possibilities.

Bernard Pratte and Co. had been one of the principal trading firms on the Missouri River since 1821, and by 1824 the company was looking at the Santa Fe trade. Joseph Robidoux was in the employ of Pratte in 1822 as a factor at the Oto post, located near Fort Atkinson on the Missouri River, and remained in the employ of the French Company, as Pratte's partnership was called, well into the early Santa Fe period. While in Pratte's employ Robidoux privately outfitted at least one Santa Fe trip and purchased company merchandise to supply the venture— his brother Antoine's 1824 caravan to New Mexico. He may also have privately backed other ventures.

Robidoux' private activities had not gone unnoticed by Chouteau and his partners; however, apparently deciding the chickens are safer if you know where the fox is, the company kept him on as an employee. Crusty old Jean P. Cabanne heartily disagreed and made no secret of his objections to Robidoux in his many letters to Chouteau. Cabanne's letters clearly revealed a hearty dislike for Robidoux, and he regularly urged his removal from the company.

In response to the rising criticism, Joseph Robidoux wrote to Pierre Chouteau, Jr., in March 1825. His letter seems almost petulant:

I have a thousand things I would like to tell you. But upon reflection I shall tell you nothing—for a good reason. You have here Mr. Cabanne who certainly forgets nothing. He speaks and writes better than I, he is your relative, friend and above all, partner, and you know very well that the best thing for me to do is to keep silent.

   I have some unpleasantness with my [illegible word]
here in regard to me making a trip to Mexico. You have
such a good memory that I need not recall to you what
we told one another about this voyage, we are all aware
of it, you permitted it to me without reluctance, you sold
me merchandise, bought my horses, etc. I had planned
this undertaking, bought everything before we had
received any news about my brother Michelle with 30
packs of beaver—and also, it was not until after his
return that Mr. Cabanne reproached [saying] I ought not
to chase two hares at the same time by taking away from
this branch of the business—because I was your en-
gage.[25]

   So Joseph Robidoux bowed his head before his
master and knuckled his brow while at the same time
insisting that Chouteau knew all along what he was
doing. The reference to "the business that I had done
at the mountain" suggests earlier private endeavors.

   Robidoux may have supplied Provost for his 1824-
25 expedition with LeClerc. Certainly he traded for his
own benefit by outfitting his brothers for Santa Fe, and
he might have invested in the ventures of others. As a
shirt-tail relative of sorts, Provost may also have been
with the Robidoux in their 1822 trading venture.

   It should be remembered that Antoine Robidoux
was in the mountains in the fall and winter of 1824-25
and with Provost's party for some of that time. Antoine
returned to Taos in February with twenty-five of Provost's men, presumably including LeClerc. This loose
association between Provost and Robidoux further
suggests the backing of the Robidoux brothers.

   The best evidence for a Provost-Robidoux connection, however, is in the letter written in December of
1826 by Bartholomew Berthold to J. P. Cabanne
concerning the necessity of ensuring the loyalty of

Provost and preventing his "reunion" with Robidoux. The letter was written in French, but the word reunion has the same meaning in both French and English. Another possibility should be considered: that Bernard Pratte and Co. supplied Provost and LeClerc with the necessary goods for their venture. Provost's position as an early employee is verified by the payment of wages due in July 1823. Dale Morgan refers to the possible backing of Provost by Robidoux in *The Rocky Mountain Journals of William Marshall Anderson*. In his earlier *The West of William H. Ashley*, he suggests that B. Pratte and Co. may have been the supplier. It is also possible that Chouteau and Pratte simply approved and thus tacitly supported the backing of Provost by Robidoux.

Back in St. Louis in that fall of 1826, after Provost insured that his cousin was properly shod for his wedding and had sufficient whiskey for a proper celebration, he made a number of purchases suggesting participation in a commercial venture of some sort. He bought 3 barrels of flour, 12 barrels (400_ gallons) of whiskey, one barrel (31 gallons) of brandy, one barrel (36 gallons) of New Orleans rum, one keg (186 pounds) of tobacco, two riding saddles and one pack saddle, one dozen shaving soap and one dozen pipes. He also bought cloth of various types and in varying quantities, but none sufficient to indicate a major trading venture.

The liquor was not of the type used in the Indian trade, although a small keg of rum was not infrequently taken along. Trade liquor was usually pure alcohol, which could produce far more drinking material per gallon transported than whiskey. The alcohol was diluted with water at the rendezvous or the trader's post and doctored usually with caramel or tobacco to give the liquor the color of whiskey.[26]

Some years later Provost did operate a tavern and inn, and both the quantity and type of purchases he made in the fall of 1826 seem far more appropriate for a "grocery," as saloons were then called, than for a major trading venture to the mountains. Surely had he intended to compete with Ashley for the mountain trade, and made such a proposal to the Chouteau interests, the correspondence between the several partners would have contained references to it; however, no such mention has been located in the Chouteau correspondence aside from Berthold's letter, which seems more concerned with keeping him in the Chouteau camp than with any competitive act by Provost.

That he did remain with Chouteau is evidenced by the ledgers of the company for January 1827. In that month the records note the purchase of a bridle by Provost and an advance of wages of $36.75 by the Osage Outfit. The services he performed were not specified, but surely he was in the field operating for the company on the lower Missouri. The Osage trade along the Missouri (in what is now eastern Kansas) had long been the province of the Chouteau interests, and the man representing the family there was Auguste P. Chouteau, Provost's leader on the ill-fated expedition of 1815-17.

Provost's commitment to the company was apparently concluded by July of 1827, for in that month he was in St. Louis, where he purchased a number of items of personal apparel: shoes, socks, black silk handkerchiefs, suspenders, a waistcoat, and cashmere pantaloons. On July 25 he was paid the balance in full for his services, a total of $413.45.[27]

What Provost did with the liquor and other items he had purchased the previous fall is unknown. The purchase of a pack saddle and two riding saddles suggests a small-scale trading venture of his own, perhaps at the same time he was working for the Osage Outfit. But why would he have purchased trade goods in October if they were not to be used until some time in the next year? It seems more likely, based on the evidence thus far uncovered, that those purchases were intended for use in a St. Louis enterprise.

Provost's future father-in-law, Lambert Salle dit Lajoie, had been granted a license to keep a tavern in 1811. The likelihood that Provost engaged in business with him is suggested by events in the years ahead. Lambert Salle dit Lajoie and family almost certainly attended the wedding of Provost's cousin that fall since the bride was a half-sister to Lambert's wife. Perhaps Provost already knew the family members. In any event, if Provost acquired an interest in Lambert's tavern, or grocery, he would sooner or later have become acquainted with his future wife, Lambert's stepdaughter Marie Rose. She was then married to another, and not to be widowed until 1828. In 1827, Provost was forty-two years old, no doubt well aware that he could not remain a trapper forever, and that he needed to make some provision for his future. A partnership in a successful tavern would provide a livelihood for those later years. From Lambert Salle's point of view, a man who enjoyed a reputation such as Provost's among the fur merchants and trappers would be a valued partner in a tavern.

Whatever his future plans might have been in 1827, after six months in St. Louis Provost abandoned the relative tameness of town life and returned to the fur trade, heading up the Missouri in 1828 as an employee of McKenzie's Upper Missouri Outfit. He probably went first to Fort Tecumseh, which was still the company's main post. Provost may have been at the fort in the spring, for Jim Beckwourth placed him at the 1828 summer rendezvous on Bear Lake. There is no reason to disbelieve Beckwourth; McKenzie was desirous of bringing the mountain trade to his new partner and employer at Fort Floyd, and he sent Provost to seek out the trappers and encourage them to trade at the new fort rather than the rendezvous. Chittenden says this occurred in the fall of 1828, but Dale Morgan places Provost among the Crow Indians at that time, also at McKenzie's order, to further the position of the American Fur Company with that nation. W. J. Ghent placed Provost's efforts among the trappers in the summer and this would fit with his presence at the rendezvous. That business and social gathering would have provided an excellent opportunity to plead the American Fur Company's case, even in the camp of the opposition.

Many mountaineers were gathered in the beautiful meadowlands at the southern end of Bear Lake, awaiting the arrival of the trade caravan, when word came of a party of mountaineers in some trouble at the north end of the lake, about eighteen miles away. According to Beckwourth, this group of thirty men was out of ammunition and a party was sent to relieve them. According to Robert Campbell, the real problem was not the lack of powder, but inferior powder which could not be counted on to fire. The powder was so bad, said Campbell, that a trapper could pull the trigger and have ample time to lay the gun down on the ground before it fired. Four trappers from the rendezvous rode to the relief of the endangered camp, which was under the leadership of Robert Campbell, with a supply of good powder.[28] Beckwourth claimed that he, "Provo and Jarvey" rode to the relief of Campbell's camp. "Provo" was, of course, Etienne, and "Jarvey" was probably Jean Baptiste Gervais.[29]

The relief party had made it through to Campbell's camp just in time; the next morning, while breaking camp, they were attacked by a large Blackfoot war party. The Blackfoot had learned of the unreliability of the trappers' powder and were emboldened to attack openly. They quickly learned that Campbell's men were no longer operating under the supposed handicap, and the loss of four Indians early in the battle convinced them to try different tactics. The battle subsided into a lengthy siege, with the mountaineers running short of ammunition, good and bad, and cut off from any way out of the willow spring to which they had repaired upon being attacked. The Blackfoot had surrounded the spring and had settled in, preferring seige tactics to a frontal assault.

It was decided that the only course was for a volunteer to break through the Indian line and ride to the main camp for aid. Campbell later said that he and a little Spaniard made the break through the Indians and led the relief party of trappers to the rescue.[30] Needless to say, Beckwourth also claimed honors for breaking through the encircling Indians to ride for reinforcements. Beckwourth's tale of derring-do is far more dramatic than Campbell's, but the problem with old Jim was that half the lies he told weren't true.

Of course, it may have been similar grandstanding on Campbell's part, when he dictated his "Narrative" forty years later, to place himself in the hero's role. Heroics of this nature do not usually fall to the leader of a group. A leader with good judgment would send others and remain at the battle to provide leadership for his men.

Provost was not otherwise mentioned anywhere in connection with the 1828 rendezvous, but in view of his mission for McKenzie and the American Fur Company, Beckwourth was probably accurate in counting him among those present. Beckwourth's recollection of other participants in various events is accurate more times than not, so it is quite likely that Provost was among those who rode into Campbell's camp the night before the battle.

Provost's appeal to trade at the AFC fort apparently made a distinct impression on the mountaineers. At the conclusion of the Bear Lake rendezvous the trappers added up what they had paid to Smith, Jackson and Sublette for their revel and for the goods necessary to carry them through the coming year. They decided that the tariff was too high and that a bit of competition would bring prices down to a more reasonable level. So in the manner of democracies everywhere, they elected a representative to carry their message to the competition. Hugh Glass, whose 1823 fight with a grizzly bear has its own unmatched place in the annals of the fur trade, soon arrived at Fort Floyd as a delegate from the hunters in the mountains.

The hunters did not want to come to the fort on the Missouri, as McKenzie had sent Provost to propose; they asked McKenzie to bring supplies from his fort to the next rendezvous instead.[31] Provost had won half the loaf and McKenzie, already eager to move into the mountain trade, seized upon Glass's invitation to mount an AFC expedition into the mountains in 1829. The company's venture away from the river was headed by William Vanderburgh and marked the beginning of an unsuccessful and sometimes disastrous twelve-year venture into the mountains. The company supply caravans were always late to the rendezvous, were never able to beat the competition's trading, and sometimes tried to compete in ways that cost lives. Success came from other quarters.

While Glass was heading for Fort Floyd, Etienne Provost moved into the Crow territory to encourage Crow trade at the new post on the Missouri and at the same time to make his fall hunt. Provost was again a "hivernan," the mountaineers' term for the trapper who spent the winter in the mountains. During this sojourn in the wilderness, he carried a Hawken rifle, made by the St. Louis firm of Sam and Jake Hawken and the standard against which all other mountain rifles were soon to be compared. Provost's is the earliest known use of that famous rifle by the mountaineers.[32] Writing to Pierre Chouteau, Jr.,from Fort Tecumseh on January 2, 1829, Kenneth McKenzie added a post-script to his letter asking Chouteau to include in the spring shipment "two rifles similar in all respects to the one made by Hawkins for Provost."[33]

It was not uncommon for the mountaineer to take up with an Indian woman who served multiple roles as companion, camp laborer, and wife. She provided the labor to cook, skin the beaver pelts, pack up the camp, and do the myriad other tasks involved in camp life, as well as warming her man's bed. Alfred Jacob Miller's 1837 rendezvous painting, *The Trapper's Bride*, immortalizes these women. That winter of 1828 Provost, forty-three years old and unmarried, reportedly took to himself a woman of the Crow Nation. There is evidence that during his years in the mountains he fathered a son with a Crow woman, in the winter of 1828-29 or 1829-30, while he was still actively trapping. Since Provost married in St. Louis in August 1829, the winter of 1828-29 seems the best bet for his liaison.

The boy's name was Nicolas; his mother's name is unknown. Little more has been learned of this mountain family of Provost's; only that Nicolas had a son, Michel, born in Canada, and both father and son allegedly served in the Civil War as bounty soldiers. Michel, Provost's grandson, was also alleged to have served with Benteen's troop as a Crow Scout during the Battle of the Little Big Horn in 1876.[34] Military records of both Civil War and Indian Scout enlistments fail to identify either man. Nor do the records of the Bureau of Indian Affairs contain any helpful information.

With the arrival of spring in 1829, Provost started downriver for St. Louis. Whatever other thoughts were in his mind as he navigated the tricky currents of the Missouri, he could not have known that Lambert Salle's daughter, Marie Rose, had been widowed during the past year.

On July 7 Kenneth McKenzie wrote a note to Pierre Chouteau, Jr., explaining that Provost had just arrived at Fort Tecumseh bound for St. Louis and was in such a hurry to continue on his way that he would hardly give McKenzie time to write a letter. He wrote that it was Provost's intent to resupply himself in St. Louis and immediately come back upriver to further trade and trap with the Crows. McKenzie added that Provost would not sell him the furs from his spring hunt, noting also, however, that Provost owed him nothing on the account books of Fort Tecumseh.[35] So, once again Provost, as he had after his Utah venture, preferred to risk transporting his pelts to the St. Louis market, where their value was higher, rather than sell them at the trading post. Provost continued downriver with McKenzie's letter to Chouteau, and by late July he was in St. Louis. The account ledgers of the American Fur Company show an entry of $100 paid to Provost on July 27 as a cash advance on his furs. The balance of $1,145.71 was credited to him on August 4.[36]

NOTES

1. Today's Provo River flowing from the Kamas Prairie, down Provo Canyon, to Utah Lake.
2. According to a story told to Samuel H. Auerbach by Orrin Porter Rockwell in Auerbach, "Old Trails, Old Forts, Old Trappers and Traders."
3. Chittenden, *American Fur Trade in the Far West*, 2: 973.
4. Weber, *The Taos Trappers*, 98.
5. Letter in Chouteau-Papin Collection, MHS.
6. Letter dated November 8, 1824, in Chouteau Collection. "Bierd" was James Baird of the 1812 McKnight company, and a trader since 1821.
7. Morgan, *Jedediah Smith*, 172.

8. "Campbell Narrative," 5, 10.

9. Morgan, *Jedediah Smith*, 187; Brooks, *The Southwest Expedition of Jedediah Smith*, 35; and, transcribed remarks of Dr. Fred R. Gowans on the site of the Green River rendezvous in July, 1984.

10. "Campbell Narrative," 12, and Brooks, *The Southwest Expedition of Jedediah Smith*, 35.

11. Morgan, *The West of William H. Ashley*, 149.

12. Chittenden, *American Fur Trade of the Far West*, 1: 280.

13. David J. Weber, "Sylvestre S. Pratte" in Hafen, ed., *Mountain Men and the Fur Trade*, 6: 367.

14. Auguste P. Chouteau had a younger brother, Paul Liguest Chouteau, and a cousin, Pierre Millicour Papin, identified in Foley and Rice, *The First Chouteaus*, 211-12.

15. Letter of Auguste Chouteau in Chouteau-Papin Collection.

16. Letter dated December 9, 1826, at Fort Lookout, Chouteau-Papin Collection.

17. Morgan, *The West of William H. Ashley*, 164.

18. At that time the lake went by several other names. Beckwourth referred to it as "Weaver's Lake" and Robert Campbell and others called it Sweet Lake or Sweetwater Lake. The latter designations were apparently used to differentiate it from the Soda Springs area just north and west which had "soda water," and the mountaineers were pleased to identify the lake with good water.

19. Janet Lecompte, "Pierre Chouteau, Jr.," in Hafen, ed., *Mountain Men and the Fur Trade*, 9: 104.

20. Sunder, *Fur Trade on the Upper Missouri*, 43.

21. American Fur Caompany Ledger M, folio 356: "Furs & Peltries to Etienne Provos: 402# Mountain beaver which we have Bought of him @ $4.00 (per pound), $1,608.00."

22. American Fur Company Ledger M, folios 353 and 371.

23. *Ibid.*, folio 357.

24. St. Mary and Joseph Church, St. Louis, Mo., Carondelet Baptisms 16 September 1826-21 November 1826.

25. Letter dated March 15, 1825, in Chouteau Collection.

26. Popular legend also has the alcohol being additionally doctored with pepper, gunpowder, and/or other spicy items to give greater kick. At least one very reputable fur trade historian, Charles E. Hanson, Jr., of the Museum of the American Fur Trade, disputes this as being highly unlikely as the Indians particularly liked the taste of whiskey, and therefore, would not accept such doctored products (from a conversation with Mr. Hanson in July, 1988).

27. Bernard Pratte and Co. Ledgers, vol. 18: 50, 53, 199, 207-8.

28. "Campbell Narrative," 28-9.

29. Bonner, *The Life and Adventures of James P. Beckwourth*, 101.

30. "Campbell Narrative," 29.

31. Myers, *Pirate, Pawnee and Mountain Man*, 216.

32. Editorial note by Charles E. Hanson in Tykal, "Etienne Provost and the Hawken Rifle," 1.

33. Letter in Chouteau-Maffitt Collection. George Frederick Ruxton provided an excellent description of the Hawken and the mountaineers' regard for it in his book *Life in the Far West*: When LaBonte outfitted himself for the mountains he "first of all visited the gun store of Hawken whose rifles are renowned in the mountains and exchanged his own piece for a regular mountain rifle. This was heavy metal, carrying about thirty-two balls to the pound, stocked to the muzzle and mounted with brass, its only ornament being a buffalo bull, looking exceedingly ferocious, which was

not very artistically engraved upon the trap of the stock." Earlier in the same narrative Ruxton wrote, "Among the trappers the Hawken was the most prized weapon in the west."

34. Letters of Roy Michel Provost to the Governor of Utah, June 17, 1964, in Utah State Historical Society, and of July 27, 1964, to Dr. LeRoy R. Hafen in the Huntington Library. Roy Michel Provost claimed to be the great-grandson of Etienne Provost through this Indian liaison. No further documentation of this claim has yet been located.

35. Letter in Chouteau Collection.

36. American Fur Company Ledgers, Book P, folio 131, and Book R, folio 129.

Trapping Beaver

Small Tobacco Twist

CHAPTER SIX
The Trapper's Bride, 1829-1830

Etienne Provost returned to a St. Louis of almost five thousand people in the summer of 1829. He must have learned quickly that Marie Rose Salle Dupuis' husband had died ten months previously. Within six weeks of his return from the mountains, on August 14, 1829, he and Marie Rose were married.[1] Provost was then forty-four and Marie Rose thirty-one.[2] She had been widowed after ten years of marriage.

Although Marie Rose Salle Dupuis was the step-daughter of Lambert Salle dit Lajoie, he always referred to her as his daughter. Lambert himself was the son of

Jean Sale dit Lajoie, one of the thirty original settlers of St. Louis.[3] Jean Sale was a trader and a member of the contingent from Cahokia that helped found the new trading post in 1764.[4] From this new post on the west bank of the Mississippi he traded with the Indians, ranging up the Missouri River and into the western Indian country to conduct his business. It was in Pawnee country that Jean Sale met his wife and Lambert's mother, Marie Rose Vidalpane.[5]

Marie Rose Vidalpane was born, apparently out of wedlock, in New Mexico in 1723 or 1726[6] to Pablo Francisco Villalpando and a woman named Martine. Pablo was born in 1710, the son of a Spanish soldier, Juan de la Villa el Pando, and Ana Maria Romero, the sister of an early settler in the valley of San Fernando de Taos. As a widow, Pablo Francisco's mother, with her children, took up residence on her brother's lands in the valley. In August of 1760, the Comanche[7] attacked the home of the Villalpando family, where a number of settlers had taken refuge. The Indians broke through the defenses, killed a great number of the defenders, including women and children, and carried fifty-seven of the survivors into captivity, among them Marie Rose. She spent the next ten years in Indian captivity. How many of those years were with the Comanche is unknown, but at some time after her capture she became a captive of the Pawnee, and it was with that tribe that Jean Sale found her by about 1767.

Having the comfort of a woman in the Pawnee village, and a non-Indian woman at that, must have been quite pleasant for Jean Sale, for he lived with Marie Rose on his trading visits for several years before bringing her to St. Louis, where he married her in 1770. In their marriage contract of July 3, 1770, Marie Rose, was identified as a widow. In this written contract they acknowledged having a son, Lambert, who had been born before they could legitimize their marriage and who was at that time about twenty months old.[8] The contract asserted unequivocally that Lambert was their legitimate heir in every respect, to share equally in their estate with any other children born of their marriage. They also acknowledged an Indian child born to Marie Rose during her captivity. By the terms of the contract, this child, Antoine, was to be raised by Sale and his wife until he was of an age to fend for himself. He was apparently given Sale's name; however, the contract specified that Antoine was to have no status whatsoever as an heir of either Jean or Marie, and no claim on either estate.[9] Heir or not, Antoine Xavier Sale was baptized on July 18, 1776. By 1800 he was dead.

Jean and Marie Rose had three more children: Pierre, born in 1771, and twins, Marie Joseph and Helene, born in 1773.[10] Marie was about thirty-four years old when she was widowed and taken captive by the Comanche. Therefore, she was in her late thirties when Antoine was born. At her marriage to Jean Sale in 1770, she was forty-four years old and Jean was twenty-nine.

In 1792 Jean Sale dit Lajoie, for reasons unknown, left his wife and family and returned to France, where he remained the rest of his life. Marie Rose lived on in St. Louis for another thirty-eight years. She died July 27, 1830, in the home of her daughter, Helene, either at the age of 104 or 107. Josiah Gregg wrote in 1844 that there were then many people still living in St. Louis who well remembered Marie Rose and with what "affecting pathos the old lady was wont to tell her tale of woe."[11]

Lambert Salle dit Lajoie was forty-three years old in 1811 when he married Madeleine Delor Cayole, the widow of Francois de Salle dit Cayole.[12] She brought six minor children to her marriage with Lambert who, by the terms of the marriage contract, were "legitimacized." Whatever the term meant in the legal phrasing of the day, Lambert referred to them as his children from that time on. Among the six children was Marie Rose; the others were Clement, Nicholas, Jean Baptiste, Marie Caroline and Marie Gertrude.[13]

When Marie Rose was twenty years old she entered into a marriage contract on July 7, 1818, and shortly thereafter married Joseph Dupuis dit Dunord in the Cathedral.[14] Two years later Marie Rose and Joseph had their son, also Joseph Dupuis dit Dunord, baptized. The next year, 1821, Grandfather Lambert gave title to a piece of property in the city to his grandson and any other children that might be born of that marriage.[15] Unfortunately, there were no more grandchildren to share in Lambert Salle's gift. The young Joseph died in 1822 at seventeen months and Marie's husband died in September of 1828, at thirty-seven, without fathering other children.[16]

To prepare for his wedding Etienne charged to his account on the B. Pratte and Co. books a new razor, razor hone, brush, shaving box, a pair of green, three-point blankets, and one pair of silk pocket handkerchiefs. He fortified himself against any unexpected expenses by drawing $55 in cash but apparently left the purchase of other forms of fortification to friends, for he bought no whiskey for this wedding.

Marie Rose had inherited the lot which Lambert had given her son, Joseph, Jr., and shortly before the wedding Lambert sold Etienne the adjoining lot. Thus Provost became a St. Louis land owner for the first time.[17] The day after the wedding Etienne and his new bride acquired a second property when Pierre Chouteau sold "Provot" a lot 50' x 150' French measure.[18] On this corner lot at Second and Lombard, about nine blocks south of the Cathedral,[19] Provost built the home which he owned for the rest of his life. He paid Chouteau $160 for this property. He also paid one "Rouply" $5 for drawing house plans and platting the house on the site. In December he paid another $2 for a survey of the property.[20]

While Etienne was preparing for his marriage, he was also making arrangements for his next trapping venture. This time he had a partner, the American Fur Company itself. He went halves with the company on an outfit for the mountains, each partner putting up $417.71. The ledgers of the company carry a separate account in that year for "Etienne Proveau's Adventure."[21] The accounts for August 10 show he bought four horses, and on the thirteenth he paid $75.00 "for Hawkens." This may have been for the purchase of rifles, but it was more likely for hardware, for in those years the Hawken brothers did as much blacksmithing work as gunsmithing. There were other entries for "2 rifles, Hawkins & Co., $50.00," and for the various and sundry items necessary to a trading venture. He took beaver traps and springs, gunpowder, lead, tomahawks, scalping knives, "Wilson's" butcher knives, vermillion, and beads. He paid advances to two men, Alexander Mathieu and Cotte Morin. These two are mentioned several times in the ledger account of Provost's "advanture," along with one Phinis Bartlett, and it may well be he had only the three men with him.

It seems clear from the dates of his purchases that he did not intend to remain long in St. Louis enjoying his marriage bed. His departure date is not known, but by September 13, just a month after his wedding, he was at Cabanne's post near the Council Bluffs.[22] In early October he was at Fort Tecumseh, where he ran into a problem in obtaining credit for additional supplies. It seems that the agent there was not aware of his partnership with the Company and Provost had no documentation of the agreement with him. Because he lacked credentials attesting to his arrangement with the Company, "but little attention was paid to his assertions" by Jacob Halsey.[23] Halsey did, however,

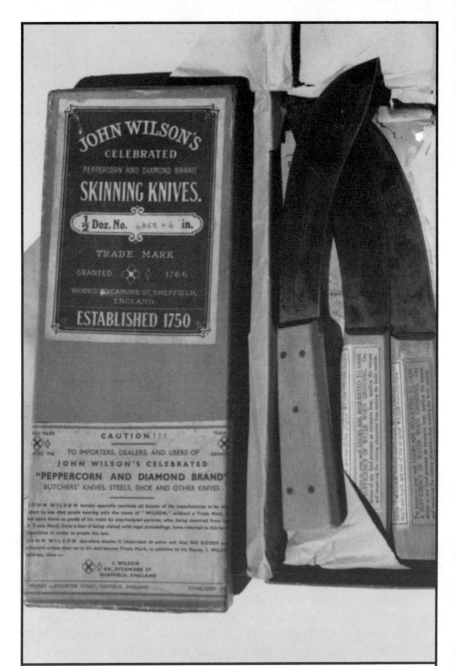

Original box of six John Wilson Knives

advance Provost what merchandise and supplies he needed, charging them against his individual account after refusing to open a partnership account.

Whether Etienne continued upriver from Fort Tecumseh to the new American Fur Company post, Fort Floyd, above the confluence of the Missouri and Yellowstone rivers, or left directly from the fort for the mountains, he once again disappeared for the winter hunt with the Crows. While he was away, Ramsay Crooks wrote to Pierre Chouteau, Jr., concerning discrepancies in the furs bought from Provost in the previous season. He advised that two packs of Provost's furs weighed ten and a half pounds less than the stated weight and that his account should be charged accordingly.

There was no lack of competition in the Crow country that winter of 1829-30. Smith, Jackson and Sublette had their various brigades roaming the mountains, and Provost's own partner, the American Fur Company, was represented by a brigade led by William H. Vanderburgh. The only information about him that winter is found in a letter of Kenneth McKenzie's of May 5, 1830, advising the recipient that Vanderburgh was expected at Fort Union about the end of June, that William Gordon was then on the Powder River with a party of four or five men, and that "Provost is with the Crows."[24]

Provost did not attend the rendezvous of 1830, which was held on the Wind River in the vicinity of present-day Riverton, Wyoming. Because of his partnership with the Company he would be expected to sell his year's catch directly to the Company either at one of the river posts or in St. Louis.

By not attending that rendezvous Etienne missed witnessing another event important in the development of the west as well as to the fur trade: William Sublette initiated the use of wagons to transport the trade goods to the rendezvous. There were ten wagons drawn by two mules each, two Dearborn carriages drawn by one mule each, and a herd of twelve cattle and a milk cow. All the wagons, four of the cattle, and the cow arrived safely at rendezvous in mid-July, the missing cattle having provided trail fare for the caravan.[25] With this expedition, Sublette demonstrated that a natural wagon road existed from St. Louis to the mountains along the Platte River; it would become the Oregon Trail.

At the rendezvous of 1830, Smith, Jackson and Sublette sold out to a new partnership of Tom Fitzpatrick, Jim Bridger, Milton Sublette, Henry Fraeb, and Jean Gervais. The new partnership was called the Rocky Mountain Fur Company.

While the annual bacchanal was under way in the mountains, Provost returned to St. Louis where the sale of the furs taken during his year in the mountains netted him $582.68 as his half of the partnership with the company;[26] not much to show for a year in the mountains, particularly with a wife to support, but the year could not by any means be considered a failure. It must have discouraged Provost, however, for that was his last independent trapping expedition. From that time on he served the American Fur Company as an employee for wages, but no longer as a trapper.

Provost may have realized that by 1830 the mountains were overcrowded and rapidly being trapped out. The demand for beaver pelts would decline each year for another decade or so, until the trade in beaver pelts would be almost dead. The loss of the European market coincided with the virtual exhaustion of the product by overtrapping. The trappers were not game managers and knew little of the natural fur cycles or the dangers of overtrapping the mountain streams. The American Fur Company was sending out its brigades in force, and coupled with those of the Rocky Mountain Fur Company operating in the mountains, their numbers made the mountains, as a mountaineer might say, downright crowded.

Provost was not to remain long in St. Louis; by the early fall of 1830 he was back upriver with the company as a hunter at Fort Union, as Fort Floyd was now called, for the Upper Missouri Outfit.[27] He was stationed at the fort through the winter, although neither the date of his employment nor term of service and wages was specified.

In the dead of winter Kenneth McKenzie sent Provost from Fort Union to Fort Tecumseh with dispatches for the agent in charge. He arrived on February 21, 1831, the same day that Robert Campbell arrived from the Yankton Sioux country. McKenzie instructed the agent to outfit Provost for the spring supply caravan to Vanderburgh, then wintering in the mountains with his brigade. All the horses of the fort that could be spared were brought to the fort from the Navy Yard.[28]

Provost needed fifty good horses; but so many were not to be found after the ravages of winter. Three days after his arrival Provost left Fort Tecumseh, with ten men and only nine horses, to find Vanderburgh on the Powder River. Over a month later, on April 1, three more men left with nineteen horses to overtake Provost, and the next day William Gordon set out from the fort with additional horses for Provost. Provost found Vanderburgh on the Green River, delivered his trade goods and supplies, and brought Vanderburgh's furs back to the river post.[29]

That meeting between Provost and Vanderburgh may have been the only gathering that could pass for a rendezvous that summer. The Rocky Mountain Fur Company did not hold one that year. Tom Fitzpatrick, who was to make the arrangements in St. Louis for the supply caravan with Jed Smith, Davy Jackson and William Sublette, had not started from the mountains until March, and when he finally arrived in St. Louis he found his suppliers en route to Santa Fe on a trading expedition of their own. He overtook them but had to accompany the caravan to Santa Fe before the wagons could be broken down and he could obtain his needed supplies. Fitzpatrick outfitted himself in Santa Fe and headed back for the mountains, far too late to make the planned rendezvous. His partner, Henry Fraeb, had been looking for Fitzpatrick and met him near the Sweetwater River. Fitzpatrick turned over the supplies to Fraeb and turned his steps eastward to St. Louis while Fraeb spent most of the fall delivering the supplies and trade goods to the RMFC men in the mountains.

After his meeting with Vanderburgh, Provost returned to St. Louis and he probably took the Company's returns with him. On August 21 he was credited with $1,000 for "services ending this summer."[29] He returned to find himself a father, his daughter Marie having been born May first, while he was in the mountains. Baptism for the baby had awaited Provost's return and took place on September twelfth.

Meanwhile, events on the Missouri River would affect the fur trade as much as anything happening in the mountains. Pierre Chouteau, Jr., had decided to use large steamboats on the Upper Missouri. It took a full summer to cordelle and pole a keelboat from St. Louis to the upper posts and float back down, so Chouteau contracted to have a steamboat built to his specifications for the Missouri River. That boat, the *Yellowstone*, made its maiden voyage in 1831. It was not as successful as hoped; low water prevented it from continuing upriver beyond Fort Tecumseh. But clearly the day of the keelboat was ended. From this year on steamboats carried the American Fur Company's employees and merchandise to the river posts and brought back the annual returns. Once the boats were in regular service, the company used the cheaper water transport to send its merchandise upriver to the trading posts and thence overland to the mountains. It was a case of penny wise and pound foolish, for although the costs were much less, river transport was invariably slower, so that the company either missed the rendezvous altogether or was so late as to miss the best trading.

NOTES

1. Parish Register, The Old Cathedral, St. Louis.

2. *Catholic Baptisms of St. Louis 1765-1840.* Marie Rose was born June 28, 1798.

3. "Salle" has also been spelled "Sale" in various records and documents, and "Lajoie" has appeared as "LaJoye," "Lejoye," and LaJoie."

4. Billon, *Annals of St. Louis,* 426.

5. Marie Rose's name has also been spelled Villalpando, Pando, and Panda in various accounts. The name and spelling used throughout are taken from her marriage contract. In New Mexico records the family name is Villalpando, and her name was Maria Rosa.

6. Accounts of her death in 1830 give her age as both 107 and 104.

7. Called Laitaine Indians in the marriage contract of 1770 between Marie Rose and Jean.

8. Born November 12, 1768, according to *Catholic Baptisms 1765-1840.*

9. Original Marriage Contract, in French, in Old Archives, vol. 3, book 1 136-38, Instrument no. 2023, MHS.

10. *Catholic Baptisms 1765-1840,* 82. Apparently Pierre and Marie Joseph died at an early age for later references identify only two children: Lambert and Helene.

11. Gregg, *Commerce of the Prairies,* 105.

12.   Also spelled Caihol.

13.   St. Louis Recorder of Deeds, Vol. C, 211: Marriage Contract between Lambert Salle dit Lajoie and Madeleine Cailhol, widow, dated February 11, 1811.

14.   Parish records, The Old Cathedral, St. Louis.

15.   St. Louis County Register of Deeds, Book K, 189.

16.   Collett's *Index to Church Registers*.

17.   St. Louis County Registrar of Deeds, Book P, 138.

18.   French measure used a 13-inch foot.

19.   Rue d'Eglise, or Church St., was also known as Second Street.

20.   St. Louis County Registrar of Deeds, Book P, 352; and American Fur Company Ledgers, Book P, folio 544.

21.   American Fur Company Ledgers, Book P, folio 542-44.

22.   Letter from J.P. Cabanne to Pierre Chouteau, Jr., September 18, 1829: "(I) have been here since the morning of the 9th. Provost did not arrive here until 4 days after me." Chouteau Collection.

23.   Jacob Halsey to Kenneth McKenzie, February 16, 1832., Letterbook of Ft. Tecumseh, Chouteau Collection.

24.   Chouteau-Papin Collection.

25.   Gowans, *Rocky Mountain Rendezvous*, 65.

26.   American Fur Company Ledgers, Book R, U.M.O. 1829 Acct., and Book P, folio 544.

27.   "Persons Employed for the Upper Missouri Outfit for the year 1830," Chouteau Collection.

28.   Deland, "Fort Tecumseh and Fort Pierre Journal and Letterbooks," 9: 147.

29.   Morgan and Harris, eds., *The Rocky Mountain Journals of William Marshall Anderson*, 21.

30.   Gowans, *Tocky Mountain Rendezvous*, 69-70.

31.   American Fur Company Legers, Book T, folio 381.

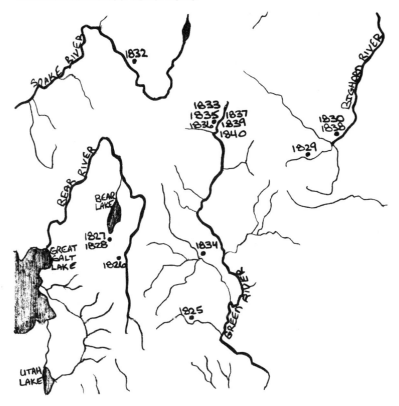

CHAPTER SEVEN
The Brigade Years I, 1831-1833

With a new daughter to get to know and a wife with whom he had spent but a few weeks of the past two years, Etienne Provost remained in St. Louis during the fall and early winter of 1831. On his way upriver to Fort Union in the late winter, he made a brief stop at Fort Tecumseh on February 20, 1832, where he was joined by one Lacharete who offered his services to Provost as a hunter for the rest of the journey to Fort Union.[1]

Provost's assignment with the company was to take the next supply caravan from Fort Union to William Vanderburgh at the summer rendezvous. At the same time Lucien Fontenelle was to come overland from the Council Bluffs to the rendezvous with supplies for Andrew Drips, who was also in the mountains that year for the American Fur Company. The arrangements for the supply trains were changed, however, and Provost was held at the fort to await Fontenelle, who was coming upriver by steamboat. The two parties would set out together for the mountains. Travel by steamboat was slow and uncertain at best, dependent upon water level and the vagaries of the river, so Fontenelle was late in arriving at Fort Union and the combined party was late in getting started. The supply caravan set out under the overall command of Fontenelle, with Provost as second in command, but it never arrived at the rendezvous at Pierre's Hole.

William Sublette had returned from the Santa Fe trading venture of the previous year, on which his partner, Jed Smith, had been killed by the Indians, and was once again ready to supply the mountaineers. He set out for the rendezvous in ample time and had the field almost to himself in 1832, for his was the only caravan to reach Pierre's Hole. Robert Campbell traveled with Sublette, not as a partner but with merchandise and supplies for his own account.[2] On their arrival Sublette and Campbell set up shop for the thirsty, beaver-rich mountaineers and took the cream of the trade while Vanderburgh and Drips waited anxiously day after day for their supply train to arrive and watched the trade slip away. They "expected a Mr. Provenu, with an equipment from Fort Union and as anxiously looked for Mr. Fontenelle, who was expected from the Council Bluffs."[3] As time passed Drips and Vanderburgh had to trade for essential supplies from Sublette and Campbell; however, they continued to hope for the arrival of their own supply train and traded for just enough to tide them over. Vanderburgh wrote to Pierre Chouteau, Jr., from the rendezvous on July 15 that the supply trains had not yet arrived but things would still be fine if they arrived by the end of the month. He commented that the failure of the American Fur Company caravan to arrive on time had given Sublette a real advantage.[4]

The most memorable event of the 1832 rendezvous at Pierre's Hole was a fight with the Blackfoot just as the gathering was breaking up. In the battle William Sublette received a wound that incapacitated him and Robert Campbell assumed command of the caravan returning to St. Louis. They returned with a total of 12,000 pounds of beaver. At St. Louis prices this was $60,000 worth of beaver pelts. The mountaineers figured beaver at sixty skins to one hundred pounds.[5] By that rule of thumb, there were 7,200 beaver pelts brought down by the Rocky Mountain Fur Company alone that year.

While Campbell and Sublette were on their way back to St. Louis, Drips and Vanderburgh set out for the Green River to backtrack the anticipated route of their missing supply trains. It was August 2 when they left Pierre's Hole and it was August 8 before they:

... discovered a party of horsemen several miles to the northward. To our great joy they proved to be (our long-expected company) headed by our old friend, Fontenelle, who had passed from St. Louis to the mouth of the Yellowstone in a steamboat and thence with pack horses to this place. He was aided by Mr. Provean in conducting the expedition. [6]

En route to the Green River and their meeting with Vanderburgh and Drips, Fontenelle and Provost had encountered the company of Captain Benjamin Bonneville, an Army officer on extended leave, who was on his first venture into the mountains at the head of a trapping expedition of some one hundred twenty men and twenty wagons. Bonneville was then building a fort

on the Green River about four miles below the spot
along the Green where Fontenelle and Provost found
Vanderburgh and Drip's brigades.[7] Bonneville's fort,
called Fort Nonsense by the mountaineers, was the
focal point of the 1833 rendezvous.

After four days of their own "rendezvous" the two
parties split. Vanderburgh and Drips headed into the
mountains for the fall hunt and Fontenelle and Provost
returned to Fort Union with the furs. Once they had
arrived back at the post on the Missouri, the furs were
loaded aboard bateaux for transport downriver. Fontenelle and McKenzie took the furs down by boat,
arriving on September 24 at Fort Tecumseh where they
remained for about three weeks before continuing to
St. Louis.[8] Meanwhile, Provost came overland from
Fort Union with a herd of horses, arriving at Fort
Tecumseh on October 4.[9] Provost left the horse herd at
the fort and continued downriver with Fontenelle and
McKenzie. Aboard the bateaux were 6,000 pounds of
beaver fur for the St. Louis market, half the amount
brought down by Sublette for the Rocky Mountain Fur
Company.[10] Those pelts, valued at $30,000, consti-
tuted but a part of the American Fur Company's trade
for the year. The Company still depended largely on the
river posts for the major portion of its annual business.
This load alone added another 3,600 pelts to those
brought down by the Rocky Mountain Fur Co. for a total
of nearly 11,000 beaver pelts brought out of the mountains. The downriver journey was made without incident and Provost was in St. Louis in the early fall.

During the winter of 1832-33 William Sublette and
Robert Campbell formed a partnership to supply the
mountaineers at the annual rendezvous, creating the
best known of the companies supplying the trade,
Sublette and Campbell.[11] Both men followed the lead of
Provost, leaving the active trapping to others but
remaining in the business in another capacity. As the

trade itself declined, there was still profit to be made in supplying those who chose to continue the hunt.

While Sublette and Campbell were forming their partnership and laying plans for the next year's supply train, Provost settled his accounts with the company and began supplying his own tavern business. A six month "grocery" license had been issued to "Achin Provou" effective in December of 1832. The first renewal was granted with the correct spelling and it was renewed thereafter at six-month intervals in Provost's name until August of 1835, at which time his brother-in-law, Clement Salle dit Lajoie, who was also known as Clement Lambert, apparently began receiving the same license and renewals. Clement continued to receive the licenses through June 1838.[12]

In the absence of records, we cannot document any earlier involvement of Provost in the tavern business. We know he was a tavernkeeper in the early 1830's and that his father-in-law, Lambert Salle, had a tavern in 1811. The merchandise Etienne had bought in 1826 was certainly more appropriate for the operation of a tavern than for home consumption and not at all sufficient for a trading expedition. The evidence suggests strongly that Provost was associated with Lambert in a tavern business, possibly as a partner. Lambert was sixty-five years old in 1833 and possibly in poor health for he died the next year. Etienne may well have felt it was time to venture out on his own.

In 1833, Provost is on record for the first time as a saloon keeper. Logic dictates that he had been involved in the business previously as an "off-season" investment. A few years hence Provost had a partnership account, Proveau and Lambert, Tavern Keeper, on the books of the American Fur Company with his brother-in-law, Clement Lambert. Finally, the shift of the license in 1835 from Etienne to Clement confirms a continuing business arrangement between the two men.

While obtaining the necessary inventory for his tavern, Etienne was also building on the corner of Second and Lombard. Whether he was adding his tavern to the home planned in 1829 or if this was the initial construction of both the home and tavern is not clear, but now his business was operated at that address. Between the early spring of 1833 and the end of June, Provost paid Lewis Clark, of Clark and Tournotte, $792.18 for his services as a carpenter and cabinetmaker in building the structure Provost used as his "grocery." In the period a restaurant was called an "ordinary," and a saloon was known as a "grocery" or "huckster shop."[13] Those which provided both lodging and spirits were "taverns" or "inns." Although Provost's initial license specified a grocery, at some later time he actually ran a tavern and inn; there are records of payment to him for the boarding of American Fur Company employees, and we may assume he took in other boarders. In 1842 he was granted a license by the County of St. Louis "to keep an Inn and Tavern at his Stand on Second Street,"[14] and the 1845 census listed eight people as residents at his address, five of whom may well have been boarders.

"The Missouri Tavern was of its own class. Identified with the vocation of Tavern keeping in Missouri are the names of some of its best known and most highly esteemed first families in the state's history."[15] Many of those who crossed Etienne's path during his years in St. Louis and the fur trade were tavernkeepers: Lambert Salle was one, Ezekiel Williams was licensed as a "grocer" in Boonville, Joseph Philibert received a tavern license in 1812, William Sublette was reported to at one time have managed the General Jackson Tavern in St.Louis, and Joseph Charless, for many years the editor of the *Missouri Gazette*, opened a tavern upon his retirement.

During the long winter months of 1832-33, while the streams were frozen in the mountains and the mountaineers were probably almost as frozen, holed up in some relatively sheltered spot, Provost remained in St. Louis establishing his business and serving as a recruiting agent for the Upper Missouri Outfit. He traveled the neighboring countryside to Cahokia, St. Charles, and Portage des Sioux seeking men for employment with the company.[16] In March he received $85.00 "on account" and $1.69 for expenses.

In the spring of 1833 Etienne readied himself to return to the upper river, probably to escort to the river posts the men he had recruited during the winter, a task he would perform regularly in later years. Also on the move that spring was Maximilian, Prince of Wied and the Baron Braunsberg, a German naturalist who traveled upriver on the company steamboats: on the *Yellowstone* as far as Fort Pierre and on the *Assiniboine* to Fort Union. With him was Karl Bodmer, a young Swiss artist who had been hired by the Prince to record the scenes of the west. Bodmer's paintings of the country, the Indians, the flora and fauna of the Upper Missouri are not only outstanding works of art but also among the most significant ethnological contributions ever made to the natural history of the west. Bodmer's illustrations depict his subjects far better than the most detailed written description ever could. As a naturalist, Maximilian directed Bodmer to produce illustrations of the natural history of the region. Bodmer's work is an exquisitely detailed source for studying the Indians of the Upper Missouri.

It must have been an interesting time for Provost, traveling aboard the *Yellowstone* with Maximilian and his party. Also on board were Pierre Chouteau, Jr., with his daughters and several of their friends, Joshua Pilcher, and John F. A. Sanford, who married into the Chouteau family and was later a partner in the company.[17]

Once on the upper river, Provost again joined Fontenelle as second in command of the company caravan, this time to the 1833 rendezvous at Horse Creek on the Green River. While Fontenelle and Provost were making their way to the Green River, Robert Campbell was well ahead of them along the trail from St. Louis with the Sublette and Campbell supply train. Sublette had taken the freight wagons upriver by flatboat, probably to the vicinity of Omaha, and then joined Campbell along the Platte River. No formal arrangement had been made between the Rocky Mountain Fur Company and Sublette and Campbell for that year, so the partners were taking their train out to rendezvous on speculation. At the same time, the RMFC men were worried about whether or not there would be a supply train to the rendezvous, so Fitzpatrick sent Henry Fraeb out either to find the trade caravan along the trail or, failing that, to continue on to St. Louis and bring back the needed supplies himself. Fraeb did find Campbell, and concluded a trade agreement with him.

Always seeming to be a day late and a dollar short when it came to the rendezvous, Fontenelle and Provost showed up with the American Fur Company goods eight or nine days after Sublette and Campbell arrived at the Green River rendezvous site.[18] As a result, "Mr. Drips had to labour under some disadvantages untill I got to him as both the others had a large supply of Liquor which as you well know is the main object with those people with whom we have to deal in this country."[19] Fontenelle reported that his late arrival probably prevented his receiving four or five packs of beaver.

Traveling with Campbell's train on his first trip to the mountains was the Scots adventurer, William Drummond Stewart, second son of the Lord of Grandtully. Provost and Stewart were to share experiences on several occasions in the years ahead, and it was Stewart who provided one of the very few descriptions of Provost.

As a second son who despised his elder brother, Stewart was destined to find his own way in the world, with little hope of inheriting the title. Stewart had entered a military career and distinguished himself at Waterloo. He later served as a mercenary in Portugal and Italy and hunted in Turkey. He came to America for adventures in the west, then regarded in Europe as the epitome of savagery and mystery, and found it so much to his liking that he returned with the rendezvous caravans for a number of years. While English to the core, and something of a condescending martinet, Stewart nonetheless succeeded in winning acceptance among the mountaineers for he displayed to them a number of times that "Thar was old grit in him, too, and a hair of the black b'ar at that."[20] For all his strange ways, that character trait earned him the respect of the mountaineers.

Provost met Stewart at the 1833 rendezvous. Stewart later described him as a "burly Bacchus" in his *Edward Warren*. Stewart also avowed that the rendezvous of 1833 was the last great gathering. While others might not concur that it was the last great revel, "According to connoisseurs of such goings-on—and there were some formidable men who attended and survived nearly all of the rendezvous— 1833 was the vintage year."[33]

The focal point of the rendezvous was the fort Bonneville had built the previous year, but the various companies were spread along ten miles of river. It was the first rendezvous at which all the companies in the mountains were represented: Bonneville at his own establishment, the American Fur Company under Andrew Drips, the Rocky Mountain Fur Company under Fitzpatrick and his partners, and a few independent traders.

The Green River rendezvous of 1833 was the first of six to be held in that same area. The rendezvous of 1839, as described by Frederick A. Wislizenus, must have been similar to the earlier Green River gatherings which Provost attended.

The Green River rises in the northwestern slope of the Wind River Mountains, flows in a southwestern direction and empties into the Gulf of California. It is a clear, rippling streamlet, abounding in trout; neither very broad nor very deep. We crossed the river and were in the acute angle formed by it and the Horse Creek (a brook coming from the northwest and emptying here into the Green River). The space between is level; the ground a loamy sand. The camping place was about two miles above the Horse Creek, along the right bank of the Green River.

What first struck our eye was several long rows of Indian tents (lodges) extending along the Green River for at least a mile. A quantity of trappers had found their way here to buy and sell, to renew old contracts and make new ones, to make arrangements for future meetings, to meet old friends, to tell of adventures they had been through, and to spend for once a jolly day. These trappers either receive their outfit, consisting of horses, beaver traps, a gun, powder and lead from trading companies and trap for small wages, or else they act on their own account and are called freemen. The latter is more often the case.

A pound of beaver skins is usually paid for with four dollars worth of goods; but the goods themselves are sold at enormous prices, so-called mountain prices. With their hairy bank notes they can obtain all the luxuries of the mountain and live for a few days like lords.[22]

Rendezvous was a time to find out which faces were missing from last year. Death was a constant companion of the mountaineer; among the many who had "gone under" since the last rendezvous was William Henry Vanderburgh, who had been killed by the Blackfoot the previous October. In July 1833, while Provost, Stewart, and the mountaineers were gathered on Horse Creek, John F. A. Sanford, Sub-Agent of Indian Affairs, reported to Governor William Clark the number of deaths of trappers at the hands of the Indians during the past season and described some causes for the problems between the Indians and the trappers. The Blackfoot alone had killed 18 or 20 men and Sanford wrote:

This is not greater than usual. This does not surprise me at all— as long as the whites are trapping in that country it will be the case. The Blackfoot chiefs have told me that I must never expect anything else so long as the whites were trapping in that country. They said, "if you will send traders to our country we will protect them well; but for your trappers, Never."[23]

The rendezvous itself was dangerous enough to life and limb, and almost every year's celebration saw the death or maiming of several of the celebrants. Fueled on mountain liquor, the party became as wild as any gathering imaginable and fights and duels were frequent. The 1833 gathering was enlivened by the lynching of a card sharp and saw a tragic circumstance of another sort when several camps were attacked by rabid wolves and a number of men bitten. At least one man died as a result of the bites.

As the rendezvous came to a close, Provost set out about August 1 to return overland to Fort Pierre by the Platte route, arriving safely on August 29. The previous year Fort Pierre had been built a short distance upstream from Fort Tecumseh to replace it as a trading post. Acting on Fontenelle's instructions, Provost took the furs downriver to St. Louis. Fontenelle had also suggested in a letter to William Laidlaw that Provost "go down to St. Louis and if agreeable to the agent at that place to try and bring into the country next winter the quantity of spiritous Liquors we shall want for next spring and sink it in a safe cache on the river plate [Platte] untill he passes with his company."[24]

Provost had been designated to command the AFC outfit to the mountains the next year, and Fontenelle was suggesting that during the winter of 1833-34 Provost smuggle liquor around the river checkpoints and cache it to be picked up in the spring on the way to the mountains.

Having once been introduced, alcohol became a staple of the trade and while perhaps decrying its use, none of the companies engaged in the mountains could afford to be the one foregoing its use. The need for liquor in the trade, the prohibitions against it by the government, and the continual efforts of the companies to evade the law comprise their own story. Kenneth McKenzie expressed the trader's attitude in a letter to Ramsay Crooks in December of 1833:

For this post I have established a manufactory of strong waters, it succeeds admirably. I have a good corn mill, a very respectable distillery and can produce as fine liquor as need be drank. I believe no law of the U.S. is hereby broken...liquor I must have or quit any pretension to trade at this post, especially when our opponents can get any quantity passed up the Mo. or introduce it as they have by another route.[25]

The proposal that Provost transport liquor upriver in the winter of 1833 is the only documented evidence that he may have undertaken such assignments for the

Company. On other occasions, when Provost was absent from St. Louis in mid-winter on an assignment for the Company, it is certainly conceivable that he might have been more than a carrier of dispatches to the upper posts.

On his way downriver to St. Louis, Etienne stopped at Cabanne's post where Joshua Pilcher was then in charge. Years later Joseph LaBarge told an interesting story involving Provost, an event he said took place in August when he was employed as a clerk at Cabanne's post and was a newcomer to both the river and the fur trade.

LaBarge and a companion were on the prairie when they were caught in the open by a band of Sioux. LaBarge, who was mounted on a slow mule, realized he could not outrun the Indians, so he sent his companion to the post for aid while he held the attackers off. The companion raced on to the post and a rescue party was sent.

On returning to the post, LaBarge found Provost there to meet Drips and Fontenelle. LaBarge said Provost, "who probably knew the western country better than any man," praised his exploit on the plains and added, "I am glad you did not show the white feather to those rascals. You are the kind of man for this country. I am going to ask Major Pilcher to let you go with me. I have need of such men." According to LaBarge, he very much wished to accompany the legendary Provost, but Joshua Pilcher had greater need of him and would not consent to his going.[26] This story would seem more likely if Provost had been bound for Bayou Salade, (South Park, Colorado) as LaBarge claimed. Since he was not, and there seems to have been little reason to recruit LaBarge merely to assist in bringing the furs to St. Louis, the story is perhaps best taken with a fair dose of salt.

Events of the next few months had major influence

on the future of Provost and the fur trade. When
Sublette returned to St. Louis with the partnership's
furs, Robert Campbell remained in the mountains and
constructed a stockade post on the Yellowstone River
about six miles by water, three by land, from the
American Fur Company's Fort Union.[27] Campbell spent
the winter there and entered into unsuccessful nego-
tiation with Kenneth McKenzie at Fort Union to sell out
the Sublette and Campbell interests on the Missouri
River to the American Fur Company. McKenzie was
rather cool to the idea and did not believe the competition of Sublette and Campbell would harm the American Fur Company interests. Rather, he believed that by
paying excessive prices for furs and reducing the cost
of goods, the Company would drive Campbell off the
river. McKenzie had already destroyed the St. Louis Fur
Company on the Missouri River by paying the exorbitant sum of $12 a pound for beaver, and had no reason
to believe he could not accomplish the same against
Sublette and Campbell.[28]

While McKenzie was sitting smugly on the Missouri
River, disdaining the Campbell offers, Sublette was in
New York talking to Astor's people directly. As in so
many things, timing was of the essence. Astor's company could whip the competition on the rivers by
paying higher and higher prices until the opposition
folded. But Astor himself intended to retire, and when
he did the company would lose his strong financial
backing and political support. The loss of Astor's
influence in the government could place Missouri's
Congressman, William H. Ashley, in a position to exert
his influence for the benefit of his old friends and
associates, the AFC's competition. In addition, the
government was troubled over the still McKenzie was
operating at Fort Union. With all the uncertainty, Astor
agreed that, in return for Sublette and Campbell giving
up all claims to trade on the Missouri River, the

American Fur Company would stay out of the mountains for the ensuing year. Since Fontenelle and Drips had already contracted with the company to supply them the next year, with Provost already designated to lead the American Fur Company caravan to the rendezvous, that arrangement was not affected.

In another development, a relative newcomer to the trade made his appearance at the 1833 rendezvous—one Nathaniel Wyeth, a Massachusetts ice merchant with grand ideas for making his fortune in the mountains. During that rendezvous Wyeth had contracted with the Rocky Mountain Fur Company to supply it at the 1834 gathering. This was not to the liking of Sublette and Campbell; with Astor out of the mountains, the partners had considered themselves free of serious competition.[29] The scene was set for the rendezvous of 1834 on Ham's Fork of the Green River, where the practical effects of a paper agreement in New York would be tested on the western ground.

NOTES

1. Daniel Lamont to Pierre Papin, March 9, 1832, Letterbook of Ft. Tecumseh and Ft. Pierre, Chouteau Collection.
2. "Campbell Narrative," 36.
3. Ferris, *Life in the Rocky Mountains*, 150.
4. Letter in Chouteau Collection.
5. "Campbell Narrative," 40.
6. Ferris, *Life in the Rocky Mountains*, 158.
7. The site is about twelve miles west of the present town of Pinedale, Wyoming.
8. "Journal of Fort Tecumseh," entries for Monday, September 24 and Monday, October 15, 1832.
9. *Ibid.*, entry for October 4, 1832.
10. *Ibid.*, entry for September 24, 1832.
11. "Campbell Narrative," 41.

12.   St. Louis County Court, Records Department Registrar City Hall, microfilm rolls F-1, F-2.

13.   Ault, "A History of Municipal Government in St. Louis, 1829-34."

14.   Registrar, City of St. Louis 1841-44; microfilm roll F-3.

15.   Stevens, *Centennial History of Missouri*, 1: 113.

16.   Anderson Journals, 346-7.

17.   Thomas and Ronnedfeldt, *People of the First Man*, 16.

18.   Letter from William Laidlaw to Pierre Chouteau, Jr., August 29, 1833, Letterbook of Ft. Pierre, Chouteau Collection.

19.   Letter from Lucien Fontenelle to William Laidlaw, written at the rendezvous, July 31, 1833, Chouteau-Walsh Collection.

20.   Gilbert, "Thar was Old Grit in Him," 61-2

21.   Ibid., 61.

22.   Wislizenus, *A Journey to the Rocky Mountains in the Year 1839*, 85-88.

23.   Letter of July 26, 1833, William Clark Papers.

24.   Letter from Lucien Fontenelle to William Laidlaw, written at the rendezvous July 31, 1833, Chouteau-Walsh Collection.

25.   Nothing more is known about this proposal, or whether or not Provost did as suggested. It may be assumed that this was a regular practice of the AFC; however, for the year 1834 the Company for the first time abandoned the river in favor of an overland route.

26.   Letter of December 12, 1833, Letterbook of Fort Union, Chouteau Collection.

27.   Chittenden, *History of Early Steamboat Navigation on the Missouri River*, 38-9.

28.   "Campbell Narrative," 43.

29.   Gowans, *Rocky Mountain Rendezvous*, 122.

Carrot of Tobacco

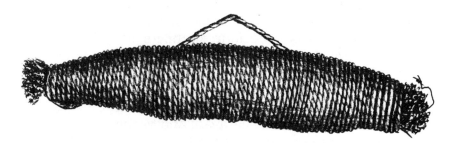

CHAPTER EIGHT
The Brigade Years II, 1834-1838

With the agreement with Astor secure on paper, William Sublette moved to strengthen his hard-won position in the mountains. Among other plans for the year, he determined to build a post near the mouth of the Laramie River where it flowed into the North Platte. Meanwhile, Astor retired, selling the Northern Department, which represented the trade along the Great Lakes and the Mississippi River, and which retained the name American Fur Company, to Ramsay Crooks. The Western Department, which now encompassed the Upper Missouri River region, was bought by Pratte,

Chouteau and Company, the old B. Pratte and Co. with a new name that more accurately reflected Chouteau's interest and influence in the company.

As the winter waned, the companies prepared for the spring caravans. This year would be unusual for several reasons. First, there were four separate companies taking the field to supply the rendezvous. What is more, this year would be documented by several mountain diarists. The four suppliers included the Sublette and Campbell caravan to supply the Rocky Mountain Fur Company and Nathaniel Wyeth, leading his train for the same purpose, and holding a contract with the company. Etienne Provost was leading the American Fur Company caravan, and Michel Sylvestre Cerre was bringing needed supplies and trade goods to Captain Bonneville. Several Methodist missionaries were traveling with Wyeth's caravan, bound for work among the Flathead Indians.[1] That instead they went on to Oregon is of no matter here.

The rendezvous of 1834 on Ham's Fork of the Green River, near present-day Granger, Wyoming, is the best documented of any of the mountain gatherings. Sublette had with him William Marshall Anderson, who kept a diary of the entire trip; and Wyeth not only kept his own journal, but he also had with him both Osborne Russell, one of the few trappers to keep a journal, and the physician and ornithologist John Kirk Townsend. Unfortunately, neither the Cerre train nor Provost's caravan had a diarist along.

Nathaniel Wyeth, the Massachussetts ice merchant, was a disciple of Hall J. Kelley, who stumped for years for the settlement of the Oregon territory. Kelley the visionary was never able to carry out his own plans, but Wyeth was a businessman more interested in the economic opportunity in Oregon than in its settlement. He envisioned a successful fur trading operation at the mouth of the Columbia River.

Wyeth had first come to the mountains in 1832, traveling with Sublette's train, and was present for the Battle of Pierre's Hole at the rendezvous that year. From the rendezvous he continued westward with Milton Sublette's trapping brigade, eventually separating from Milton and making his way to the Hudson's Bay posts on the Pacific coast. After a winter among the British, Wyeth returned eastward for the rendezvous of 1833 on the Green River, where he contracted to supply the Rocky Mountain Fur Company at the 1834 rendezvous. Tom Fitzpatrick even put down a deposit of earnest money with Wyeth. So, in 1834, Wyeth was starting for the rendezvous with every expectation of selling out his trade goods and merchandise to the RMFC and establishing himself as a power in the trade.

Travelers to the mountains usually started from St. Louis which, in the spring of 1834, was the commercial center for the entire northwest and to the visitor "wore an obvious garland of prosperity."[2] John Townsend and Thomas Nuttall, an English botanist, arrived to join Wyeth's company to the rendezvous. Nuttall was sponsored by his employer, Harvard College, and Townsend was sponsored jointly by the American Philosophical Society and the Academy of Natural Sciences, both of Philadelphia. They sought Wyeth out for guidance in outfitting themselves for the journey, and with his assistance they selected "several pairs of leathern pantaloons, enormous overcoats, made of green blankets, and white wool hats with round crowns, fitting tightly to the head, brims five inches wide, and almost hard enough to resist a rifle ball."[3]

Provost was also making up his outfit that spring. This year the American Fur Company's supply train would, for the first time, take the overland route to the rendezvous. The "Invoice of merchandise sent to Lucien Fontenelle in charge of Etienne Proveau to be sold in the Rocky Mountains for account and risks of U.M.O.

1834" lists four pages of the supplies and trade goods bound for the rendezvous. His cargo, valued at $7,256.06, included 198 gallons of alcohol, 100 beaver traps with chains, cloth of various types, shawls of both cotton and wool, socks, green goggles, "warranted scalpers knives" (50 dozen of those dandies), a dozen lead pencils, handsaws, files, awls, beads, and vermillion.

Of particular interest were "6 steel mounted rifles, Hawken" at $20 each.[4] This is the only record of Hawken rifles being taken to a rendezvous as trade items.[5] Also taken along for trade were ten other "steel mounted rifles," at $17.50 each. This was the noted "Northwest Gun," probably the most numerous weapon in the mountains. The name was not a brand; it referred to a style of weapon manufactured by a great number of gunsmiths. No other gun ever enjoyed such widespread use over so long a period of time. The fur companies sold them at the trading posts, the traders carried them into the various Indian nations, and they were given by the thousands to the Indians as treaty payments by the government.[6]

In April the time was right for the caravans to get under way. Their departure was dependent upon the greening of the prairie grass; leaving too early would bring the trains to the grassland before it was sufficiently high to sustain the animals. Since Provost did not have a journalist with him, the comments from the diaries of Wyeth, Anderson, Townsend and Osborne, who preceded Provost over the same route by only a few days, must convey a sense of the overland route as experienced by all trains that summer.

Wyeth and his caravan left Independence on April 28, the first of the four trains to pull out. There were 70 men and 250 horses in the company. Wyeth and Milton Sublette were at the head of the column followed by "the men in double file, each leading with a line, two horses heavily laden." Each pack animal carried 160 pounds of cargo made up of two 80 bales. Townsend found the departure was "altogether so exciting that I could scarcely contain myself. Every man in the company seemed to feel a portion of the same kind of enthusiasm; uproarious bursts of merriment, and gay and lively songs were constantly echoing along the line" (p. 31).

William Sublette's train did not leave Independence until May 5 and spent the first night twenty miles out on the prairie at Sapling Grove. Wyeth's party was somewhere ahead of them on the trail, and Sublette was determined to overtake him. But that night he shared the campsite with the parties of Provost and Cerre.[7] Provost was not mentioned again in the journals of the various supply trains to rendezvous but, Anderson wrote that their parties had "the same destination as ourselves."

Anderson and Townsend provide some interesting insights into the conduct of a caravan of considerable size traveling over the plains. Parties of such size ran little danger of an Indian attack, but nevertheless, caution was exercised at all times. The Indians might not attack, but they would steal horses if the opportunity arose. Townsend described the making the evening camp:

Captain W[yeth] rides around a space which he considers large enough to accommodate it, and directs where each mess shall pitch its tent. The men immediately unload their horses and place their bales of goods in the direction indicated, and in such a manner, as in the case of need, to form a sort of fortification and defence. When all the messes are arranged in this way, the camp forms a hollow square, in the centre of which the horses are placed. The guard consists of from six to eight men, and is relieved three times each night, and so arranged that each gang may serve alternate nights (p. 33).

The men were divided into messes of eight members, each mess having an experienced "captain" who received the group's daily ration each morning. One man was chosen as cook for the group. Alertness was an obvious requisite for the night watch, and if a member was found asleep on watch, he was made to walk for three days. Townsend noted that in the early days of the march that penalty was rarely enforced; however, as the caravan advanced farther onto the prairie and the danger increased, so did adherence to the rule.

They traveled about twenty miles a day. This was about all the distance that could reasonably be covered, considering the load of each pack animal and the heat of the plains, which was making itself more evident as the days wore into summer. In Sublette's train, once on the trail, "we were kept in strict military order and marched double file. Those first ready took their places next to the commander."[8] Sublette's procedures for night camp were very similar to Wyeth's; presumably they were standard among all plains travelers.

At night, according to Townsend, the horses were brought into the hollow square and picketed:

To stake or fasten a horse for the night, he is provided with a strong leathern halter, with an iron ring attached to the chin strap. To this ring, a rope of hemp or plaited leather, twenty-two feet in length, is attached, and the opposite end of the line made fast with several clove hitches around an oak or hickory pin, two and a half feet long. The top of the pin or stake is ringed with iron to prevent its being bruised, and it is then driven to the head in the ground. For greater security, hopples made of stout leather are buckled around the forelegs (p. 32).}

Within two weeks Sublette made up the distance lost by his later departure and he passed Wyeth in the dark of a prairie night. Once ahead, he never relinquished his lead, arriving first at the rendezvous as he had planned from the beginning. He was not about to lose the hard-won position he had negotiated with Astor. Townsend wrote, "It seems rather unfriendly to run by us in this furtive way, without even stopping to say good morning, but Sublette is attached to a rival company, and all stratagems are deemed allowable when interest is concerned. It is a matter of some moment to be first at rendezvous" (p. 41). Wyeth's own journal made little of the fact Sublette had passed him. He wrote, under the date of May 12, "in afternoon started and in about 8 mils found a camp of Sublettes for nooning."[9]

On the fifteenth of May one of Wyeth's men came to the Sublette camp with a letter Wyeth hoped to have sent ahead with the faster caravan for delivery to Fitzpatrick at rendezvous. He was attempting to regain the advantage and protect his contract with Fitzpatrick. He had written on May 12, the day he discovered Sublette had passed him:

To Thos Fitzpatric or Co. In the Rocky Mountains: Wm Sublette having passed me here, I am induced to write you by this opportunity and hope you will get it. You may expect me by the 1st July at the rendesvous named in your letter to Milton [Sublette]. I am not heavily loaded and shall travell as fast as possible and have a sufficient equipment of goods for you according to contract. Cerre will be much later than me, and also the Am. Fur Co.[10]

Once the supply trains had passed beyond Grand Island (Nebraska) on the Platte River, the parties began to see buffalo "by thousands and tens of thousands." Anderson described "the Platte, from two to three miles wide, and fully knee-deep" (p. 95), and passed judgment on the prairie dog: "if barking can make them so, these comical little sons of bitches will be dogs to all eternity." Farther up the Platte, the parties came to what Anderson and Townsend both called "the chimney," indicating it had not yet received its later sobriquet, Chimney Rock.[11] Anderson also referred to it cryptically as "E.P.," initials of the translated and bawdy Indian name for the cylindrical formation.[12]

On May 31, Sublette's party, still in the lead, was camped on the banks of the Laramie River. Here they began construction of the post that was intended to be the foundation of Sublette's position as supplier for the mountain trade. According to William Anderson, once the first logs had been laid:

A friendly dispute arose between our leader and myself as to the name. He proposed to call it Fort Anderson, I insisted upon baptizing it Fort Sublette, and holding the trump card in my hand, (a bottle of champagne) was about to claim the trick. Sublette stood by, cup reversed, still objecting when Patton offered a compromise which was accepted and the foam flew, in honor of Fort William, which contained the triad pre names of clerk, leader and friend (p. 109).}

Sublette left Patton and a group of men on the Laramie to complete the fort and pushed on to rendezvous, arriving at Ham's Fork on June 15. Wyeth's party was two days behind, arriving on June 17.[13]

Within a few days all the caravans had arrived and were stretched for miles along the river. Anderson visited the camp of the American Fur Company, located about eight miles below Sublette's camp at the junction of Ham's and Black's Forks of the Green River. He particularly enjoyed the rice and plum puddings offered him, which had been made from ingredients

Green River, Oregon

brought out by Provost. There were few times that the mountaineers could enjoy luxuries such as puddings and bread of any sort. The rendezvous gave them the opportunity to enjoy salt, sugar, and various spices as well.

The rendezvous was a disaster for Wyeth because Fitzpatrick and his partners refused to honor their contract with him.[14] They defaulted, willingly it seems, on the advance payment made to him and did business with Sublette and Campbell, as Sublette had intended all along. Wyeth, bitterly disappointed and blaming Sublette for undermining him, abandoned the rendezvous and moved to a site on the Snake River where he built a trading post that he named Fort Hall after one of his partners.

John Kirk Townsend's views of the rendezvous varied, depending upon his mood of the moment. Just before arrival, he was looking forward to the gathering where "All will be mirth and jollity, no doubt." Just five days later, while recuperating from an illness, he wrote:

These people with their obstreperous mirth, their whooping and howling, and quarreling, added to the mounted Indians who are constantly dashing into and through our camp, yelling like fiends, the barking and baying of savage wolf-dogs, and the incessant cracking of rifles and carbines, render our camp a perfect bedlam. I (lie ill) and am compelled to listen to the hiccoughing jargon of drunken traders, the sacre and foutre of Frenchmen run wild, and the swearing and screaming of our own men (p. 82).

That sounds like the view of a man with a fierce headache. Later on Townsend felt better and was somewhat more tolerant in his remarks. Dale Morgan had a more amiable view of the rendezvous, which has come down in history as a month-long orgy of drunkenness and carousal:

It must be remembered that there were no kegs of applejack stowed away under mountain roof beams for the long winter nights, no taverns for convivial tippling, no opportunities for Saturday night or country fair blowouts. If a mountain man was going to treat his comrades, show himself a good fellow and generous withal, he had to do it at the rendezvous. The excesses of a whole year were compacted into a few weeks; and the mountain men took perverse pleasure in shocking onlookers. Indians at the rendezvous were their friends, and as friends might be treated. Over the whole history of the rendezvous, no red visitors were debauched or impoverished by alcohol. Such incidents rather attended the trade for buffalo robes, especially on the High Plains, after the fort building epoch began.[15]

Morgan's assertion that during the mountaineer period alcohol was not used to take advantage of the Indian in trading is borne out by Alfred Jacob Miller's observations of the 1837 rendezvous. He noted that when an Indian was overcome by drink, he would be "overpowered, knocked down and secured from mischief."[16]

Shifting organizations were ever the game in the fur trade. Early in the 1834 rendezvous, while Provost sat comfortably on the sidelines and watched the goings-on among those groups lacking the powerful backing of Chouteau and the American Fur Company, Henry Fraeb and Jean Baptiste Gervais sold their interest in the Rocky Mountain Fur Company to their other partners, opening the way for the formation of a new partnership, Fitzpatrick, Sublette and Bridger. And as if that was not enough for one rendezvous; further negotiations between the various companies resulted in the merger of the new Fitzpatrick, Sublette and Bridger

with Fontenelle, Drips and Company into a new partnership called Fontenelle, Fitzpatrick and Company.

The new partnership bought Fort William on the
Laramie from Sublette and Campbell together with
their territorial rights and the right to deal with Pratte,
Chouteau and Company. Sublette and Campbell agreed
not to supply any competitors, and retired from the
mountain trade.[17]

On reflection, Sublette seems to have gained nothing from his agreement with Astor. The American Fur
Company train for 1834, with Provost at its head, had
been permitted to operate as agreed. Then, the accom-
modation worked out for 1835 permitted the Chouteau
interests, as Astor's successors to the western trade, to
supply the new company. Thus the American Fur
Company interests never did actually leave the mountains and seemed to have gained the best of both
worlds.

Don Berry provides a rationale for Sublette's actions in his *A Majority of Scoundrels*, which he readily
admits is a purely personal view arrived at as a result
of his research. Berry believes that Sublette acted
somewhat less than honorably: that he agreed with
Astor to bring about the collapse of the Rocky Mountain
Fur Company. Sublette held the notes of the RMFC,
and there was no way the company could pay its debt
at the current price for beaver pelts. To bring about the
collapse of the company, it could not be permitted any
cash surplus with which to pay its debts. Therefore,
Sublette must be first to rendezvous, pushing Wyeth
out of the picture. Possibly Sublette used his position
as creditor to force the RMFC to deal with him rather
than Wyeth, because if the company had dealt with
Wyeth at the much lower prices promised, it would
have had sufficient cash flow to pay its debt and remain
a viable entity. Berry contends that Astor and Sublette
planned the collapse of the RMFC so the American Fur

Company could re-enter the mountains in 1835 following expiration of the limitation agreement.[18]

This is what eventually happened, with the partnership first reforming and then merging with Fontenelle and Drips, backed by Chouteau, although Dale Morgan did not support the rationale of Berry. Morgan wrote in his introduction to *The Rocky Mountain Journals of William Marshall Anderson* that "Astor's 'trust' did not bring the Rocky Mountain Fur Company to its knees by unrelenting competition, to remain in victorious possession of the mountain scene; and Sublette did not throw away the Rocky Mountain Fur Company like an orange squeezed dry, no longer of any use to him" (p. 30).

As the 1834 rendezvous drew to a close, William Anderson had to decide whether to remain in the mountains with the trapping brigades and return to St. Louis the following spring, or to return immediately with William Sublette. Anderson decided to stay, and Sublette set out on July 10 without him. By late July, however, Anderson had changed his mind and was ready to leave the mountains after all, so he joined the American Fur Company party that would soon be returning to St. Louis. Now, for the first time, we have a contemporary account of Provost's activities, or at least activities in which he participated. Because Anderson chose to return with this party, when he wrote in his journal of events on the return trip, Provost, who was taking the company's furs back, was there.

On August 6 the various groups went their intended ways, with Jim Bridger leaving for the fall hunt with his brigade of about fifty men, including Kit Carson. Anderson moved into Fontenelle's camp to be ready for the next day's departure. "This is the day & sacred & prosperous be it, of our return. There is a most general joy on the occasion."[19]

On the return, the party laid over one day to hunt buffalo to provision their march. That night the discussion around the campfire turned to the discovery of the Great Salt Lake. Some credited William H. Ashley; however, it was said "by good authority" that Ashley had never seen the lake. "Tis believed the credit, if there is any in the accidental discovery of a place, is due to Weaver [Weber] or Provost." [20] Unfortunately, Anderson does not attribute any comments to Provost himself, although he surely must have stated when he had seen the lake.

Some days later the company passed an abandoned Pawnee camp and the discussion turned to the various Indian tribes and their numbers. In his journal Anderson refers to, "My informants, Mssrs. Fontenelle, Fitzpatrick & Provost," in recording the various estimates of population for the different tribes.

On September 11 the group came to the ruins of old Fort Atkinson on the Missouri River and dropped downriver to Cabanne's Post, where they found both Joshua Pilcher and Jean P. Cabanne. Anderson was pleased to return to civilization: "to see men with boots & shoes on, to dine at a table and to eat with forks again is a right pleasant thing" (p. 209).

Cabanne accompanied the party downriver to Fontenelle's post, Bellevue, where they prepared to send the returns to St. Louis by boat. Fontenelle wrote to Chouteau advising that in a few days he would be sending the returns down by water and that he was leaving the matter of insurance on the furs to Chouteau, although he himself considered it unnecessary to insure the shipment for "the boat will be very strong, and will have a double crew formed of the very best kind of voyageurs under the eyes of Mr. Cabanne and the superintendence of Etienne Provost."[21]

The boats were under way on September 18, two canoes lashed together and powered by six paddlers.

There were seventeen men in the party, including Provost, Cabanne, Anderson, and Fitzpatrick. The trip was largely a matter of avoiding the snags and sawyers in the river and navigating the many twists, turns, and bends the Missouri made in its rush to join the Mississippi. On reaching Lexington, the party beached and spent the night. Anderson showed something of an appreciative eye for both society and the ladies:

I have again supped at a tavern amidst village philosophers, pedantic doctors and sage looking lawyers. Our dirty coats and greasy breeches seemed to offend their nice eyes and delicate noses—God help them! A few white squaws were quite a treat. Happily too, the first I have seen is worth seeing—a fat healthy looking amiable countenanced lady—the wife of Major Ryland (p. 220).

Soon thereafter a minor rebellion and desertion reduced their voyageurs by half and the two boats separated, each now being paddled by its own crew. They arrived at St. Charles on September 29, where Anderson left the party to travel overland to St. Louis. It was forty miles by river to St. Louis, but only nineteen by land. Anderson could have been describing no one but Provost when he wrote as the final entry in his journal:

Never again, perhaps, shall I hear the facetious and characteristic command of: "fumez la pipe" from our weatherbeaten, bronzefaced Canadian Charon, when he willed that his galley boys should rest—His other dites' 'Gardez aux rames" attrape les chicot, & a hundred & one such sayings will sound in the ears of my memory for many an hour unborn—Adieu old friend—adieu! you have piloted me through many a straight—you have safely brought me over many a hidden danger (p. 227).

Provost arrived in St. Louis without further incident and delivered the furs to the warehouses of Pratte, Chouteau and Company. In November he was credited on the books of the company with $611.15, which appears to be the balance due him after taking out cash payments to his wife during the past eight months and debits for regular purchases of "rhum," sugar, coffee and the other merchandise necessary to the running of his tavern.[22] Historians have assumed that his wife managed the tavern in his absence, but based on the evidence presented earlier, it would appear far more likely that his brother-in-law, Clement Lambert, managed the business in Provost's absence.

A story had circulated in St. Louis during the summer of 1834 to the effect that Provost's train had been attacked by Indians on its way to the rendezvous. The *Missouri Republican* for August 26, 1834, reported a correction by a "gentleman who reached this city from the mountains" that Provost's party "had not been attacked by, nor had they a fight with the Pawnee Indians last spring."

Provost returned to learn of the death of his second daughter, Marianne, the previous June.[23] High infant mortality was a fact of life in the 1800's. The records suggest a high incidence of cholera deaths that year, not in epidemic proportions, but far greater than normal. Besides Etienne's daughter, Jean Baptiste Provost and his wife, the couple whose wedding Etienne had attended, both died in that year. Cholera may have been the cause for all three deaths.

Provost became involved in a lawsuit little more than a month after returning home. He brought a civil action of trespass against Trudeau LeBlond and Antoine Guion, charging that on November 1 they:

with force and arms made an assault on him the said Provost and him [they] *then and there did beat strike*

*wound knock down kick and trample upon and other
wrongs to him the said Etienne then and there did to the
[illegible] damages of the said Etienne and the said
Etienne saith he is injured and hath sustained damages
to the amount of Two thousand dollars and therefore he
brings his suit.*

LeBlond and Guion filed a counterstatement through
their attorney, turning the whole story around. They
were merely innocent victims of Provost's assault, and
in the defense of their persons they "did necessarily and
unavoidably a little beat strike wound knock down and
trample upon" the plaintiff, Etienne Provost.[24]

Trial was set for the November term of the court, but
the sheriff could not locate LeBlond and Guion to serve
the papers. The case was reset for the March term of the
court. March came, but still the trial did not take place.
The matter was postponed from court term to court
term at six-month intervals until the December term of
1836. Then the case finally came before the judge, but
history shall never know the full story, for though the
defendants were present with their attorney, "the said
plaintiff although solemnly called, comes not but makes
default." As a result, the judge dismissed Provost's suit
and assessed against him the charges and costs of the
defendants.[25]

Why Provost failed to appear to press his suit in
court cannot be determined. The account of his activities in the year 1836 is sketchy; sometime between
December of 1836 and February of 1837 he made a
fifty-one-day trip to the Council Bluffs. Thus he may
have been gone when the court convened, but he could
have had other reasons for not appearing.

Returning to 1835, we can learn very little of Provost's activities during the year. On March 31 he
bought the lot from his brother-in-law that Clement
had inherited from his father and which adjoined the

lot inherited by Provost's wife. Soon thereafter, in early April, he was working at Boonville with Jean Cabanne. Whatever work Provost was performing for him, Cabanne was not at all pleased with his crew, for he wrote Chouteau that "Fontenelle's men get drunk whenever they have the chance, a little less now because I have limited them to a half-gallon a day. Provot, who is a master drunkard, tells me that it was Fontenelle's intent to treat them well."[26]

In May Etienne was back in St. Louis when he and his wife sold the property that his father-in-law had sold to them in 1829. In the body of the deed his name is spelled properly, yet where he made his mark his name is written, "Akin Probo."[27]

During the summer of 1835 he was sent to Fort William, newly renamed Fort Lucien by Fontenelle, Fitzpatrick and Company. It appears he was working with Robert Campbell and Lucien Fontenelle, helping transfer the fort from Sublette and Campbell to the new partnership. He seems to have remained in the mountains throughout the fall. Whether he spent the entire time at Fort Lucien, still more popularly called Fort William, or ventured to the posts on the Missouri is not recorded, but he was paid $900 for his services by the Rocky Mountain Outfit in 1835, which indicates that his efforts in the field were on behalf of the new partnership of Fontenelle, Fitzpatrick and Company. Had he been working for the Missouri posts, part of his wages would have been covered by the Upper Missouri Outfit.

As 1835 drew to a close, Kenneth McKenzie wrote from Fort Union to Ramsay Crooks in New York with a grim picture of life as a trader:

Could I but fancy myself seated opposite to you by your own comfortable fireside with a bottle of your excellent port on a small table between us, we should see the bottom of it before I had recounted to you half my adventures by "flood and field" since we parted last summer. Coming down to sober reality I am alone in a smoky room, the thermometer 15 below zero, and although my ink is not frozen, my pen will neither move so nimbly, nor my ideas flow so freely as I would desire when writing to my good friend Ramsay.[28]

The demand for beaver pelts was rapidly diminishing every year after 1833, and it was necessary to look for other means of trade to support the river posts. After turning Fort William over to its new owners, Robert Campbell had come downriver in a Mackinaw boat with a load of buffalo robes.[29] In a letter from Fort Union to Alexander Culbertson, dated May 5, 1835, and probably written by Kenneth McKenzie (the signature is illegible), Culbertson is advised that "As the beaver trade for the last three years has been regularly declining it appears to me that our own sheet anchor will be the Robe Trade."[30]

By January of 1836, Provost was back in St.Louis. William Sublette wrote to Robert Campbell that "the two Prevoes" had left Fontenelle at Liberty where he was sending whiskey up to the Black Snake Hills (St. Joseph, Missouri).[31] Sublette related "Old Prevoes Tale" to Campbell, the essence of which was that Fitzpatrick had spoken to Provost about selling the fort on the Laramie if a satisfactory arrangement could be worked out and that Fontenelle would join Provost and some others in a venture.[32] If Fitzpatrick was talking in selling out, then within a year of its organization the new partnership was foundering. And such seems to have been the case for by the summer of 1836 the partnership of Fontenelle, Fitzpatrick and Company was in such bad shape that Chouteau sent Joshua Pilcher to Fort Lucien to buy them out and preserve what he could of his investment.[33]

With the arrival of spring in 1836, Provost left St. Louis with Toussaint Racine for another trip to Fort William (Lucien). Whether they joined Pilcher on his mission to buy the fort, or whether they were on a mission of their own is not known. Once at the fort they separated and Racine accompanied Pilcher to the rendezvous of 1836 at Horse Creek, where Pilcher succeeded in buying the business of the partnership, including Fort Lucien. Once the sale was completed, Fitzpatrick settled some of his accounts by issuing drafts on the company against the partnership account. The drafts included one to Toussaint Racine for $320, less any advances, and another to him for $150 for "his trip to Fort Lucien with Proveau."[34] Racine and Provost must have gone to the fort on some business for Fontenelle, Fitzpatrick and Company rather than for the Chouteau interests, although to some extent they were the same since Chouteau was backing the company. By early July he had returned to St. Louis where, on July 11, he was paid $225 for his "trip this spring to Ft. Lucien," again charged to the account of the Rocky Mountain Outfit.[35]

In the winter of 1836 he was again on the trail, this time for fifty-one days to the Council Bluffs and back. He had left by the end of December and had returned by mid-February of 1837. The trip may explain his failure to keep his court appearance, but the purpose of this mid-winter journey is unknown. Undoubtedly he carried company dispatches to be passed on to the upper posts; possibly he was also smuggling alcohol above the Bluffs.

The winter dispatch express was very important. It left St. Louis for Fort Pierre with dispatches for all the posts on the upper river. Provost may have carried the dispatches on the first leg of that journey to the Council Bluffs, where another rider took them on to Fort Pierre. The river posts, in turn, sent riders down to Fort Pierre, where the messengers exchanged dispatches. The upriver express brought news of St. Louis to the isolated posts together with instructions for the conduct of the next year's trade. The river posts notified St. Louis of their supply needs for the spring shipment and of the conditions in their various territories. The dispatches were, "intrusted only to those in whom the company had absolute confidence."[36]

Provost returned to St. Louis, probably attending to his tavern business until the arrival of spring once again directed the Company's thoughts toward the provisioning of its mountain brigades. In charge of the supply train to the 1837 rendezvous was Thomas Fitzpatrick, with Provost as his trail boss. This was the expedition that included as second in command William Drummond Stewart, still adventuring on the plains. Stewart brought a New Orleans artist he had employed to record scenes of the expedition. The artist was Alfred Jacob Miller, Baltimore-born and Paris-trained.

While the rendezvous of 1834 is unquestionably the one best documented in the journals and diaries of the participants, the 1837 gathering is the only one depicted visually. Miller was free to paint what he wished, and Stewart's only complaint seems to have been that Miller was not prolific enough.[37]

Miller began sketching and painting from the time the caravan left St. Louis, and his scenes of the train fording rivers and crossing the plains, of the camp on the prairie and at rendezvous are marvelous depictions of the mountaineer's life. Miller was, as Catlin and Bodmer were not, a deliberate artist-chronicler of the fur trade. Nowhere else can be found scenes of the Indians parading for the mountaineers, as they did in honor of Stewart, and no other artist recorded the Indians and trappers both at play and work. Equally important, Miller provided detailed commentaries to accompany his sketches that are far more descriptive of mountain life and of the mountaineers than the writing of so many diarists and journal keepers who faithfully recorded the day-to-day events but had not the imagination to comment on what they observed. Of a scene depicting the caravan rushing to the river to drink he wrote, "The question may be asked why we did not take water along with us? The answer is that it would have been an innovation on established custom. Nobody did any such thing— it was looked on as effeminate, to say nothing of the rough jests with which the reformer would be pelted."[38] He also described the breaking of camp at sunrise, the noon rest, and a threatened attack by Indians:

We descried one of our hunters returning to the camp at full gallop. His speech was to the purpose, "Injins all about—thar will be some raising of h'ar,—as sure as shootin." At this juncture it would have been a good study (if the matter had not been so serious) to watch the countenances of the various men. The staid indifference of the old trappers ready for any emergency, the green-horns (braggarts of the campfire) pale about the gills and quite chopfallen. No boasting now! Monsieur Proveau, subleader, with a corpus round as a porpoise, revolving in his mind what was to be done.[39]

Shortly thereafter the anticipated horde of Indians descended upon the caravan, and Miller describes them with an artist's eye: "painted without regard to harmony of color." After the usual threats a parley was held, and the Indians departed with a blackmail payment of tobacco and other goods.

In describing the camp preparing for dark, Miller wrote:

The point of view is from Monsr. Proveau's Tent—and the

time near sunset. The men have been quietly preparing their evening meals. Mo'sieur P. adipose and rotonde— "larding the lean earth as he walks along"— now raises both hands to his mouth and with stentorian lungs bawls out something like, "Attrapez des Chevaux"— the men immediately rise and run towards a cloud of dust from which the horses are seen emerging,— these are being driven in by the horse-guards from their range, some 2 or 3 miles, and the men secure each their own by lariats trailing on the ground from their necks,extending some 15 feet,— thence they proceed to their pickets, where they are secured for the night, with sufficient range to permit their grazing until morning.[40]

These are the only references to Provost in Miller's commentaries, and the paintings they accompany are the only depictions identified with him.

In June the caravan arrived at Fort William, and here Miller painted the only views ever made, both inside and out, of the original post built three years earlier by William Sublette. The fort stood on a rise of land on the west bank of the Laramie River, about a mile up that river from its junction with the North Platte. The exact site has never been determined by archeological excavation; however, the best evidence places it on what became the parade ground of the U.S. Armys post, Fort Laramie.[41]

Leaving Fort William on June 27, forty-five men and twenty carts headed for the mouth of Horse Creek, where the rendezvous was again to be held. The mountaineers had been gathering since early June, but Fitzpatrick did not arrive with the supplies until July 18.[42]

Once at the Green River site, the fourth of six rendezvous to be held on Horse Creek, Miller continued his painting of mountain scenes, and as a field note to one of his paintings wrote a valuable description of the

Interior of Fort Laramie

rendezvous:

*This was our ultima thule, our final destination. Here we
rested for a month under the shadows of the great spurs
of Wind River Mountains, encamping among 3000 Snake
and other Indians who had all assembled at this place
for a special purpose, viz. to trade buffalo robes and
peltries for dry goods, ammunition, tobacco, etc. It truly
was an imposing, animated and unique sight. The white
lodges of the Indians stretching out in vast perspective,
the busy throng of savages on spirited horses moving in
all directions, some of them dressed in barbaric magnifi-
cence.*

*The first day is given up by established custom to a
species of Roman saturnalia. King Alcohol is in great
demand and attainable, although selling at that time
here at $64 per gallon. It sets the poor Indian frantic,
sometimes causing him to run amuck, when he is
overpowered, knocked down and secured from mischief. Gambling, ball playing, racing and other amusements are in the ascendant.*

*On the second and succeeding days all this is changed.
The American Fur Company's great tent is elevated and
trading goes briskly forward. Here the trapper gets his
outfit and gangs of them depart under a "bourgeois" for
the beaver streams.*

*From this place we also made excursions to the charm-
ing lakes that form a chain through the upper portions of
the mountains for the purpose of making sketches of the
scenery.*[43]

At this gathering Jim Bridger was presented with
what many, Miller included, have called a full suit of
armor. Actually it was a cuirass, or steel vest, and

helmet with plume, presented to Bridger by Stewart. Miller painted Bridger on his horse wearing this armor. Miller also recorded a judgment on Bridger's social graces: "It is sad to record the infirmities of great men but my impression is that we saw [Bridger] one evening reeling from the commander's tent where 'high jinks' had been held, evidently having eaten too much dinner."

Fitzpatrick and Provost returned to St. Louis with the company peltries, only to find that the Panic of 1837 had dramatically depressed fur prices, which would finally hit bottom in 1843 and 1844. Provost was paid $600 for his services to the Rocky Mountain Outfit.

While Provost, Miller, Stewart, and compatriots were enjoying their summer gathering on Horse Creek, a smallpox epidemic moved up the Missouri wreaking havoc among the Indian tribes with no immunity or resistance to the dread infection. The Company sent Provost up the river to assess the damage wrought on the Indian tribes and the anticipated effect on the 1838 trade.

There are several myths regarding the origin of the epidemic, one being that a disgruntled former employee of Pratte, Chouteau & Co. placed infected clothing aboard the company steamboat. This clothing was allegedly stolen by a Mandan Indian when the boat was moored at Fort Clark near the Mandan villages, thus initiating the outbreak of illness. No less a person than General Bernard Pratte, Jr., took partial blame for the outbreak in another, similar version of the story. General Pratte, who was then captain of the steamboat *St. Peters*, said that the upriver voyage included a man who had caught and recovered from the smallpox. He remained on board, his wages "being a temptation to continue the voyage." The end of this story is similar to the first: a Mandan Indian stole the man's blanket, thus infecting whole nations.[44]

Laramie Fort

The infected and stolen blanket story originated with a letter written by the subagent for the Mandan at Fort Clark, one Fulkerson by name, to Governor Clark, advising him of the outbreak of the disease and relating the stolen blanket story. Governor Clark questioned not only the truth of Fulkerson's story but whether it had even been written from Ft. Clark. It appeared to Clark that the letter had been written from Fulkerson's home near St. Louis and was a complete falsehood.[45] True or not, the tale was picked up and repeated, being told by, among others, the worthy naturalist and artist John James Audubon, who felt constrained to moralize on the consequences of theft, and Hiram M. Chittenden.

What actually did happen? The best evidence indicates the following sequence of events: As General Pratte had related, about two weeks after the steamboat had left St. Louis a deckhand on the *St. Peters* came down with a fever. The true nature of his illness was not evident for several days, during which time Pratte had refused at least once to put the man ashore. By the time it became clear that the man had smallpox, others on board had been infected; when the steamboat reached the Council Bluffs agency, there were a number of people on board who were highly contagious. At the Bluffs three Arikara women boarded to return to their village upriver near Fort Clark, and these innocent women rather than a Mandan thief carried the infection to the Mandan villages.[46]

From this point the effects of interwoven contacts spread the disease. Infected trade goods and supplies were unloaded at one post; passengers and goods came aboard to become exposed to the disease and then disembark farther upriver. In this manner, through the regular commerce of the river, the infection was passed from one post and Indian village to another all the way to Fort Union. It required no special or deliberate effort.

The Indians unwittingly contributed to the spread of the disease. When they were warned of the danger, they accused the traders of trying to cheat them of their annuities, which were aboard the *St. Peters*, and refused to stay away from the posts.

At Fort Union a group of young Blackfoot braves, engaged in the Indian national sport of horse stealing, scaled the fort's walls and drove out a band of horses. The company men gave chase, caught the Indians, recovered the horses, and unwittingly passed on the pox. Indian warfare also contributed to the spread of the epidemic. In the fall, the Skidi Pawnee attacked a band of Oglala Sioux, taking captives who were infected. As a result, roughly one quarter of the entire Pawnee nation fell victim to smallpox.

With the onset of cold weather the ravages of smallpox lessened on the upper river. In December, 1837, Provost was sent to the Council Bluffs both to carry the dispatches for the upper posts and to obtain whatever information he could of the damage worked by the epidemic among the Indians on whom the company now depended for their trade. James A. Hamilton wrote to Chouteau on January 23 advising that he expected Provost's return momentarily and that he hoped the news would be better than the last information, for Jacob Halsey had submitted a report the previous November that painted a rather grim picture.

On February 25, 1838, Hamilton was able to write to Chouteau, "Late last evening Provost arrived and this morning (Sunday) we have been all occupied in perusing the melancholy details of plague pestilence and devastation, ruined hopes and blasted expectations." Provost had brought back the first real information as to how widespread the devastation was, and Hamilton was able now to report accurately to Chouteau. Less than a fourth of the Blackfoot had survived, the Mandans were almost destroyed, and half the Arikara nation was gone. Etienne also brought back word that the Assiniboine survivors were hostile, as Halsey had mentioned in November, and threatened vengeance. But the Blackfoot, for so many years the scourge and terror of the trapper, had become humbled and submissive; they begged the traders not to desert them. Provost also brought the news that "The Bull's Back Fat survives and is as warm a friend as heretofore."[47] The Buffalo Bull's Back Fat, whose portrait had been painted in 1832 by George Catlin,[48] was the head chief of the Blood tribe, one of the three main branches of the Blackfoot.

Hamilton also relayed to Chouteau Provost's estimates of the buffalo robes to be garnered in the coming season: 1,600 from the Sioux, who were but minimally affected by the smallpox, 800 from the Blackfoot and 300 each from the Crow and Assiniboine. The beaver trade was expected to be about the same as the previous year.

In 1838, Pratte, Chouteau & Co. again underwent a reorganization and name change to become Pierre Chouteau, Jr. & Co. The company reached an agreement with Bent, St. Vrain & Co., which was headquartered on the Arkansas River, dividing the trading territory above and below the South Platte River. This left Chouteau with a vast territory including present-day Wyoming and Montana, with Fort William and Fort Union controlling it. Etienne Provost once again went to the rendezvous, held this year on the Popo Agie River at its junction with the Wind River. It appears that this change of location after three years on the Green River was intended to mislead the Hudson's Bay Company, which had managed to attend every rendezvous to date. If such was the intent, it didn't work; the HBC people showed up as usual.

The company supply train was under the command

of Andrew Drips, since Tom Fitzpatrick was not going to the mountains that year. What position Provost held on this expedition is not known, but one of the several missionaries in the group, Cushing Eells, wrote "the guide mounted on a large and distinguishably white mule led the way."[49]   Was he describing Provost? Miller's paintings suggest that Etienne preferred mules, and it is possible that he served as guide for the train and perhaps also as second in command. William Drummond Stewart was along again, on his last adventure before returning home to Scotland to assume the inheritance and his duties as Lord of Grandtully, which had finally come his way with the death of his brother. The caravan included women this year, the wives of several missionaries en route to their post among the Indians.

No doubt the rendezvous was toned down somewhat in the presence of white women, and missionary wives at that. The women also added a culinary dimension to the camp not found in earlier rendezvous. To vary the steady diet of hump ribs and boudins, one wife at rendezvous "this afternoon made a couple of pies, chopped the meat with a butcher knife on the back of a cottonwood tree which Mr. S. pealed off. Rolled the crust with a crooked stick in a hollow bark, baked them in the tin baker out of doors in the wind." [50] She wrote that despite the disadvantages of crooked sticks, wind, and no doubt dust, the pies were good.

Other, more delicate, problems of sharing a tent with another couple were overcome with some discretion. One wife wrote that "Mr. and Mrs. S. went out and were gone several hours, so husband came & made me quite a pleasant visit." On the next day she noted, "Husband looks more happy than I have seen him in a long time."[51]

Provost was paid $500 for his services to the Rocky Mountain Outfit in 1838. When he left the rendezvous that year, it was for the last time. He never again returned to the mountains, although he would be many times up and down the Missouri for his employer in the years ahead. That year, the beaver trade was in deeper trouble than ever. Barely 2,000 beaver and otter pelts were traded at rendezvous, and there were only 125 trappers, both free and hired, in attendance. Despite the problems, the Rocky Mountain Outfit kept a brigade in the field over the winter of 1838-39 and supplied the rendezvous of 1839. Chouteau sent Andrew Drips to the Green River in 1840 on a journey more speculative than not, and the rendezvous of that year was but a pale imitation of its predecessors. Robert "Doc" Newell, who had been a mountaineer for some eleven years at this time, described the rendezvous of 1840 most succinctly: "times was certainly hard no beaver and everything dull."[52] It was also the sixteenth and last rendezvous.

NOTES

1. The missionaries were Jason Lee, his nephew Daniel Lee, Cyrus Shepard, C. M. Walker and P. L. Edwards.
2. Sunder, *Bill Sublette, Mountain Man*, 138.
3. Townsend, Narrative, 11.
4. American Fur Company Ledgers, Book Y, folio 6.
5. Editorial note by Charles E. Hanson, Jr., in Tykal, "Etienne Provost and the Hawken Rifle," 1.
6. Hanson, *The Northwest Gun*, 2.
7. Anderson, *Anderson Journals*, 73.
8. *Ibid.*, 80n.
9. Wyeth, *The Journals of Captain Nathaniel J. Wyeth*, 67.
10. Anderson, *Anderson Journals*, 82n.
11. Many of the landmarks of the Oregon Trail were not named by the mountaineers but by the later

emigrant parties or surveyor parties such as Fremont's of 1842.

12. Anderson, *Anderson Journals*, 102. Morgan, noting that Wyeth referred to it as "the chimney or Elk Brick," suggested that Wyeth was either "obtuse of ear or had a certain sense of humor."

13. Gowans, *Rocky Mountain Rendezvous*, 134-35.

14. Wyeth wrote in his journal: "and much to my astonishment the goods which I had contracted to bring to the Rocky Mountain fur Co. were refused by those honorable gentlemen."

15. Anderson, *Anderson Journals*, 33.

16. Carl Russell, "Rendezvous Period," 38.

17. Ibid., 26, 29-30.

18. Berry, *A Majority of Scoundrels*, 352-53.

19. Anderson, *Anderson Journals*, 174.

20. Ibid., 194. The quotation is from his diary; in his journal he wrote "credit, is due to Mr. Provost of St. Louis," making no mention of Weber.

21. Anderson, *Anderson Jounrlas*, 214n.

22. American Fur Company Legers, Book X, folio 56, "Etienne Proveau, Tavernkeeper" account.

23. Collett's *Index to Church Registers*.

24. St. Louis Circuit Court Records, November Term, 1834, No. 32.

25. St. Louis Circuit Court, Book 8: 154.

26. Letter dated April 7, 1835, in Chouteau Collection.

27. St. Louis Recorder of Deeds, May 18, 1835, 408.

28. Letter dated December 10, 1835, Letterbook of Fort Union, Chouteau Collection.

29. "Campbell Narrative," 46.

30. Letterbook of Fort Union, Chourteau Collection.

31. The "two Prevoes" were not identified but were certainly Etienne and probably Constant.

32. Letters of January 31 and February 9, 1836, Campbell Papers, MHS.

33. Anderson, *Anderson Journals*, 30.

34. Hafen, *Broken Hand*, 159, 160 n., and Hafen, "Etienne Provost," in Hafen, ed., *The Mountain Men and the Fur Trade*, 6: 381.

35. American Fur Company Legers, Book X, folio 56.

36. Chittenden, *History of Early Steamboat Navigation on the Missouri River*, 41.

37. McDermott, "Miller," 8.

38. Ross, *The West of Alfred Jacob Miller*, plate 132.

39. *Ibid.*, Plate 76.

40. *Ibid.*, Plate 197.

41. Warner, *The Fort Laramie of Alfred Jacob Miller*, 2, and letter of Merrill J. Mattes in Gregory M. Franzwa's *Maps of the Oregon Train*, 106.

42. Gowans, *Rocky Mountain Rendezvous*, 191, 199.

43. Carl Russell, "Rendezvous Period of American Fur Trade," 38.

44. Pratte, "The Reminiscences of General Barnard Pratte, Jr.," 59-71.

45. Dollar, "The High Plains Smallpox Epidemic of 1837-38," 33.

46. *Ibid.*

47. Letter to Pierre Couteau, Jr., in Chouteau-Papin Collection.

48. Halpin, *Catlin's Indian Gallery*, endpaper.

49. Gowans, *Rocky Mountain Rendezvous*, 208.

50. *Ibid.*, 220.

51. *Ibid.*, 228.

52. Johanson, ed., *Robert Newell's Memoranda*, 39.

Bone-handled knife made by
Wm. Coreaves & Son circa 1830

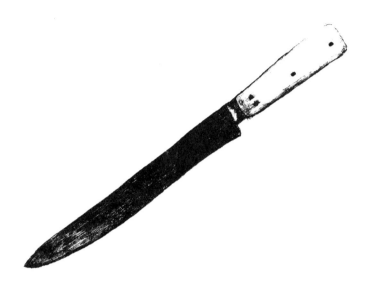

CHAPTER NINE
The Guide Years, I, 1839-1840

When Provost returned to St. Louis in the late summer of 1838, he was fifty-two years old. Even if the rendezvous years were not rapidly coming to a close, he might have considered ending the grueling trek to the mountains because of his age. Instead he now began a new career with the Chouteau interests which was just as demanding of strength and endurance as anything he had undertaken before. For most of the remaining years of his life, Provost continued to recruit new men for the company and escort them to the river posts each spring aboard the company steamboat. In the winter of 1838-39, he made a month-long trip to Arkansas, perhaps to recruit men for the company. He was advanced $40 for the trip, and in January returned the unused $6.[1]

And there was other, more arduous, employment as well in the years ahead. Escorting the new recruits to the river posts took very little time, and if there was nothing else for him to do, then his employment for the year ended with the boat's return to St. Louis. So the company used his vast knowledge and experience in other ways. After delivering the men to the posts, he often served as camp conductor or guide to various private expeditions in the Upper Missouri area, with his wages paid by the private party.

The American Fur Company frequently took on the aspects of a travel agency in St. Louis. No agency was better equipped to supply and transport anyone to the Upper Missouri country. And any good will the company services generated could counterbalance constant criticism of the company's monopolistic tendencies. Powerful government forces supported the Company; and equal forces supported the opposition. So the Company served its own interests when it assisted outside groups by furnishing supplies, transportation, and guides for their ventures—all paid for by the expedition, of course. The public relations effort succeeded admirably.

The Company had arranged George Catlin's travel to the Upper Missouri in 1832 and had again assisted in 1833-34 when Maximilian and Bodmer made their journey. In both instances the company provided transportation and all necessities and amenities at the various river posts and maintained accounts for them on the company books.

In 1839, Joseph Nicholas Nicollet and John Charles Fremont came to St. Louis to outffit a new expedition for the river for which Provost served as camp conductor. The previous year Nicollet had led a government sponsored expedition up the Mississippi to survey and map the southeastern portion of the immense triangle of land lying between the Mississippi and Missouri rivers. He was funded for a second year, and he intended to go up the Missouri by steamboat to Fort Union and from there to travel overland to Devils Lake, in present-day North Dakota, to survey the rest of the area between the great rivers for a new map.

Nicollet, an astronomer and cartographer born in Savoy, France, in 1786, lived and worked in the United States from 1832 until his death in 1843. His map and report of his expeditions contributed greatly to the geographic knowledge of the U.S.[2] John C. Fremont, a young lieutenant in the Topographical Bureau's Corps of Engineers, served Nicollet as second in command on both expeditions.

Fremont also oversaw the government funds for the expedition, which he began spending on supplies even before his appointment to serve a second year with Nicollet was confirmed.[3] In March of 1839, he was advised not only of his appointment to continue with Nicollet but also that a credit of $5,000 had been established with Pierre Chouteau & Co. for his use in supplying the party.

Nicollet had intended to take the steamboat all the way to the Yellowstone, but river conditions conspired to prevent that. The pilot of the steamboat was Joseph LaBarge, beginning his long career on the river at age twenty-four.[4] Nicollet's party of eight boarded the steamboat *Antelope* in early April, and they disembarked sixty-nine days later at Fort Pierre. Low water had delayed them, and Nicollet had to get under way overland as soon as possible, so he scrapped the idea of continuing to the Yellowstone and decided to set out from Fort Pierre.

On the river journey, Fremont wrote that "once

above the settlements of the lower Missouri, there were
no sounds to disturb the stillness but the echoes of the
high-pressure steam pipe, which travelled far along
and around the shores, and the incessant crumbling
away of the banks and bars, which the river was
steadily undermining and destroying at one place to
build up at another."[5]

Of the original members of his expedition Nicollet
wrote:

*I had brought up with me from St. Louis only five men,
who for my purposes were certainly worth ten. Four
among them had proved themselves by numerous voyages across the prairies, as well as voyages over the
Rocky Mountains. One of them was Etienne Provost,
known as 'L'homme des montagnes' - the man of the
mountains.*"[6]

At Fort Pierre Nicollet sought additional men and
supplies. The fort could only spare six men to accompany the party. The lack of men did not unduly concern
Nicollet and Fremont at that point, for during the
previous year's expedition they had arranged that a
party of reinforcements would meet them on the Riviere
a Jacques (James River).[7] This, however, was not to be.
Nicollet might not have been overly concerned, but as
the Brays noted, "The importance and danger of this
expedition into the Indian country of the arid northern
plains was acknowledged by the presence in the party
of Etienne Provost, perhaps the most famous of the
'mountain men' who had started in the fur trade with
Pierre Chouteau, Jr. in 1815 and knew the west from
Santa Fe to Canada probably better than any living
man.'"[8]

On July 1, Provost, whom Nicollet had promoted to
the position of "headman," reported that all was in
readiness, and Nicollet issued the orders to get under

way. They numbered nineteen, including the leaders, with thirty-three horses and ten carts. Among the recruits were William Dixon and Louison Freniere, both half-breeds and well known as horsemen, hunters, and experienced guides.[9] On this expedition Provost served as the camp conductor, responsible for the orderly management of the camp and its safety, for choosing campsites, for organizing messes and watches and the myriad details that insured the smooth operation of the expedition.

Although Nicollet had said the post could only spare him six men, the party obviously picked up an additional five men from somewhere. Two were a "Mr. May" and an unnamed companion who joined them at the fort, and a third was William Dixon who was hired by Nicollet on the way upriver, not at the fort.

On leaving Fort Pierre, it took a day and a half for the company to cross the now-swollen Missouri from the west bank to the east. From there they journeyed north toward Devils Lake. On the way, Fremont and Freniere would often ride ahead of the caravan and at such times, Fremont wrote, he liked "to lie in careless ease on the grass by a pond and be refreshed by the breeze which carried with it the fragrance of the prairie" (p. 56).

The reinforcements expected at the James River never materialized. Faced with the choice of continuing with his limited company or giving up his plans for the year, Nicollet determined to go on. He expressed both trepidation at what lay ahead and at the same time a great confidence in the ability of his small band, with the combination of their experience and firepower, to overcome or avoid any difficulty.

Shortly thereafter, the party found itself in the middle of a buffalo surround being conducted by a band of Yankton and Sisseton Sioux. Rather than move the wrong way and find themselves on the receiving end of a buffalo drive, Nicollet moved his men to the Indian camp area. Fremont reported in his journal that after moving to the Indian camp:

We were invited to eat in the lodges of the different chiefs; the choicest, fattest pieces of buffalo provided for us, and in return they were invited to eat at our camp. The chiefs sat around in a large circle of buffalo robes and blankets, each provided with a deep soup plate and spoon of tin. The first dish was a generous pot-au-feu, principally of fat buffalo meat and rice. With the first mouthful each Indian silently laid down his spoon, and each looked at the other. After a pause of bewilderment the interpreter succeeded in having the situation understood. Mr. Nicollet had put among our provisions some Swiss cheese, and to give flavor to the soup a liberal portion of this had been put into the kettles. Until this strange flavor was accounted for the Indians thought they were being poisoned (p. 61).

In late July, the stifling heat forced them to cut the daily marches short. The loaded horses were unable to take the strain, so the party limited its travel to the early morning and the late afternoon when the heat lessened. Another problem was the mosquitoes. Fremont wrote, "So virulent were they that to eat in any quiet was impossible, and we found it necessary to use the long green veils, which to this end had been recommended to us by the fur traders. Tied around our straw hats the brims kept the veils from our faces, making a space within which the plates could be held" (p. 62).

As the expedition approached the vicinity of Devils Lake their precautions increased; a number of Indian bands known to be hostile frequented the area. The horses were tied close to hand at night, as much a precaution for the horses' safety as their own. The guard was doubled during the night hours, and each man slept with his rifle at the ready. Their arrival at the lake after these precautions and fears was almost anticlimactic. They encountered no Indians, and spent more than a week peacefully making measurements and observations.

As they completed their tasks at Devils Lake, Nicollet was feeling some anxiety over the passage of time. The delays caused by the low water, the river crossing, and the extreme heat had consumed too many days of the brief summer of the northern prairies. The party still had a long way to go; the men's enlistment was fast running out; and the onset of cold weather was near. On the return route, they had planned to divide the party, with the larger group returning to Fort Pierre and the rest continuing with Nicollet. It was mid-August before the trails separated and all the men hired at Fort Pierre returned to the fort. Nicollet kept only those men and supplies necessary to finish the expedition. Writing to Pierre D. Papin at the time of the separation, Nicollet said that, "without exception I am pleased with my men."[10]

Provost remained with Nicollet to the end of the trip. They traveled southeast to Fort Snelling on the Mississippi, then down to Prairie du Chien. There they waited for Fremont, who had taken a survey party inland and was supposed to rejoin them momentarily. They eventually despaired of his arriving before the river froze, so they left for St. Louis on November 1. Fremont finally arrived at Prairie du Chien and, desiring to rest a few days, declined passage on the steamboat then loading for St. Louis. He was to regret that decision, for the river froze shortly thereafter and river travel ended until spring. Fremont had to make his way overland through the snow to St. Louis.

Once Nicollet and the men with him had returned to St. Louis, Provost received payment of $783 for his services as camp conductor. He was paid at the rate of

$3 per day from March 1 to November 16.

With his return from the Nicollet expedition, Etienne turned his thoughts to his local interests. On December 17, Etienne and Clement Salle dit Lajoie paid $36 for a license to run a grocery for a period of six months beginning December 24.[11] In 1840 a new account was opened in the ledgers of the American Fur Company for "Proveau and Lambert, Tavern Keepers." The account continued only through that year, the last entry being made on December 15. After that, either the formal partnership broke up or their accounts were kept elsewhere. The grocery license was renewed in June under Lambert's name only, and in December under Provost's only.[12]

The population of St. Louis had almost tripled in ten years and by 1840 there were 16,469 residents. The city directory for 1840-41 listed "H. N. Provost" as operating a grocery at the corner of "Second and Lumber," clearly Etienne at Second and Lombard. Elsewhere in the city, P. Chouteau & Co. had opened new offices and a warehouse on Laurel Street overlooking the levee. Company names may change, but no matter for it was still popularly called the American Fur Company. That year Chouteau sent Andrew Drips to the rendezvous with a caravan of goods without having made any prior arrangement. The rendezvous was a failure, as has been already noted in the comments of Robert "Doc" Newell: "times was certainly hard no beaver and everything dull."[13]

Etienne Provost spent most of 1840 managing his tavern and was not employed by the American Fur Company in any capacity. It is one of the few years in which he took no part in the company's business, and it may be that he stayed at the tavern because Clement Lambert, who was himself reasonably well known as a guide and mountaineer during these years, was on the prairie. Provost did not spend the entire year in St.

Louis, though; in the fall he was engaged as guide for a hunting party to the plains of western Kansas.

In mid-August seven British Army officers from Canada arrived in St. Louis on leave of absence from their military duties to engage in a buffalo hunt. Lieutenant William Fairholme, who had but recently arrived in Canada, kept a journal of the entire expedition.[14] The Britishers left Montreal in July and came to St. Louis by rail and water through Niagara, Buffalo, the Great Lakes, and Chicago.

As their steamboat approached St. Louis, the many chimneys of the city's manufacturing concerns created a smoky pall which hung constantly over the city in the humid August heat. Once ashore, the officers set out to see the city and to arrange for their expedition. One of their first stops was the shop of Kenneth McKenzie, who at that time was a St. Louis liquor merchant. He had been forced to leave Fort Union on the Upper Missouri over the incident of the still he had operated there, and had taken up residence in St. Louis. McKenzie offered them every assistance, and they thought him quite civil and obliging.

The following day the group learned that "Mr. McKenzie procured for us an excellent conducteur, in fact one of the head conducteurs of the American Fur Company, by name Provost, and he promised to engage for us 7 other Canadians." Provost was to receive $80 per month as "conducteur" and his seven men were to be paid $20 a month, which included an extra $5 per month to relieve the British adventurers of the onerous task of standing night guard. Among the seven men hired by Provost were two of his nephews.[15] The names were not given, but they must have been from his family rather than his wife's since the journal refers to the hiring of "Canadians." Perhaps one was the "Constant Provost" whose name soon begins appearing in Company records.

Feeling satisfied with their accomplishments of the day, the British officers enjoyed a good meal at the hotel. Lieutenant Fairholme wrote that afterwards, "following the example of the natives we lounged about the door of the hotel smoking and talking with the numbers of idle well dressed men who are always to be found about an American bar; in fact, all business in the States is carried out over a glass of Mint Julep or Sherry Cobbler" (p. 33). Perhaps it was during one of these barroom conversations that Fairholme ran across an earlier acquaintance, General Robert Patterson, an American and former militia officer who was then a prominent Philadelphia merchant, investor, and politician. Patterson was invited to join the expedition and gladly accepted. In succeeding days he helped outfit the party.[16] Provost also assisted, and on August 20 charged to McKenzie's account the purchase of various small items "per Proveau for English Men."[17]

The party made its way overland to Westport, where it would obtain any last-minute supplies and animals before setting out over the prairie. The hunters learned quickly the secret of dealing with their French-Canadian engages. Fairholme explained, "The grand point in any expedition with Canadians is to get away, no matter how short a distance, you make a beginning, before starting is spent in taking leave of their friends and they are seldom perfectly sober when the hour for moving arrives" (p. 39).

Fairholme became ill while en route to Westport, and at Jefferson City he separated from his companions to continue by steamboat, intending to rest and join them later in Westport. Another officer also became ill, dropped out of the company altogether, and returned to Canada. Fairholme had fairly well recovered by the time he reached Westport, but he was unable to find his companions in the town. He did not rejoin them until several days later when, after searching the prairie, he finally came upon them at Caravan Grove on the Santa Fe Trail.[18] Once the party was re-assembled it included 19 men, 44 horses and mules, 8 oxen, 3 dogs and 4 wagons by Fairholme's count (p. 73).

The expedition moved west rapidly because Fairholme had learned in Westport that the buffalo herds were much farther west than expected. As they moved over the prairies, they were enthralled by the numbers and variety of wildlife they encountered, and Fairholme waxed poetic over the cry of the geese passing overhead. They relaxed at their campsites, enjoying the company and the meals prepared by Henry, their Negro cook, who was believed to have been with the Lewis and Clark expedition.[19] One evening, Fairholme wrote;

Old Provost and Henry related to us some stirring incidents of Indian Warfare of which they had seen a great deal, having lived a great part of their lives among the Indians and in the Rocky Mountains. Provost on many occasions had had very narrow escapes and was wounded in several places (p. 85).

On September 27 the hunters saw their first buffalo, and lost it. They were giving chase when it just disappeared from view. Henry insisted that it was an Indian dressed in a buffalo skin to spy on the hunting camp. Soon thereafter they came upon buffalo aplenty, and the young lieutenant's journal for many pages reports little but the many chases they enjoyed. The American, Patterson, had brought along a lance with which to spear a buffalo, but he never used it during the hunt.

On one occasion a wagon broke a wheel, and Lieutenant Fairholme was quite impressed with Provost's ability to improvise repairs in the field. Fairholme noted that Provost wrapped the broken wheel and spoke with wet rawhide from a freshly killed buffalo, and as the hide dried it shrank around the wheel, holding it together better than steel.

October brought frosty mornings and chilly air to the plains, and the travelers returned eastward toward the settlements. On the evening of October 22, there was the smell of burning in the air and a few ashes fell on their dinner. A strange glare they had watched all day on the eastern horizon became, with darkness, a glow in the sky.

Provost informed them that it was a prairie fire, but a long way off. As the glare increased, however, so did the group's anxiety, and Fairholme and another walked to the top of a hill where they "saw the most grand [spectacle] that can well be conceived. The whole horizon from north to south was one wall of fire" (p. 157). The two men decided that the wind was moving the fire in their direction and returned to the camp to advise Provost to take some precautionary measures. Provost returned to the hilltop with them, and after viewing the distant blaze said it would pass them by and was of no concern: "ce n'est rien - le vent change"— it's nothing, the wind is changing.

Time, and a very short time at that, proved him wrong. As the evening progressed the fire continued to burn in their direction. All hands, Provost included, turned out to protect the camp against the onrushing fire. They tried to make a firebreak across the top of the hill above their camp, but time was not in their favor. They estimated the fire to be moving at five miles an hour and Fairholme charged that "Provost's obstinacy in neglecting to take precautions in time became more pregnant with danger." They were only half done with their preparations when the fire closed in over the top of the hill. With the destruction of their camp imminent, they freed the animals, which immediately headed for the middle of the stream that backed the camp.

Ultimately the camp was saved not so much by human effort as by the rocky hillside above it. The hillside was so gravelly that the grass was sparse and would not sustain the fire, which moved off to the north and away from their camp. The next day, as they continued eastward, they rode through ash and smoke for a distance of seventeen or eighteen miles.

Arrival in Westport was cause for both celebration and disappointment. The engages were entertained so generously by the townspeople that by the time the tales of their adventures had been sufficiently repeated for all listeners, the men were in no condition to work. The officers had hoped to sell their equipment, horses, and mules in Westport, but the prices offered were so low that they decided to sell most of the animals and wagons in Independence.

Once the returning company arrived in Independence, the town crier announced an auction for the sale of the wagons, mules, and remaining equipment. Their few remaining horses were sold; however, they could not get even a fair bid on the mules and wagons. Rather than concern themselves further with the mules, they signed them over to Provost for $200 in partial payment of his wages.

Because of the time consumed disposing of their gear, the adventurers had missed the St. Louis steamboat at Independence, so they bought a scow on which they floated the Missouri for three days. They hunted game and bought milk, bread, and honey from settlers along the riverbank, all of which must have been an enjoyable idyll in the beautiful late fall weather.[20] Before leaving Independence, they had tried to enlist some of their men to assist in handling the flatboat, but only one took them up on the offer. Fairholme presumed that Provost had persuaded the others to assist him in taking his wagons and mules home. The British officers sold the scow at Glasgow and took passage to

St. Louis on a steamboat. Meanwhile, Provost and his assistants began the overland trek to St. Louis where he presumably sold his wagons and mules to obtain his wages in dollars.

NOTES

1. Anderson, *Anderson Journals*, 349.
2. *Nicollet*, 1.
3. *Fremont Expeditions*, 1: 70.
4. *Nicollet*, 28.
5. *Fremont Expeditions*, 51.
6. "Nicollet's Account," *South Dakota Historical Collections*, 10: 112-113.
7. *Fremont Expeditions*, 1: 50.
8. *Nicollet*, 28.
9. *Ibid.*, 52.
10. Letter of August 19, 1839, Chouteau Collection.
11. Registrar of St. Louis County, Microfilm F-2, 299.
12. Ibid., 330, 362.
13. Newell, *Robert Newell's Memoranda*, 39.
14. Sunder, "British Army Officers on the Santa Fe Trail," 148n. Fairholme was born in 1819, and received his commission in February 1840.
15. Fairholme Jounral, 32, 73.
16. Sunder, "British Army Officers on the Santa Fe Trail," 150.
17. American Fur Company Legers, Book BB, K. McKenzie account.
18. Sunder, "British Army Officers on the Santa Fe Trail," 152.
19. The only Negro with Lewis and Clark was Lewis' servant York.
20. Sunder, "British Army Officers on the Santa Fe Trail," 154.

Mackinaw Boat

CHAPTER TEN
The Guide Years, II, 1841-1844

The available records do not give any hint as to what success Provost enjoyed in selling the mules and wagons from the buffalo hunting expedition. It appears that he sold them himself for there are no entries in the ledgers of the Company that would indicate it bought them from him.

After his year off from the Company he spent the next two years, 1841 and 1842, serving the company in various capacities and at the same time continued to manage his tavern. In February 1841, Etienne and his wife attended the wedding of their niece, Helene Gibeau.[1]

In the spring of 1841 Provost once again escorted the company recruits upriver and was gone from April to July of that year. His partner, Clement, if partners they were still, was away for thirty-three days in June and July as an engage and part-time cook on John Charles Fremont's survey of the Des Moines River.[2]

To protect itself from loss by desertion the company made payment of wages to recruits conditional upon a certain term of service. To accomplish the transfer of funds to the river posts, the company credited Provost on its books with the salaries due the recruits he was bringing upriver, and he carried the credit to the appropriate post where it was transferred to that post's books. Among the new company trappers and hunters were a "C. Prevost," and an "M. Prevost," who might have been the nephews hired by Provost for the buffalo hunt the previous year.

While Provost was escorting his new company engages upriver, the plains that he knew so well were again changing. The first of more than 300,000 people who would travel Sublette's wagon route west in the next twenty years was the Bidwell-Bartleson party of 1841. Fifty-eight strong, they headed over the prairies; twenty-four split off at Soda Springs, looking for California without the least idea of how to get there. The remaining thirty-four continued on to the valley of the Willamette River in Oregon.[3] As far as the Soda Springs they had been most fortunate: Thomas Fitzpatrick was guiding a party of Catholic missionaries and the wagon train joined with them to take advantage of Fitzpatrick's experience.[4]

Toward the end of July, Provost returned to St. Louis from the Upper Missouri, and the company settled with him on July 27. Possibly later that year, but more likely early in the new year, he was sent on a thirty-eight day trip to the Bluffs carrying the express for the company. He was given $35 for expenses, and on his return in mid-February turned back 87 cents of unused expense money. He also turned back the Spanish saddle and saddlebags the company had furnished, and he was paid $57 for his time.

In the spring of 1842, he again took his charges upriver, and his unabashed admirer Joseph LaBarge observed Provost's talent for handling the rough characters bound for the upriver posts. Once the company recruits were aboard, LaBarge likened the situation to a herd of cattle in which one must be recognized as herd boss. Provost would arrange to determine this champion early on, thus saving much fighting and argument during the rest of the trip. He would form a ring on the deck, and each of the bullies and braggarts was made to step into the ring in front of the passengers and their fellow engages and demonstrate his prowess against all challengers. One by one they fell, until one man emerged as victor. Him Provost would proclaim the champion, and he was given a red belt to wear for the rest of the trip.[5]

On the return downriver that year the steamboat ran out of water at Fort Clark. The river just wasn't deep enough to permit the boat to continue to St. Louis. The logbook of the American Fur Company kept by the boat's captain, Joseph Sire, presents an interesting glimpse of the problems encountered on that trip downriver. In many respects it serves to illustrate the unending problems that faced a steamboat captain on the Upper Missouri in any year. If it wasn't low water or obstructions in the river's course, it was the lack of firewood—and oftimes all three.

Mon., 6/13 We have no more wood. Mr. Picotte and Provost go with the men to look for some where I don't think they will find any.

Sun., 7/11 (low water) I send all the men with Mr. Picotte and Prevost to the other side to make a canoe so that, in case the water does not rise this week, Mr. Picotte can go to the fort. When Provost comes back he tells me that in the channel he found 3-4 feet.

Tues., 7/12 Messrs. Picotte and Provost will leave tomorrow in a canoe and Provost will bring me back a mackinaw barge.

Wed., 7/13 Messrs Picotte and Provost leave after dinner for Ft. Pierre.

Fri., 7/22 Prevost appears at the pointe with a Mackinaw barge and he come aboard.

Tues., 8/12 We decide to leave at dawn. I have left Provost with 3 of my men to bring down another barge loaded with packages (robe packs) and tongues.

Captain Sire and the passengers returned to St. Louis in one Mackinaw boat, and Provost was left in charge of another to bring down the season's returns. Provost ran into some unidentified difficulty and the boat sank with its cargo of approximately 2,600 robes, 4,000 buffalo tongues, and various other skins and castors.[6] In late September Pierre Chouteau, Jr., was informed that "Proveau arrived yesterday evening by steamboat. You will recall he lost his barge on the 15th near Weston. It was worth about $8,000."[7] A salvage attempt was undertaken, but it resulted in the recovery of only 405 robes.

On October 1 Provost was paid $280 for his services from April to September, a rate of $50 per month. This was considerably less than the $1,400 per season he was earning a few years before, but he was now fifty-seven years old and times were difficult. The effects of the 1837 depression were just now being felt in St.

Louis and along the rivers.

On his return to St. Louis, Provost discovered that in his absence the family had lost a lawsuit or, rather, defaulted by failure to appear in court, just as Etienne had failed to appear in his suit against LeBlond and Guion. In this instance the suit was against one Sullivan Blood for trespass, apparently having to do with the question of Jean Sale dit Lajoie having actually established residency on the property granted him following the founding of the trading post in 1764. The plaintiffs in the suit were the surviving heirs of Lambert Salle dit Lajoie and their spouses. The case came to court in July, and while Blood was represented by his attorney, the plaintiffs were absent. The judge dismissed the case, directing that the costs and charges of the defendant were to be paid by the plaintiffs. Clement Lambert was absent from the court hearing because he was with Fremont as camp conductor on his 1842 expedition to map the Oregon Trail.

Provost was listed in the city directory for 1842 as residing at the corner of Second and Lombard, and his occupation as "clerk." [8] In March of 1842 he had been granted a license "to keep an Inn and Tavern at his Stand on Second Street for one year from the seventh day of March."[9] Since both he and Clement were gone for some months, perhaps Etienne's wife did take an active role in the management of the tavern. During the winter Etienne continued managing his tavern and recruiting for the company. He would once again make the steamboat voyage to the Company posts once the ice was out of the rivers.

In late March of 1843, John James Audubon arrived in St. Louis, having arranged with the company for transport up the Missouri to obtain specimens and make drawings. He had with him Edward Harris, his good friend and companion on earlier ventures; Lewis M. Squires; an artist, Isaac Sprague; and a taxidermist,

John G. Bell. After consulting with the company, Audubon was hopeful of securing Provost's services as his guide.

Initially the party stayed at the Glasgow House, the second-best hotel in St. Louis at that time. They were appalled at the $9 per week charge for a room. To conserve his limited funds, Audubon moved in with his brother-in-law, Nicholas Berthoud until he could board the steamboat, and the other members of the party found quarters across the Mississippi near Edwardsville, Illinois.

If Audubon thought the hotel rates were outrageous, he was far more favorably impressed with the cost of various food items. In his letters he wrote of eggs costing 5 cents a dozen, the "best beef" but 3 cents a pound, canvasback ducks for 12 cents each and geese for 10 cents. He spent considerable time in St. Louis while awaiting the steamboat's departure. In his view, St. Louis was "a large town with about 20,000 inhabitants and looks well from the river but the streets are somewhat narrow and houses rather low."[10]

Arriving in St. Louis shortly after Audubon and his party, Sir William Drummond Stewart had returned to the United States for one last great adventure. He planned a magnificent safari to the plains with himself in the role of a grand mogul and with many young British and American gentlemen along as his loyal subjects. To Stewart's everlasting disappointment, the young gentlemen refused to altogether submit to the tyrant's will.

Stewart invited Audubon to accompany his entourage, and for some time Audubon wavered between accepting Stewart's invitation or the Chouteau offer of transportation up the Missouri. Audubon finally decided to travel up the Missouri but indicated that he would join Stewart somewhere in the mountains and return overland with him. That plan was not to be; he returned to St. Louis by boat. Audubon wrote a description of Stewart as a "rather tall, very slender person [who] talks with the lisping humbug of some English nobles." He also wrote of Stewart, "No one here can understand that man, and I must say that in my opinion he is a very curious character."[11]

Audubon was disappointed to find that natural history was of little interest to those whom he met in St. Louis, and he was astonished to find that even those who had spent years in the mountains knew little about any animals other than those worth riding, trapping, eating, or avoiding.

By the end of March, the weather was still quite cold and the work could not be completed on the drydocked American Fur Company steamboat *Omega*, which was to take the Audubon party and Provost upriver. The boat would not be ready until the latter part of April. While waiting, Audubon continued to arrange for his expedition and wrote to his friends that:

We may per chance have an old Voyager who has been in the trade for 29 years and in the employ of the Chouteaux. He may go with Lieut. Fremont, USA, with whom he made a partial engagement. If not succeeding in that quarter, when he has disposed of the Trappers, we may have him return with us in a Mackinaw boat, built expressly for us 25 feet long and 12 beam. This Mr. Provost is an excellent waterman &c and is known by all the Indians as being in the employ of the company.[12]

Shortly after the *Omega's* start upriver Audubon wrote that Provost would be returning with his party.

Captain Joseph Sire wrote Chouteau assuring him that everything possible would be done for the Audubon party's comfort, short of delaying the boat. The expedition was soon able to move on board the steamboat, where Audubon and the others in his party each had a stateroom in the Ladies' Cabin. Audubon's was 8' x 10' with a double bed and a stove, luxurious by his measure.

The steamboat finally got under way on April 25, but not before noon because most of Provost's charges were drunk and it took the better part of the morning to get them on board. As the boat pulled away from the levee, the new recruits saluted its departure with shouts, yells, and the firing of their guns.[13] Once on the river with no chance of deserting, the new men were mustered on the deck, the roll was called, and each was given a blanket containing his clothing for the trip, "somewhat scanty and of indifferent quality." While on board, they were not allowed to eat in the cabin with the other passengers; rather, they were each issued one pint of corn, "and as much fat or lard or fat pork as will render it soft and eatable. This is cooked in large boilers and is poured in wooden trenchers that accommodate one gang each (10 or 12 men)."[14]

River travel was never easy, and just above Fort Leavenworth the boat ran aground. The captain put the hands to work to dislodge the boat by hauling on a cable run to the shore; however, after a few hours of unsuccessful effort, the cable broke and the boat was forced to lay to overnight on the sandbar. The next day a new cable was run out. After some considerable effort the boat was pulled free, but by then the wind was so strong that it was impossible to navigate, so again the boat was delayed, laying to along the lee bank until the wind abated sufficiently for the steam boilers to overcome its effect. On arrival at Bellevue, Audubon noted in his journal that there they found the "brother-in-law of old Provost, who acted as clerk in the absence of Mr. Sarpy."[15].

The Audubon party had two principal complaints about the journey upriver: first they had understood that the steamboat would stop two hours before nightfall each day to take on wood, and instead it was stopping briefly at every opportunity, no matter the time. Audubon and Harris had planned to use those two-hour periods to collect specimens. They found their plans horribly disrupted because they could not be prepared to go afield on the spur of the moment and on those few occasions on which they did, they were uncertain how much time was allotted. Second, when they did go afield, so did the new hunters, and the hunters, as Harris observed in his journal, were:

very much in our way on our shooting expeditions. We find these men (who are scarcely any of them old trappers) to be the worst shots we have ever seen, with either rifle or shot gun, and how they are to subsist in the woods after they are turned loose to shift for themselves is not easy to conceive (p. 17).

Joseph LaBarge was pilot of the *Omega* on this trip, and later he told another Provost story, this one involving Audubon's expedition. LaBarge obviously had a great admiration for Etienne and loved to tell tales in which Provost bested someone or showed his mettle. In recounting this trip, LaBarge also revealed a considerable dislike for Audubon and his associates, and in this tale he took pleasure in Provost's besting Mr. Prou, Audubon's botanist. According to LaBarge, Prou had bragged that he could identify any plant in that country just from the leaf and stalk, even if he had never before seen it. LaBarge has Provost saying, "You may think so, but I will undertake to prove that you are mistaken; for I know a plant that grows in this country whose name you will not be able to tell even with the aid of your books." Soon thereafter Provost located several new corn shoots sprouting from some kernels the Indians had dropped the previous winter. Carefully wrapping a shoot in soil and concealing the kernel, he brought this specimen to Prou who was completely baffled by the plant. He acknowledged defeat and allowed it was most certainly a new species. "Provost then, with provoking gravity, pulled away the dirt around the roots and finally disclosed to the astonished scientist - a kernel of *corn.*"[16]

On May 31 the boat arrived at Fort Pierre, where Provost's engages and about half the cargo were put ashore. The passage from St. Louis had taken thirty-six days, a new record despite Edward Harris' exasperation at the inconsistent and indefinite estimates of travel time and dates of arrival given to him by the boat's officers. He was most impatient at what he believed was an overly long trip. "It certainly requires time and patience to ferret out truth in this world, and more particularly I think in this far western world," he wrote (p. 24). It was almost another two weeks of river travel from Fort Pierre to Fort Union, and the *Omega* finally arrived there on June 12. They had bested the previous record for river passage from St. Louis by fifteen days.

Audubon was impressed by the vast numbers of game he found at Fort Union; within three miles of the fort he noted twenty-two mountain rams in one flock, numerous "Grisley" bears, and wolves beyond counting. The days at Fort Union were filled with hunting for sport, for meat, and for Audubon's specimens. The diaries of both Audubon and Harris are replete with references to hunting, and many of their entries contain comments about Provost and his prowess as a hunter. Early in their stay at the fort, Provost demonstrated a whistle to imitate the cry of a fawn, for use in hunting deer. Audubon was so impressed that he made several references to Provost's use of his whistle.

On one occasion, Provost went across the river with several of the fort's hunters and by use of his "bleating whistle" succeeded in killing two does. He then "drew them to a tree and hung his coat near them while he returned for help to bring them to the fort. The hunters have a belief that a garment hung near game freshly killed will keep the wolves at bay for a time."[17] This time proved the exception to the rule, for when Provost returned he found a dozen wolves just finishing up the second doe. All he recovered was one ham, which he brought to the fort.

Audubon wrote in his journal on June 29, "Provost told me (and he is a respectable man) that during the breeding season of the Mountain Ram, the battering of the horns is often heard as far as a mile away, and that at such times they are approached with comparative ease." Provost imparted many other facets of western life to Audubon during their months together. He told Audubon of the beaver, which were now so scarce, and observed how few the mosquitoes were in that summer. He told him that wolves were often killed by wild horses and described how a horse would defend himself against a wolf. One day a dog was killed for dinner. Audubon tried it and wrote that he found it, "fully equal to any meat I ever tasted. Old Provost had told me he preferred it to any meat, and his subsequent actions proved the truth of his words" (*Journal*, July 12, 1843).

In mid-July, Audubon, Bell, Alexander Culbertson (in charge of Fort Union), Harris, Owen, Squires and Provost undertook a trip to the Yellowstone River seeking bighorn sheep, elk, and beaver. They took both a skiff and horses and established a base camp some distance up the Yellowstone. Shortly after the camp was established, and after Provost had taken a bath in the river, a violent storm came up. All but Provost were kept busy securing the tents and gear. They all became soaked in the process; however, "Old Provost" had taken shelter under a shelving bank on the river and stayed dry throughout the storm. Once the storm passed, he returned to camp, stretched out on the wet ground, and was soon asleep.

After two days on the Yellowstone, all of the party except Provost and Squires returned to the fort. They kept the skiff and continued to hunt up the Yellowstone. It was another three days before they returned to the fort, having had an enjoyable time but no hunting success. They had tried for two days to trap a beaver, with no luck; Provost hunted bighorn, with no luck, and Squires missed his only shot at a large bighorn ram.

The differences between the experienced mountaineer and the greenhorn were captured by an incident Audubon described in his journal on August 6:

When Bell was fixing his traps on his horse this morning, I was amused to see Provost and LaFleur laughing outright at him. These old hunters could not understand why he needed all those things to be comfortable. Provost took only an old blanket, a few pounds of dried meat, and his tin cup, and rode off in his shirt and dirty breeches. LaFleur was worse off for he took no blanket, and said he could borrow Provost's tin cup; but he, being a most temperate man, carried the bottle of whiskey to mix with the brackish water.

On August 16 Audubon and his band, with Provost as their pilot, set off from Fort Union to return to St. Louis, a trip that would take them two months.

Regrettably, Edward Harris seems to have lost interest in keeping his journal once the party started downriver. His record of this part of the trip is sketchy at best, limited to a record of specimens obtained and the dates and times of their arrival at the various posts along the river. Audubon continued his writing, however, and at one point described in great detail how Provost set a trap for a beaver they detected along the river. Provost's experience notwithstanding, no beaver was taken.

Audubon last saw Provost October 18, the day before the party reached St. Louis. The boat landed at St. Charles to obtain some bread and other supplies for the forty miles of river yet to be covered. Audubon wrote merely that "Provost became extremely drunk, and went off by land to St. Louis."[18]

For his services to Audubon, Provost was paid $214, at a rate of $50 per month. He received another $78.33 from the Upper Missouri Outfit for escorting the new trappers upriver.[19]

At about the time Provost was on the upper river readying Audubon's Mackinaw boat for its trip downriver, in St. Louis Clement Lambert received a license to keep an inn and tavern "at his stand" on the corner of Second and Lombard streets. This raises a question about the relationship between Provost and Clement Lambert as partners. This license to Clement was for the operation of a tavern and inn in Block 43, whereas Provost's home and tavern were "catty-corner" across the street in Block 49. Whether they were each now operating a tavern or had just moved the partnership location is uncertain. The books of the Company still carried an account for "Etienne Proveau, Tavernkeeper" which was active in December of 1843.

The St. Louis *Daily Missouri Republican* for Tuesday, April 30, 1844, announced the recent completion of the American Fur Company's new steamboat, *Nimrod*. The boat was 150 feet long on the deck and had a beam of 26 feet. Under the command of Captain Cerre, it was described as being "as commodious and well arranged as that of any boat of her class on the river." The paper also reported that the boat was departing that day for the Yellowstone, carrying supplies and about 120 hunters and trappers for the mountains.

Among the passengers on the *Nimrod* was Armand Fouche, Comte d'Otrante. Fouche was the second son

d'Otrante

of Joseph Fouche, Minister of Police and Duc d'Otrante under Napoleon, and while he did not actually inherit the title until his older brother died in 1862, the few American references to him call him the Comte d'Otrante. He was at that time forty-four years old and the voyage was solely for pleasure. He had with him his own retinue of servants from France and traveled in the grand manner. And his guide for his grand tour of the Upper Missouri country was Etienne Provost.

Provost was again escorting his recruits upriver and worked fifty-five days for the company in this capacity. Then for the six months from June 23 to December 24 he was in the service of d'Otrante, for which he received $300.

Nothing is known of d'Otrante's expedition beyond the fact that he went as far as Fort Union. Whether he remained in that vicinity and hunted close by as Audubon had in the previous year, or whether he ventured farther afield with Provost is completely unknown. No record of his journey— no narrative, diary or other account— has been located.[20] In January of 1845 the *St. Louis Weekly Reveille* reported that:

The Count d'Otrante, who started from St. Louis last May, arrived at Fort Leavenworth some three or four weeks since from his trip to the Rocky Mountains. He returned in most robust health, and loaded down with trophies of his skill as a hunter. Nothing like a tour of the prairies.

Where Fouche spent the winter is not certain, but most likely it was in St. Louis. In the spring of 1845 he was again a passenger on the Company boat, the *General Brooke.*[21]

When Etienne Provost returned home from his 1844 expedition with d'Otrante in late December, he found himself faced with another lawsuit, only this time he was a defendant.

NOTES

1. Parish Records, Cathedral of St. Louis, MHS microfilm, roll no. 72. Provost and his wife were listed as witnesses.

2. *Fremont Expeditions*, 110,111. Voucher issued to Clement Lambert, July 23, 1841, for services from June 23 to July 22.

3. Franzwa, *Maps of the Oregon Trail*, 1.

4. Morgan, *The Great Salt Lake*, 117.

5. Chittenden, *History of Early Steamboat Navigation on the Missouri River*, 128-29.

6. Suner, *The Fur Trade on the Upper Missouri, 1840-1865*, 46-47.

7. Sharpy to Chouteau, September 29, 1842, Chouteau Collection.

8. J. H. Sloss, *St. Louis Directory*, 1842.

9. Registrar, City of St. Louis, Microfilm F-3.

10. Audubon, *Audubon in the West*, 13, 37-38.

11. *Ibid.*, 47, 57.

12. *Ibid.*, 46-47. Nothing in the Fremont journals indicates that he had contemplated utilizing Provost's services that year.

13. *Harris Journal*, 16.

14. Audubon, *Audubon in the West*, 66.

15. Audubon, *Journals*, entry for May 9, 1843.

16. Chittenden, *History of Early Steamboat Navigation on the Missouri River*, 152-53.

17. *Audubon Journal*, entry for June 23, 1843.

18. Audubon, *Journals*, 2:175

19. American Fur Company Ledgers, Book GG, folios 267, 350.

20. Letter of December 4, 1984, to the author from Madame Th. von Stedingk, a grand-niece of Armand Fouche. Fourche's life itself seems to be something of

an enigma. He apparently left his home in Stjarnholm, Sweden, sometime in 1840 or 1841 and was gone for four years without telling anyone where he was going or when he would return. He made no provisions for support of his estate or servants. Family legend has it that he went to Canada, and if such is the case he apparently went to St. Louis from there.

21. Barry, *The Beginning of the West*, 507. Nothing more is know of d'Otrante in this year.

Our Camp

Hudson's Bay Company Ax
circa 1833

CHAPTER ELEVEN
The Final Years, 1845-1850

Second street in 1845, the St. Louis thoroughfare on which Etienne Provost maintained his home for thirty years:

SECOND STREET— The cross streets which run from Main to this, are of a mixed character— Olive containing printing offices, Justice Offices, and Pine containing also, Justices and Lawyers Offices; Locust is nearly the same. (note: the traveler speaks of the lower end of these streets toward the water.)

Second street begins to display a distributive and accessary commercial character, very mixed in character, for in it are found some private dwelling houses, manufacturers, fruiterers, locksmiths and artizans— also, tributary to the arts and literature, as lithographic and engraving businesses; house painters, dry goods and grocery stores.[1]

In 1845 the city directory listed H. N. Provost as residing at the corner of Second and Lombard but failed to identify his occupation. This year his home was in jeopardy, however, for one Elizabeth Hughes had filed suit claiming that in 1819 her deceased husband had purchased not only the property now owned by Provost but also contiguous lots owned by two others named as defendants in the suit, and that she had a dower interest in the property. Her claim was against the lot which Provost had bought from Pierre Chouteau in 1829 at the time of his marriage.

Provost was upriver with the Comte d'Otrante at the time the suit was filed, so the papers were served by "leaving a true copy of it and the Petition at the usual place of abode of Etienne Provot with a white person of the family over the age of fifteen years." The matter dragged on through 1845, with various depositions and filings and was not settled until February of 1846, when Hughes advised the court that she would no longer press her suit and voluntarily offered to pay the costs of the defendants.[2] Whether she had become convinced she could not win or had reached an out-of-court settlement with Provost and his neighbors is not known, but her willingness to pay costs and charges suggests some sort of agreement had been reached between the parties.

St. Louis conducted a census in 1845. According to that talley, there were eight people residing in Provost's household, and Provost's immediate family consisted of three—himself, his wife, and his daughter. Of the others, two were males between ages ten and eighteen, one was a female under age ten, one a female between twenty-one and forty-five, and the fifth came under the category "children 6 to 15 y'rs at school." The additional five suggests that he was still operating his boarding house at Second and Lombard.

As usual, Provost escorted the new recruits upriver. This year he continued in the Company's service and was again at Fort Pierre on November 2 to take the Company returns down to St. Louis. He was detained for a week in hopes that Honore Picotte would arrive to accompany him; however, Picotte had not shown up and Provost was sent on since the season was then so far advanced.

From the 1830's until at least 1845 Provost had been buying shares in land lying along the Des Moines River in present-day Iowa, described as the "half-breed lands." The ledgers of the Company carry a record of payments for some of these purchases under the account of "Etienne Proveau, Tavernkeeper" for the years 1843 and 1845,[3] and in his will, written in 1839, he made reference to shares in the "half-breed Sac and Fox lands" so he had been buying real estate for a number of years prior to 1843.

There is no indication that he ever made any attempt to either sell or develop his holdings. Perhaps he bought them on speculation, anticipating a profit some years in the future. Interestingly, some of the land Provost bought was near Nauvoo, then the home of the Church of Jesus Christ of Latter-day Saints, the Mormons. It may be that it was here he met Orrin Porter Rockwell, whose comments about Provost and his trading posts have been noted.

Etienne Provost disappears from any records in the year 1846 and may well have remained home with his family and his business. A City Guard was formed that year for the protection of the city, but even had he wanted to, Etienne could not have joined because membership was forbidden to anyone who was "directly or indirectly interested in any tavern, inn, coffee house, beer house or tippling house."

The Oregon question was settled in 1846 by the Buchanan-Packenham Treaty. The treaty fixed the U.S-Canadian boundary at the 49th Parallel, which was an extension of the already existing boundary to the Continental Divide on the eastern slope of the Rocky Mountains. The argument over the territory had raged hot and heavy before the issue was finally settled.[4] By 1846 emigrants were crossing the plains in ever greater numbers to take up residence in the fertile valleys of Oregon, which up to that year were not under the flag of either nation. Peaceful settlement was highly desirable to the American government, for although occupancy gave strength to the American claim, the United States was also facing conflict with Mexico at the same time and a war with England was the last thing the U.S. wanted.[5]

The St. Louis city directory of 1847 lists "Ettienne Provot," as a mountain trader with his residence at 244 S. Second St. In April of 1847, "P. Chouteau & Co." received a bill for $10 for passage on the steamboat *Little Missouri* "for Mr. Provost from Kansas Landing to St. Louis"[6] which suggests he may have been up the Missouri in the early spring carrying dispatches for the company.

In the late spring Etienne went again to the upper river with his recruits, this time on the steamboat *Martha*, leaving St. Louis on May 15. The captain was his old admirer Joseph LaBarge, who provides another tale of Provost on this voyage. A band of Yankton Sioux was at a trading post near Crow Creek awaiting their government annuity, which was on board the *Martha*. For some reason the Indian agent chose to give them only part of their due, telling them the rest would be handed over at Fort Pierre. The Indians objected that it made no sense to be required to make a long trip to receive what was already there on the boat. The agent was adamant, however, and the goods were not released. The Sioux acquiesced but remained dissatisfied.

Some ten or twelve cords of wood were stacked for use of the steamboat, and Captain LaBarge wished to get it aboard, fearing the Indians would burn it the moment the boat left. The Sioux refused to let the wood be loaded without some payment, which LaBarge was compelled to provide, and then:

Etienne Provost who was employed on these trips to take charge of the rough and turbulent mountain men, was asked to attend to the loading of the wood as there might be trouble. Provost came up on the boiler deck and sat down by LaBarge, saying: "We are going to have some fun before that wood is on board." He then shouted, "Woodpile! Woodpile!" and enough men rushed to the bank to take the whole woodpile at once.

As the men carried the wood aboard, the Indians assaulted them, either to create an incident or to bully them into abandoning the wood. They succeeded admirably; the men were frightened into dropping the wood and retreated back aboard.

Provost lay back and roared with laughter, saying, "I told you we should see some fun." He then went out himself onto the bank where the Indians were, and said, "Now, men, come out here and get this wood." They came and loaded up. "Now go on board," he said, and they went entirely unmolested. Provost went last, and before descending the bank, turned toward the Indians and asked them: "Why don't you stop them? Are you afraid of **me**?" *The truth is they were afraid of him. They knew him well and respected him, and understood that he would stand no foolishness.*[7]

Later that same day, however, the still-disgruntled Sioux attacked the boat and gained control of the entire forequarter before LaBarge drove them off by threatening to use a small cannon he had on board.

It becomes more difficult to follow the activities of Etienne Provost in this year because of a second Provost, Constant, who is now often mentioned in the records of the Company. Constant Provost may well have been a relative of Etienne.

The Letterbook of Fort Pierre from early December of 1847 through April of 1848 contains numerous references to "Proveau" being expected momentarily, to his being sent out with goods, and to a variety of other activities on behalf of the Company. A problem arises in that the December references identify only the last name, whereas after the first of the year the full name, Constant Proveau, appears in the letters. No entries were located in the Company records of any payments to Etienne in 1848, and considering his age, it certainly seems more likely that it was Constant, and not Etienne, struggling through the snow on the Upper Missouri during the winter of 1847-48.

Company records and age (sixty-three) notwithstanding, Etienne Provost was a tough old bird, and one cryptic reference places him on the river in 1848. John Palliser, an English adventurer who traveled the Upper Missouri area in 1847 and 1848, met Provost at the Minataree village (Ft. Berthold) sometime in the late spring/summer of 1848.[8] In his book on his travels, Palliser writes of hunting the Grizzly bear and notes:

Although in general, the bear easily vanquishes his less formidable opponent, the buffalo, I heard a very well authenticated instance related by old Provost at the Minataree, in which both parties suffered so severely as mutually to resign the conflict, move off a little way in opposite directions, and lie down and die (281-82).

Thus it may be presumed that Palliser heard this tale, and undoubtedly others of Grizzly bear hunts and other mountain adventures, from Provost at Ft. Berthold near the Minataree village. So enthused did he become that he apparently left the fort to undertake his own hunt prior to the arrival of the annual steamboat.

It is not until six pages later, and now, according to Palliser, late July, that "the American Fur Company's steamer *Martha* arrived from St. Louis at the Minataree's Post" (287). Despite Palliser's statement, this was actually the return leg of the journey, en route to St. Louis. The *Martha* had left St. Louis on the upriver journey on May 9.[9] The record at this point is very confused, and it has not been possible to determine if Provost was aboard the *Martha* when it departed St. Louis, or if he had wintered on the upper river, and was not awaiting passage home down river. The absence of any identified company payment to him in 1848 compounds the confusion. The company records are split among so many entities, however, that the possibility cannot be overlooked that an entry was simply missed. All that can be said with seeming surety is that he met John Palliser at Ft. Berthold on the upper river in the Spring of 1848. The *Martha* had departed the mouth of the Yellowstone on June 29, and arrived in St. Louis on July 14, 1848, so Palliser's statement of a late July arrival is in error.[10]

Nothing else is known of his activities for 1848, but in 1849 he was again upriver, this year on the steamboat *Amelia.* In late June the steamer passed St. Joseph on its upriver voyage, and in early August was at Fort Pierre on the downriver leg of the journey. From

the fort the agent wrote to "Messr. P. Chouteau & Co."
advising that "Mr. Provost who is now on board the
Amelia will return with Cap Finch in charge of the men
he is well known to you as an efficient man in that
capacity. Should the old man wish to return and you
feel disposed to employ him he might be useful at Ft.
Pierre."[11]

The letter is couched in language very supportive of
Provost and seems to be an appeal to Chouteau that
favorable consideration be given to hiring him. Either
Chouteau was not so disposed or Provost did not wish
to return, for this was his last trip up the river.

On July 3, 1850, Etienne Provost died in St. Louis
in his sixty-fifth year. The cause of his death was not
recorded; however, the evidence indicates he died of
causes incident to his age, possibly a heart attack. In
his estate papers there is a bill for his final medicines
and included among them were items such as lauda-
num, an opium derivative used to alleviate pain, and
stimulants such as whiskey and brandy. The *Missouri
Republican* for July 4, 1850, reported simply:

*Died. Yesterday afternoon, about 4 o'clock Mr. Etienne
Provot, an old resident of this city.*

*The friends and acquaintances of the family are invited
to attend his funeral, This afternoon at 4 o'clock from his
late residence on the corner of Lombard and Second
streets, to the Cathedral burial ground.*[12]

The year before St. Louis had suffered from an
epidemic of cholera and the illness was still present in
the city, although not to its previous extent. Had
Provost died of cholera his friends and acquaintances
would not have been extended the invitation to attend
the funeral.

Where Provost was buried, or more accurately

where his grave is today, remains an unanswered question. The third Cathedral burial ground, the New Catholic Cemetery, just opened in Rock Springs, was the only Catholic burial ground in use in 1850, and Provost was certainly buried there. Rock Springs cemetery was to become a truly forgotten piece of land despite the fact that between 1849 and 1854 approximately 5,000 burials took place there. By around 1890 it was more or less abandoned and around 2,000 of its bodies had been moved. Still, 3,000 bodies remained.[13]

There is no record of Provost having been moved to Calvary Cemetery after it opened in 1853, so he must still lie under whatever now exists at Dunkin and Sarah streets. His wife is buried in Calvary in a family plot purchased by her son-in-law.

In April of 1839, just prior to going out with Joseph N. Nicollet on his mapping expedition, Provost had written a will. He named his wife executrix of his estate and bequeathed to her all his property, both real and personal. This will was disallowed by the probate court, which ruled that the "said instrument is not duly proved to be the last will and testament of said Etienne Provot, deceased."[14] No records explain the reason for this questioning of the will.[15]

An inventory of his estate valued his furniture and other personal items at $78.95, and cash on hand was $102.70. The inventory of real estate showed ownership of the lot on which his home stood, various parcels of unimproved land in Iowa totaling 627 1/4 acres, 13 lots in the town of Keokuk, and one lot in Nashville, "by deed of partition between Patrick Walsh & wife and the said Etienne Provost." Those in Iowa would seem to be the "half-breed lands" of some years earlier, and it appears he held an undivided half interest in them with Walsh. Oddly, the inventory makes no reference to a partnership or interest in a tavern, nor to any furnishings associated with a tavern.

On July 29 his widow attested that she and her daughter Mary were the only living heirs of "Ettiene Provot" and that he had died without a will, "except an instrument in writing purporting to be a will of the deceased which has been rejected by the Judge of Probate aforesaid."[16]

Expenses of the estate eventually took all the cash and property assets: taxes for 1850 and 1851 took almost half, and there was $54 for the coffin and shroud, $2 for shaving the deceased, $6 for the burial service, $3 for the clergyman in attendance at the cemetery, $7.20 for candles for the funeral service, $1.50 for a carriage, and $1 for medicine. Along with the laudanum and medicinal liquor, the medicines included such items as vinegar, mustard, flax seed, rice, and ginger oil. Seemingly not much to show for sixty-five years of a life such as few men had ever lived, but many a mountaineer left no legacy but his bones along some mountain stream.

NOTES

1. A Walk in the Streets of St. Louis in 1845," *Missouri Historical Society Collections*, vol. 6., 1928-31.

2. St. Louis Circuit Court Records, Book 15, 312, 459; Book 17, 85.

3. American Fur Company Ledgers, Book GG, folios 190, 350.

4. The emotions of the argument, if not the reasoning, were well expressed by a "howling tiger of the great west" who, according to the *New Orleans Picayune* in 1844, said:

*Whar, I say **whar** is the individual who would give the first foot, the first outside shadow of a foot of the great Oregon? There aint no such individual. Talk about*

*treaty occupations to a country over which the great
American eagle has flown! I scorn treaty occupation.
Some people talk as though they were affeerd of England.* **Who's** *affeered? Hav'nt we licked her twice, and
can't we like her again? Some skeery folks talk about the
navy of England (and) that she is the* **mistress** *of the
ocean. Suppose she is -- aint we the* **master** *of it? Can't
we cut a canal from the Mississippi to the Mammoth
Cave of Kentucky, turn all the water into it, and dry up
the d--d ocean in three weeks! Whar, then, would be the
navy? It would be* **no whar.** *There never would have
been an Atlantic Ocean if it hadn't been for the Mississippi, nor never will be after we've turned the waters of
that big drain into the Mammoth Cave.*

So much for the reasoned approach to diplo-
macy. Typed copy of an item in *Niles Register*, vol. 66:
114, April 20, 1844; Morgan Collection, Utah State
Historical Society.

5.   A good summary of the politics of the treaty may
be found in Bernard DeVoto's *1846, Year of Decision.*

6.   Original bill in Chouteau-Maffitt Collection.

7.   Chittenden, *History of Early Steamboat Navigation of the Missouri River*, 178-80.   Dale Morgan and
LeRoy Hafen both place this incident in 1848, but a
careful reading of Chittenden's account (pg. 177) puts
it squarely in 1847.

8.   Palliser, *Solitary Rambles*, 83. Palliser indicates
he arrived at Ft. Berthold on April 1, 1848

9.   Barry, *The Beginning of the West*, 766

10.   Gray: "Honore Picotte, Fur Trader," *South Dakota History*, pg. 198, and Barry, *The Beginning of the
West*, 766.

11.   Letterbook of Fort Pierre, August 2, 1849, Chouteau Collection.

12.   LeRoy Hafen, "Etienne Provost," in Hafen, ed.,
The Mountain Men and the Fur Trade of the Far West, 6:

385n.

13. Keller, "City Cemeteries" quoting from the *St. Louis Post Dispatch* of September 29, 1951.

14. City of St. Louis Probate File No. 3242, Etienne Provost.

15. In his sketch of Provost, Hafen said the will was denied by the widow, but he failed to explain why, in "Etienne Provost," Hafen, ed., *The Mountain Men and the Fur Trade of the Far West*, 6: 387.

16. City of St. Louis Probate File No. 3242, Etienne Provost.

EPILOGUE

Etienne Provost's importance to the American fur trade is based on his being a strong figure in the early days of the trade whose influence was considerable; a man to be reckoned with by the corporate leaders shaping the direction of the fur industry. His strength lay in his capacity as a field leader; he was never one of the corporate board.

He was a French-Canadian by birth who lived most of his life in this country. For all his many years of residence, however, we do not know how well he spoke English, or even if he spoke it at all. Joseph LaBarge tells stories of Provost in which his English, when quoted, is impeccable, yet William Marshall Anderson, Alfred Jacob Miller, and William Fairholme quoted his remarks in French.

By way of understanding this anomaly, LaBarge, himself, was of French-Canadian origin and spoke French from birth, so it is undoubtedly in that language that he and Provost conversed. The perfect English of his Provost stories may well be attributed to Chittenden, who cast LaBarge's translated tales in the classical English style of the day. Anderson also spoke fluent French, and his reported conversations with Provost were likely conducted in that language. We may assume that as an educated British officer, Lt. Fairholme was also capable of handling a conversation in French. Thus there is no direct evidence that Provost spoke anything but his native language, although if that were the case, surely he learned sufficient English to get along among the Americans with whom he worked.

It was the independent side of the trade, however, that was primarily English speaking. The American Fur Company interests operating out of St. Louis were basically French: the Chouteaus, Cabanne, Berthold, Fontenelle and others, as well as the working level of the trade, the engages, who were almost all of French-Canadian origin.

Provost's early forays into the fur trade with Philibert, Chouteau, and deMun between 1814 and 1817 were undistinguished, but they provided a training ground for his entry into the Santa Fe trade in the early 1820's. It was during these years in New Mexico as an independent trader that he made his reputation.

I am convinced that Provost was deeply involved in the Santa Fe trade long before his well-known trapping venture of 1824. Returning to Santa Fe with the trade caravan of the Robidoux brothers in 1822, gave Provost an excellent opportunity to evaluate the opportunities that might exist for him as an independent trapper. The record verifies that he was in Santa Fe at least by 1823, when he returned with a message for the American authorities from the Mexican government. Circumstances suggest that he had been there even earlier.

By 1826 Provost's reputation was well established among the St. Louis fur merchants. Ceran St. Vrain referred specifically to Provost in his 1825 letter to Bernard Pratte, and Jean P. Cabanne called Provost a key to preventing what he viewed as William H. Ashley's move to corner the southwest market. Cabanne expressed his conviction that Provost was the one man who could compete with Ashley in the southwest. In 1826 Bartholomew Berthold wrote that Provost's loyalty was essential to the Company's welfare and referred to him as the soul of the hunters in the mountains. Interestingly, all those laudatory comments emanate from one place or another in the Chouteau camp: St. Vrain was backed by Pratte and Chouteau in 1825; Cabanne and Berthold were partners with them. Provost was clearly a mover and a shaker in the eyes of the Chouteau interests during those early years in New Mexico and important in Chouteau plans for the development of the business.

He remained allied to the Chouteaus throughout his career. Records indicate that Provost was in the employ of Chouteau as early as 1823; quite possibly he was backed by Chouteau either directly or indirectly in his 1824 partnership with LeClerc. He sold his furs to Chouteau on his return from the mountains in 1826 and shortly thereafter became an employee of the Pratte, Chouteau partnership which had just become allied with Astor's American Fur Company. He remained in the employ of that company until his death, and in 1829 his reputation was such that the company entered into a separate partnership agreement with him.

Even after his days as an active trapper ended, Provost remained a mainstay of the Company. In 1828 he was chosen to persuade the Crow Indians to bring their pelts to the AFC post on the Missouri River. He brought the supply trains to the brigades in the mountains and returned the harvested pelts to St. Louis. In 1834 he captained the first AFC supply train to follow the overland route to the mountains. It was Provost who was sent by the AFC on special assignments to the Upper Missouri country. He was a competent and reliable man, one who would carry out any task with dependability. He was recommended as guide or camp manager to various independent expeditions, and in every instance the leaders expressed high regard for both the reputation which preceded him and the competence with which he fulfilled his responsibilities. Whether or not one believes Joseph LaBarge's tales of Provost's prowess, one must believe that Provost had an ardent admirer in LaBarge and that the stories were a reflection of the general regard in which Provost was held by his peers.

He was as much a pathfinder as Jed Smith and even preceded Smith in 1824 and 1825 when he ranged the lands north of Taos, in western Colorado and northeastern Utah. He trapped and traded through that area for two years and should be credited with the discovery of the Great Salt Lake.

Were there a grave and headstone for Etienne Provost, he could ask for no better epitaph than these words:

> *He could remember when it was new, and a man setting foot on it could believe he was the first one, and a man seeing it could give names to it.*
>
> A. B. Guthrie, *The Big Sky.*

BIBLIOGRAPHY

Articles

"A Walk in the Streets of St. Louis in 1845." *Missouri Historical Society Collections* 6 (1928-31).

Auerbach, Herbert S. "W. A. Ferris in Utah." *Utah Historical Quarterly*, IX (Jan.-Apr. 1941).

___. "Old Trails, Old Forts, Old Trappers and Traders." *Utah Historical Quarterly*, IX (Jan.-Apr. 1941).

Ault, Frederick C. "A History of Municipal Government in St. Louis" I-X (1808-63). St. Louis Public Library, 1942.

Becknell, Thomas. "Journals of Captain Thomas Becknell." F. A. Sampson, ed. *Missouri Historical Review* IV (1909-10).

Behrman, Rev. E. H. , "The Story of the Old Cathedral." *Parish of St. Louis IX, King of France*, nd.

Bingham, Henry Vest. "The Road West in 1818." *Missouri Historical Review* Xl (1946).

DeLand, Charles Edmund. "Editorial Notes on Old Fort Pierre and Its Neighbors." *South Dakota Historical Collections* (1902).

___. "Fort Tecumseh and Fort Pierre Journal and Letterbooks." *South Dakota Historical Collections* IX (1918).

deMun, Jules. "The Journals of Jules DeMun." Thomas Maitland Marshall, ed. *Missouri Historical Society Collections* V (1927-28).

___. "Letter of Jules DeMun to Governor William Clark" (Nov. 25, 1817). *Missouri Historical Society Collections*.

Dollar, Clyde D. "The High Plains Smallpox Epidemic of 1837-38." *The Western Historical Quarterly* VIII, #1 (1977).

Drumm, Stella M. "Etienne Provost." in *Dictionary of American Biography*, 15. New York: Charles Scribner's Sons. 1935.

___. ed. *Glimpses of the Past.* (9 vols., 1933-42) Missouri Historical Society.

Faatz, Mabel. "Final Resting Place? Not Quite!" *St. Louis Genealogical Society Quarterly.* (1976).

Fremont, John Charles. "Fremont's Story, 1838-39" (excerpts). *South Dakota Historical Collections* 10 (1920).

Gilbert, Bil. "Thar Was Old Grit In Him." *Sports Illustrated* (Jan. 17, 1983).

Hafen, LeRoy. "Etienne Provost, Mountain Man and Utah Pioneer." *Utah Historical Society Quarterly* XXXVI, No. 2 (1968).

___. "Mountain Men Before the Mormons." Speech given before the Utah Historical Society May 10, 1958. *Utah Historical Society Quarterly* XXVI (1958).

Hanson, Charles E., Jr., and Veronica Sue Walters. "The Early Fur Trade in Northwestern Nebraska." *Nebraska State Historical Society*, 57, No.4 (1976).

Keller, Janet. "City Cemeteries." *St. Louis Home*, Vol. 4, No. 3, March 1984.

Kennedy. "Kennedy's Sectional Map of St. Louis with Street Directory." St. Louis: Alex McLean, 1859.

Kennerly, James. "Diary of James Kennerly 1823-1826." Edgar B. Wesley, ed. *Missouri Historical Society Collections*, 6 (1928-31).

Loiselle. *The Loiselle Marriage Index. Index to Marriage Records in Quebec, 1642-1963.* Salt Lake City. LDS Genealogical Library. nd.

Mattison, Ray H. "Fort Union - Its Role in the Upper Missouri Fur Trade." Reprint from *North Dakota History*, 29 (Jan.-Apr. 1962).

McDermott, John Francis. "Miller." *American Scene* IV, No. 3 (1962).

Morgan, Dale L. "The State of Deseret." *Utah Historical Society Quarterly* VIII (1940).

___. "A New Ashley Document." *The Westerners' New York Posse Brand Book* 12, No. 4 (1966).

___. "Utah Before the Mormons." *Utah Historical Society Quarterly* XXXVI (1968).

___. notes. "Santa Fe and the Far West." Reprinted 1949 for Glen Dawson from *Niles Register* XLI (1841).

Nadon, Pierre, David Lee, Antonio Jurkovich and — Duffet. "Fort Chambly Interpretation Papers." Parcs Canada. 1966.

Nicollet, Jean N. "Nicollet's Account." *South Dakota Historical Collections* X (1920).

Ogden, Peter Skene. "Peter Skene Ogden's Journal of His Expedition to Utah, 1825." David E. Miller, ed. *Utah Historical Society Quarterly* XX (1952).

Pratte, Bernard Jr., "The Reminiscences of General Bernard Pratte, Jr." From the *Missouri Republican*, 1879. *Missouri Historical Society Bulletin* (Oct. 1949).

Primm, James Neal. "Henry Shaw: Merchant Capitalist." *Gateway Heritage*, 5: No. 1 (Summer, 1984) Missouri Historical Society.

Russell, Carl P. "Wilderness Rendezvous Period of the American Fur Trade." *Oregon Historical Quarterly* XLII (Mar., 1941).

Sunder, John E. "British Army Officers on the Santa Fe Trail." *Missouri Historical Society Bulletin*, 23. (Jan. 1967).

Tykal, Jack B. "Etienne Provost and the Hawken Rifle." *The Museum of the Fur Trade Quarterly*, 19: No. 2 (1983).

Ulibarri, George S. "The Chouteau-DeMun Expedition to New Mexico, 1815-17." *New Mexico Historical Review* 36, No.4 (1961).

Voelker, Frederick E. "Ezekiel Williams of Boon's Lick." *Missouri Historical Society Bulletin* VIII, No. 1 (1951).

Williams, Ezekiel. "Letter to the Editor of the *Missouri Gazette* published Sept. 14, 1816.

Books

Alter, J. Cecil. *Jim Bridger*. Norman. University of Oklahoma Press, 1979.

Anderson, William Marshall. *The Rocky Mountain Journals of William Marshall Anderson*. Dale L. Morgan and Eleanor Towles Harris, eds. San Marino: The Huntington Library, 1967.

Angus, Alexander D. *Old Quebec in the Days Before Our Day*. Montreal: Louis Carrier, 1949.

Auclair, Armand. *Chambly: Its History and the Sidelights on its History*. Chambly, Que.: Information Chambly Enr., 1974.

Audubon, John James. *Audubon in the West*. John Francis McDermott, ed. Norman: University of Oklahoma Press, 1965.

Audubon, Maria. *Audubon and His Journals*. 2 vols. With Notes by Elliott Coues. London: John C. Nimmo, 1897.

Barry, Louise. *The Beginning of the West*. Topeka: Kansas State Historical Society, 1972.

Bell, John R. *Journal of the S. H. Long Expedition*. Harlin M. Fuller and LeRoy R. Hafen, eds. Glendale: The Arthur H. Clark Company, 1973.

Berry, Don. *A Majority of Scoundrels*. New York: Harper and Brothers, 1961.

Billon, Frederick L. *Annals of St. Louis in Its Early Days Under the French and Spanish Dominations*. St. Louis: Nixon Jones Printing Co. (printed for the author), 1886.

___. *Annals of St. Louis in Its Territorial Days, 1804-1821*. St. Louis: Nixon Jones Printing Co. (printed for the author), 1888.

Bonner, Thomas D. *The Life and Adventures of James P. Beckwourth.* Lincoln: University of Nebraska Press, 1981

Canadian Department of the Interior. *Guide to Fort Chambly.* Canadian Department of the Interior, 1922.

Carson, Kit. *Kit Carson's Autobiography.* Milo Milton Quaife, ed. Lincoln: University of Nebraska Press, 1970.

Carter, Clarence Edwin, ed. *Territorial Papers of the United States Louisiana-Missouri Territory, 1815-1821.* Vol. 15. Washington: USGPO, 1951.

Catholic Baptisms of St. Louis, 1765-1840. St. Louis: St. Louis Genealogical Society, 1982.

Chardon, Francis A. *Chardon's Journal at Fort Clark, 1834-1839.* Annie Heloise Abel, ed. Pierre: Department of History, State of South Dakota, 1932.

Chittenden, Hiram Martin. *History of Early Steamboat Navigation on the Missouri River: Life and Adventures of Joseph LaBarge.* 2 vols. New York: Francis P. Harper, 1903.

___. *A History of the American Fur Trade of the Far West.* 2 vols. Stanford: Academic Reprints, 1954.

Chouteau, Auguste. *Fragment of Col. Auguste Chouteau's Narrative of the Settlement of St. Louis.* St. Louis: Mercantile Library Association, Geo. Knapp & Co., 1858.

Cleland, Robert Glass. *This Reckless Breed of Men.* New York: Alfred A. Knopf, 1950.

Cline, Gloria Griffen. *Exploring the Great Basin.* Norman: University of Oklahoma Press, 1963.

Clokey, Richard M. *William H. Ashley: Enterprise and Politics in the Trans-Mississippi West.* Norman: University of Oklahoma Press, 1980.

Clyman, James. *James Clyman, Frontiersman.* Charles L. Camp, ed. Portland: Champoeg Press, 1960.

Dale, Harrison Clifford. *The Ashley-Smith Explorations and the Discovery of a Central Route to the Pacific, 1822-29* Cleveland: The Arthur H. Clark Co., 1918.

DeVoto, Bernard. *The Year of Decision: 1846.* Boston: Little Brown and Company, 1943.

Devoy, John. *A History of the City of St. Louis and Vicinity.* St. Louis: John Devoy, Publisher, 1898.

Edwards, Richard, and M. Hopewell. *The Great West and a Complete History of St. Louis, 1764-Present Time.* St. Louis: *Edwards Monthly, A Journal of Progress,* 1860.

Faherty, William Barnaby, S.J. *Two Centuries of St. Louis Catholicism, 1766-1967.* St. Louis: Piraeus Publishing, 1973.

Ferris, W. A. *Life in the Rocky Mountains.* Paul C. Phillips, ed. Denver: Old West Publishing Co., 1940.

Fetter, Richard. *Mountain Men of Wyoming.* Boulder: Johnson Publishing Company, 1982.

Foley, William E., and David C. Rice. *The First Chouteaus; River Barons of Early St. Louis.* Urbana: University of Illinois Press, 1983.

Flint, Timothy. *Recollections of the Last Ten Years in the Valley of the Mississippi.* George R. Brooks, ed. Carbondale: Southern Illinois University Press, 1968.

Forssell, Nils. *Fouche: The Man Napoleon Feared.* Anna Barwell, trans. New York: Frederick A. Stokes, nd.

Fowler, Jacob. *The Journal of Jacob Fowler.* Elliott Coues, ed. Minneapolis: Ross & Haines, Inc., 1965.

Franzwa, Gregory. *Maps of the Oregon Trail.* Gerald, Mo.: Patrice Press, 1982.

Fremont, John Charles. *The Expeditions of John Charles Fremont.* Vol. I. Donald Jackson and Mary Lee Spence, eds. Urbana: University of Illinois Press, 1970.

Frost, Donald McKay. *Notes on General Ashley, the Overland Trail and South Pass.* Worcester: American Antiquarian Society, 1945.

Ghent, W. J. *The Early Far West: A Narrative Outline 1540-1850.* New York: Longmans, Green & Co., 1931.

Gilbert, Bil. *Westering Man.* New York: Atheneum, 1983.

Goetzmann, William C., and Joseph C. Porter. *The West as Romantic Horizon.* Omaha: Center For Western Studies, Joslyn Art Museum, 1981.

Gowans, Fred R. *Rocky Mountain Rendezvous.* Provo: Brigham Young University Press, 1976.

Gregg, Josiah. *The Commerce of the Prairies.* Norman: University of Oklahoma Press, 1954.

Hafen, LeRoy. *The Mountain Men and the Fur Trade of the Far West.* 10 vols. Glendale: The Arthur H. Clark Co., 1968-1972.

___. *Broken Hand.* Denver: The Old West Publishing Co., 1973.

___. and Ann W. Hafen. *Old Spanish Trail.* Glendale. The Arthur H. Clark Co., 1954.

Halpin, Marjorie. *Catlin's Indian Gallery.* Washington: The Smithsonian Institution, 1965.

Hanson, Charles E., Jr. *The Hawken Rifle: Its Place in History.* Chadron, Neb.: The Fur Press, 1980.

___. *The Northwest Gun.* Lincoln: Nebraska State Historical Society, 1981.

Harper, Frank B. *Fort Union and its Neighbors on the Upper Missouri.* Great Northern Railway Co., nd.

Harris, Edward. *Up the Missouri with Audubon: The Journal of Edward Harris.* John Francis McDermott, ed. Norman: University of Oklahoma Press, 1951.

Houck, Louis. *A History of St. Louis.* 3 vols. Chicago: R. R. Donnelley & Sons, 1908.

Irving, Washington. *The Adventures of Captain Bonneville, U.S.A.,* Stuyvesant Edition. New York: G. P. Putnam's Sons, 1849.

___. *Astoria*. New York: G. P. Putnam's Sons, 1861.

James, Thomas. *Three Years Among the Indians and Mexicans*. New York: J. B. Lippincott Co., 1962.

Jensen, Andrew. *Encyclopedic History of the Church of Jesus Christ of Latter-day Saints*. Salt Lake City: Deseret News Publishing Co., 1941.

Jensen, Marinus. *History of Provo, Utah*. Provo: New Century Printing Co. (printed for the author), 1924.

Johnson, Overton, and William H. Winter. *Route Across the Rocky Mountains*. Carl L. Cannon, ed. Princeton University Press, 1932.

Lavender, David. *The Fist in the Wilderness*. Garden City: Doubleday & Co., 1964.

Luttig, John C. *Journal of a Fur Trading Expedition on the Upper Missouri, 1812-1813*. Stella M. Drumm, ed. St. Louis: Missouri Historical Society, 1920.

Martel, Jean Claud, and Marie a Solange Sinclair. *Dictionnaire National des Canadiens Francais, 1606-1760*. Montreal: Institut Genealogique Drouin, 1977.

Maximilian, Prince of Wied. *People of the First Man*. Davis Thomas and Karin Ronnefeldt, eds. New York: E. P. Dutton & Co., 1976.

McDermott, John Francis. *The French in the Mississippi Valley*. Urbana: University of Illinois Press, 1965.

Meras, E. Jules, trans. *Memoirs Relating to Fouche*. New York: Sturgis & Walton Co., 1912.

Merritt, John. *Baronets and Buffalo*. Missoula: Mountain Press Publishing Company, 1985.

Miller, Marilyn McKeen, and John Clifton Moffitt. *Provo: A Story of a People in Motion*. Provo: Brigham Young University Press, 1974.

Morgan, Dale L., Supv. *Provo: Pioneer Mormon City*. Portland: Workers and Writers Program for the WPA: Utah, Binford and Mort, 1942.

___. *Jedediah Smith and the Opening of the West*. Indianapolis: The Bobbs-Merrill Company. 1953.

___.ed. *The West of William H. Ashley*. Denver: Old West Publishing Co., 1964.

Mumey, Noley. *The Life of Jim Baker*. New York: Interland Publishing Co., 1972.

Myers, John Myers. *Pirate, Pawnee and Mountain Man.* Boston: Little Brown and Co., 1963.

Newell, Robert. *Robert Newell's Memoranda.* Dorothy O. Johansen, ed. Portland: Champoeg Press, 1959.

Nicollet, Joseph N. *Joseph N. Nicollett on the Plains and Prairies*. Edmund C. Bray and Martha Coleman Bray, eds. St. Paul: Minnesota Historical Society Press, 1976.

Ogden, Peter Skene. *Peter Skene Ogden's Snake Country Journals, 1824-25 and 1825-26*. Vol. 13. E. E. Rich, ed. London: The Hudson's Bay Record Society, 1950.

___. *Peter Skene Ogden's Snake Country Journals, 1827-28 and 1828-29*. Vol. 28. Glyndwr Williams, ed. London: The Hudson's Bay Record Society, 1971.

Oglesby, Richard Edward. *Manuel Lisa and the Opening of the Missouri Fur Trade*. Norman: University of Oklahoma Press, 1984.

Palliser, John. *Solitary Rambles of a Hunter*. London: John Murray, Albermarle St., 1853.

Phillips, Paul Chrisler. *The Fur Trade* 2 vols. Norman: University of Oklahoma Press, 1967.

Quigley, Martin. *St. Louis: A Fond Look Back*. St. Louis: The First National Bank in St. Louis, 1956.

Robidoux, Oral Messmore. *Memorial to the Robidoux Brothers*. Kansas City: Smith-Grieves Co., Printer (printed for the author), 1924.

Ross, Alexander. *The Fur Hunters of the Far West*. Kenneth A. Spaulding, ed. Norman: University of Oklahoma Press, 1956.

Ross, Marvin C. *The West of Alfred Jacob Miller (1837]*. Norman: University of Oklahoma Press, 1951.

Russell, Osborne. *Journal of a Trapper.* Aubrey L. Haines, ed. Portland: Oregon Historical Society, 1955.

Ruxton, George Frederick. *Ruxton of the Rockies.* LeRoy Hafen and Mae Reed Porter, eds. Norman: University of Oklahoma Press, 1979.

___. *Life in the Far West.* LeRoy Hafen, ed. Norman: University of Oklahoma Press, 1981.

Sanborn, Margaret. *The Grand Tetons.* New York: G. P. Putnam's Sons, 1978.

Scharf, John Thomas. *St. Louis City and County.* 2 vols. Philadelphia: Louis H. Everts & Co., 1883.

Schulte, Paul C. *The Catholic Heritage of St. Louis.* St. Louis: np, 1934

Sloss, J. H. *St. Louis Directory.* St. Louis: Charles N. Hammond Printers, 1842, 1848.

St. Louis Genealogical Society. *Catholic Baptisms in St. Louis, 1765-1840.* St. Louis: St. Louis Genealogical Society, 1982.

Stevens, Walter B. *Centennial History of Missouri.* St. Louis: S. J. Clark Publishing Co., 1921.

Stewart, William Drummond. *Edward Warren.* London: G. Walker, 1854.

Stuart, Robert. *On the Oregon Trail.* Kenneth A. Spaulding, ed. Norman: University of Oklahoma Press, 1953.

Sunder, John E. *Bill Sublette Mountain Man.* Norman. University of Oklahoma Press, 1959.

___. *The Fur Trade on the Upper Missouri 1840-1865.* Norman. University of Oklahoma Press, 1965.

___. *Joshua Pilcher; Fur Trapper and Indian Agent.* Norman: University of Oklahoma Press, 1968.

Tanguay, Cyprien. *Dictionnaire Genealogique des Familles Canadiennes.* New York: AMS Press, 1969.

Thomas, William L. *The History of St. Louis County, Missouri.* 2 vols. St. Louis: The S. J. Clarke Publishing Co., 1911.

Townsend, John Kirk. *Narrative of a Journey Across the Rocky Mountains to the Columbia River.* Lincoln: University of Nebraska Press, 1978.

Twitchell, Ralph Emerson. *Spanish Archives of New Mexico.* Cedar Rapids: The Torch Press, 1914.

Tyler, Ron, ed. *Alfred Jacob Miller, Artist on the Oregon Trail.* Fort Worth: Amon Carter Museum, 1982.

Vandiver, Clarence A. *The Fur Trade and Early Western Exploration.* Cleveland: The Arthur H. Clark Company, 1929.

Victor, Frances Fuller. *The River of the West.* vol. I. Winfred Blevins, ed. Missoula: Mountain Press Publishing Co., 1983.

Warner, Robert Combs. *The Fort Laramie of Alfred Jacob Miller.* Laramie: University of Wyoming Press, 1979.

Weber, David J., ed. and trans. *The Extranjeros.* Santa Fe: Stagecoach Press, 1967.

___. *The Taos Trappers: The Fur Trade in the Far Southwest, 1540-1846.* Norman: University of Oklahoma Press, 1980.

Whitney, Orson F. *History of Utah.* 4 vols. Salt Lake City: Geo. Q. Cannon & Sons, Co., 1892.

Wishart, David J. *The Fur Trade of the American West, 1807-1840.* Lincoln: University of Nebraska Press, 1979.

Wislizenus, Frederick A. *A Journey to the Rocky Mountains in the Year 1839.* Glorietta, N Mex.: The Rio Grande Press, 1969.

Wyeth, Nathaniel. *The Journals of Captain Nathaniel J. Wyeth.* Fairfield: Ye Galleon Press, 1969.

Yount, George C. *George C. Yount and His Chronicles of the West.* Charles L. Camp, ed. Denver: Old West Publishing Co., 1966.

Government Documents

American State Papers, Vol. 3, *Indian Affairs*. House Document 140, 14th Cong., 1st sess. Washington.

Benton, Thomas Hart. "Regulation of the Fur Trade, 1826." Senate Document 58, 19th Cong., 1st sess. Washington, 1826.

City of St. Louis Circuit Court Records, St. Louis, Mo. 1834, 1845.

City of St. Louis Probate Files. St. Louis, Mo., 1850.

Eddy, Frank W. (Supervisor), et al. *The Archeological Mitigation Program and Excavations at Site 5MF605, Brown's Park National Wildlife Refuge, Moffat County, Colorado.* U.S. Department of the Interior Study. Boulder: Science Applications, Inc., 1982.

Fremont, J. C. (Brevet Captain). *Report of the Exploring Expedition to the Rocky Mountains in the Year 1842 and to Oregon and North California in the Years 1843-'44.* House Document No. 166. Washington: Blair and Rives, Printers, 1845.

List of Lands Granted By the Crown in the Province of Quebec from 1763 to 31 December, 1890. Quebec: Printed by Order of the Legislature, Charles-Francois Langlois, Printer, 1891.

Marriage Record, Book I, Part I, St. Louis County (1808-1836). Recorder of Deeds, St. Louis.

Message From the President of the United States. Senate Document 90, 22d Cong., 1st sess. Washington, 1832.

Monroe, James. *Message from the President of the United States Relative to the Arrest and Imprisonment of Certain Americans at Santa Fe.* House Document 197. Washington. E. De Krafft, 1818.

Rapport de L'Archiviste de la Province de Quebec. Quebec: Provincial Government (annually 1920-77).

Recorder of Deeds, St. Louis County, St. Louis, Mo.

St. Louis County Court Records Department Registrar. 1835-38.

St. Louis Courthouse Papers, St. Louis, Mo.

St. Louis Missouri Census, 1845 St. Louis, Mo.

Storrs, Augustus. *Answers to Certain Queries Upon the Origin, Present State and Future Prospect of Trade and Intercourse Between Missouri and the Internal Provinces of Mexico.* Senate Documentt 7, 18th Cong., 2d sess. Washington: Gayles and Seaton, 1825.

U.S. Census Records, 1850. Washington, 1850.

Manuscripts

"A Journal History of the Church of Jesus Christ of Latter-day Saints". History Library, LDS Church (microfilm). Salt Lake City.

"A Journal of the Proceedings of the Legislature of the Territory of Louisiana - Commencing June 3, 1806." St. Louis Mercantile Library.

Alley, John Richard, Jr. "The Fur Trapper and the Great Basin Indian." Master's thesis, University of Utah, 1978.

American Fur Company Ledgers. Missouri Historical Society, St. Louis.

Ashley, William H. "Journal of William H. Ashley." Chouteau Papers. Missouri Historical Society, St. Louis.

Billon, Frederick L. Collection. Missouri Historical Society, St. Louis.

Boileau, Rene. "Notarial Records of Chambly, 1803-1842." Archives Nationales du Quebec, Montreal.

Chouteau Papers. Chouteau Collection. Missouri Historical Society, St. Louis.

Chouteau-Mafit Papers, Chouteau Collection. Missouri Historical Society, St. Louis.

Chouteau-Papin Papers, Chouteau Collection. Missouri Historical Society, St. Louis.

Chouteau and Sarpy Ledgers. Chouteau Collection. Missouri Historical Society, St. Louis.

Clark, William. Papers. Missouri Historical Society, St. Louis.

Cline, Gloria Griffen. Collection. University of Nevada, Reno.

Collett, Oscar. [*Index to St. Louis Archives, 1766-81*]. St. Louis Cathedral Archives, 1912-1913.

___. *Collet's Index to St. Louis Church Registers*. No. 24, Baptisms, No. 25, Marriages; No. 26, Burials. Transcribed by Francis W. Douglas or Mrs. E. Boyd Ware. St. Louis, 1916-18.

Cragin, F. W. "Cragin Far West Notebooks." Pioneer's Museum, Colorado Springs.

deMun, Jules. Papers. Missouri Historical Society, St. Louis.

Dougherty, John. Letter to William Clark. Superintendent of Indian Affairs Letterbook, 1830-32, Kansas State Historical Society, Topeka.

Fairholme, William. "The Journal of Lieutenant William Fairholme, 1840." The Huntington Library, San Marino.

Fayel, William. "A Narrative of Col. Robert Campbell's Experiences in the Rocky Mountains Fur Trade from 1825 to 1835." Missouri Historical Society, St. Louis.

Gamble, Hamilton Rowan. Papers. Missouri Historical Society, St. Louis.

Grise, Antoine. Notarial Records of Chambly, 1756-1785. Archives Nationales du Quebec, Montreal.

Grise, Jean Baptiste (fils). Notarial Records of Chambly, 1785-1796. Archives Nationales du Quebec, Montreal.

Hafen, LeRoy. Collection. The Huntington Library, San Marino.

Hodiesne, Gervais. Notarial Records of Chambly, 1739-1764. Archives Nationales du Quebec, Montreal.

Hudson's Bay Company Archives (microfilm). Public Archives of Canada, Ottawa.

Journal of Fort Pierre. Chouteau Collection. Missouri Historical Society, St. Louis.

Kelly, Charles. Papers. Utah State Historical Society, Salt Lake City.

LaBarge, Joseph. "Logbook of the American Fur Company." Steamboat Papers. Missouri Historical Society, St. Louis.

___. "Logbook of American Fur Company Steamboat *Nimrod.*" Steamboat Papers. Missouri Historical Society, St. Louis.

Leguay, Francois (fils). Notarial Records of Chambly, 1793-1807. Archives Nationales du Quebec, Montreal.

Letterbook of Fort Pierre. Chouteau Collection. Missouri Historical Society, St. Louis.

Letterbook of Fort Tecumseh. Chouteau Collection. Missouri Historical Society, St. Louis.

Letterbook of Fort Union. Chouteau collection. Missouri Historical Society, St. Louis.

McEnnis, Michael. "Recollections." Cemeteries Collection. Missouri Historical Society, St. Louis.

___. "Cholera, 1849." Cemeteries Collection. Missouri Historical Society, St. Louis.

Mexican Archives of New Mexico (MANM). State Records Center and Archives, Santa Fe.

Morgan, Dale L. Collection. Utah State Historical Society, Salt Lake City.

Parish Records, The Old Cathedral. Basilica of St. Louis the King, St. Louis.

Parish Register: Paroisse de St. Joseph de Chambly, Diocese de St. Jean. Archives Nationales du Quebec, Montreal. Also on microfilm in Genealogical Society of Utah, Salt Lake City.

Parish Register: St. Mary and Joseph Church, St. Louis. Carondelet Baptisms. Missouri Historical

Society.

Philibert Family Papers. Missouri Historical Society, St. Louis.

Provost, Etienne (deponent). Deposition Taken at St. Louis, Mo., December 20, 1841, in Support of Claim of August Chouteau and Jules deMun Against the Mexican Government. National Archives, Washington.

Quebec District, Judiciare de Montreal, Greffes de Notaires. Public Archives of Canada, Ottawa.

Salle, Jean dit Lajoie. Marriage Contract of Jean Salle dit Lajoie and Marie Rose Villalpando. Instrument No. 2023, Old St. Louis Archives. Missouri Historical Society, St. Louis.

Selkirk Papers. Public Archives of Canada, Ottawa.

Shaw, Henry. Papers. Botanical Garden Archives. St. Louis.

Spanish Archives of New Mexico (SANM II). State Records Center and Archives, Santa Fe.

St. Louis Church Register: Baptisms. Missouri Historical Society, St. Louis.

Newspapers

Daily Missouri Democrat. St. Louis.
Daily Missouri Republican. St. Louis.
Missouri Gazette. St. Louis.
Missouri Intelligencer. Franklin, Mo.
Missouri Republican. St. Louis.
St. Louis Daily Globe. St. Louis.
St. Louis Enquirer. St. Louis.
St. Louis Gazette. St. Louis.
St. Louis Post Dispatch. St. Louis.
The Saint Louis Weekly Reveille. St. Louis.
The St. Louis Republic. St. Louis.

INDEX

Abbott, Samuel 45
Adams-Onis Treaty of 1819 56
Allen, Alfred 35 n26
Allen, Ethan 4
Alvarez, Manuel 35 n20
American Fur Company 45, 73, 76, 97, 100, 106, 118, 128, 132
Anderson, William Marshall xxix, 122, 133, 135
Ashley, William H. xxv; forms expedition 45, 50, 58, 60-61; Ashley's Fort 68; Cabanne's report of Ashley's party 70; Sells out 1826 71; Alleged falling-out with Provost 72-73, 99; Reaches agreement with AFC for 1827 74; Congressman 118; Question of seeing Great Salt Lake 134
Astor, John Jacob xxvi, 13, 45, 73, 118
Astoria 14
Atkinson, General Henry 61
Audubon, John James 173, 178-79
B. Pratte & Company 40, 45, 69, 73-74, 81
Baird, James (Beard) 35 n26, 42, 70
Baronet (or Barony) 31
Bartlett, Phinis 97
Baum, Peter 35 n26
Bear Lake rendezvous/fight with Blackfeet, 1828 84
Beaubien, Charles 35 n20
Beckwourth, James (Jim) 65 n52, 70-71
Becknell, William 41, 48, 52
Bell, John G. 174, 179
Bent, St. Vrain & Co. 150
Bernard Pratte and Co. 79, 81
Berthold, Bartholomew 74, 80
Bissonett, Joseph dit Bijou 21-22, 30, 32, 35 n20
Bizet, Antonio 30
Blood, Sullivan 173
Bodmer, Karl 111
Bonavia, Commandante General Bernardo 24
Bonneville, Captain Benjamin L. E. 107, 113, 122
Bourassa, Marie Anne 2
Bourguignon, Charles 30
Braunsberg, Baron (see also Maximilian) 111
Bridger, James xxv, 45, 49, 100, 133, 145-46
Brizar, John Batisti 30
Bruffee, James 74
Buchanan-Packenham Treaty, 1846 190
Buffalo Bull's Back Fat 150
Bullock, Thomas xxiii
Cabanne, Jean P. 40, 70, 79-80, 134-35, 138
Campbell, Robert 70, 84-85, 101, 106; commands 1832 return caravan 107; partnership with Sublette 108, 112; builds Ft. William (on the Yellowstone) 1833 118; Works with Provost 138, 139; Old Prevoe's Tale 139

Carriere, Michael 31
Carson, Christopher (Kit) 133
Catlin, George 156,
Cayole, Francois de Salle dit 95
Cayole, Madeleine Delor 95
Cerre, Michael Sylvestre 122, 125
Chambers, Samuel 35 n26
Chambly, Captain Jacques de 3
Chambly, Quebec 1
Champlain, Jean Baptiste 21
Charboneau, Toussaint 31
Charless, Joseph 110
Chouteau, Auguste 13-14, 17
Chouteau, Auguste P. 20, 24-28, 73
Chouteau, Pierre, Jr. xxvi. 13, 70, 76-77, 79, 96, 102, 111
Chouteau's Island 26
Cisdelle, Joseph 30
Clark and Tournotte 110
Clark, Lewis 110
Clark, William 13, 148
Clyman, James 52
Cohen 26, 31
Columbia Fur Co. 44, 73, 76-77
Commandante General at Durango 24
Commercial Trading Company 11
Constant, Agnes Delor 78
Cook, Thomas 35 n26
Cooper, Benjamin 42
Crooks, Emilie Pratte 73
Crooks, Ramsay 73, 99, 116, 121, 138
Culbertson, Alexander 139, 179
deManse, Teniente Coronel Don Pedro Maria 28
deMun, Jules 20, 24-28,
Deposition of 1817 29
Derport, Francois 30
Devils Lake 157, 160-61
Dixon, William 159
D'Otrante, Comte (see Fouche,

Armand)
Drips, Andrew xxv, 106-08, 113, 151-52, 162
Duchesne 35 n20
Dudley, S.S. 44
Dupuis, Joseph dit Dunord 96
Dupuis, Marie Rose Salle 83, 93
Eells, Cushing 151
Fairholme, Lieutenant William 163-64
Ficio, Baptisti 30
Fitzpatrick, Sublette and Bridger 131
Fitzpatrick, Thomas xxv, 45, 52, 100-102, 113, 123, 127, 135, 139-41, 146, 151, 170
Fontenelle, Drips and Company 132
Fontenelle, Fitzpatrick and Company 132, 138-39
Fontenelle, Lucien B. xxv, 106-08, 112, 116, 134, 138-39
Fort Chambly 16, 1, 3-4
Fort Floyd (Union) 77, 86
Fort Hall 130
Fort Laramie 143
Fort Lucien 138-40
Fort Nonsense 108
Fort Pierre 115, 178
Fort Snelling 161
Fort Tecumseh 45, 76, 78, 101-02, 108
Fort Union 77-78, 101, 149, 178
Fort William 128, 132, 143
Fort William (on the Yellowstone) 118
Fouche, Armand 181
Fowler, Jacob 42-43
Fraeb, Henry 100, 102, 112, 131
Fremont, John Charles xxiv, 156-57, 159, 161, 170, 173
French Company, The 79
Freniere, Louison 159
Fulkerson 148

Gardner, Johnson 54, 60
General Company of Lake Superior and the South 11
General Store, The 11
Gervais, Jean Baptiste (Jarvey) 84, 100, 131
Glass, Hugh 86
Glenn, Hugh 42
Gordon, William 9, 101
Grenie 23, 35, n20
Guerin, Francois 69
Guion, Antoine 136-37
Halsey, Jacob 97, 149
Ham, Zacharias 52
Ham's Fork (of the Green) 122, 128
Hamilton, James A. 149
Harris, Edward 173, 177, 179
Hawken rifle 86, 97, 124
Hawken, Jake 86
Hawken, Sam 86
Henry, Andrew xxv, xxix, 13, 45, 70
Henry, Negro cook 165
Higbee, John S. xxiii
Horse Creek 112, 143
Huddart, William 48
Hudson's Bay Company 10, 44
Hughes, Elizabeth 188
Jackson, David 71, 101
James, Thomas 41
Jarvey (see Gervais, Jean Baptiste)
Kelley, Hall J. 122
Kipp, James 44
Kittson, William 54
LaBarge, Joseph 117, 157, 171, 177, 190-92
Lacharete 105
LaFleur 180
Laidlaw, William 44, 116
LaLande 35 n20
Lambert, Clement (see Salle, Clement)

Lamont, Daniel 44
LeBeau, Magdeline 2
LeBlond, Trudeau 136-37
LeClerc, Michael (Francois) 22, 33, 46, 52
Ledoux 35 n20
Lefargue, Jean Baptiste 21, 23
Legris, Pierre 30
Leroux, Antoine 35 n20
Leroux, Helene (Salle) 95
Leroux, Pierre 35 n20
Lesperance, Pierre 21, 32
Levanway (see Livernois)
Lewis 31
Lewis, Meriwether 13
Lewis, Reuben 13
Liguest, Pierre Laclede 17
Ligueste 73
Lisa, Manual 13, 20, 39
Livernois, Joseph 35 n20
Mainard, Marie Anne 2
Martine 94
Mathieu, Alexander 97
Mauant, Francois 30
Maximilian, Prince of Wied 111
May, Mr. 159
Maynez, Don Alberto 25
McDonough, Michael 35 n26
McKenzie, Kenneth 44-45, 76-77, 86, 88, 99, 101, 108, 116, 118, 138, 163
McKnight, John 41
McKnight, Robert 21, 23
Menard, Anne Salle dit Cayolle 34
Menard, Louis (1) 19
Menard, Louis (2) 19
Menard, Marie Anne (see Mainard)
Menard, Marie Francoise Robidou 19
Miami Company, The 11
Miers, Charles 35 n26
Miller, Alfred Jacob xxi, 141-43,

145

Millicoure 73

Mines, William 35 n26

Morin, Cotte 97

Morgan, Dale L. xxix, 81, 130-31, 133

New Catholic Cemetery 195

Newell, Robert "Doc" 152

Nicollet, Joseph N. 156-60

Nolan 35 n20

Northern Department, AFC 121

Northwest gun 124

North West Company 10, 14, 44

Nuttall, Thomas 123

O'Fallon, Benjamin 46, 61

Old Prevoe's Tale 139

Ogden, Peter Skene 51, 53

P. Chouteau & Co. 150, 162

Pacific Fur Company 13

Paket, Francois 30

Palliser, John 192

Pando, Juan de la Villa el 94

Paquet, Marie Louise 2

Parish of St. Joseph of Chambly 1, 14

Patterson, Robert 164

Philibert, Joseph 21-26, 110

Phillebers Company 21

Picotte, Honore 44, 171-72

Pierre Chouteau, Jr. & Co. 150

Pierre's Hole 106-07

Pilcher, Joshua 40, 111, 117, 134, 139-40

Pratte, Bernard 18, 40, 47, 146

Pratte, Chouteau and Company 121, 132, 136, 150

Prevost, C. 170

Prevost, M. 170

Prou, Mr. 177

Proveau, Etienne, Tavernkeeper 181

Proveau and Lambert, Tavern Keeper 109, 162

Provo River xix, 49

Provo, City xix

Provos Fork 50

Provost, Albert 2, 5

Provost, Antoine 12

Provost, Barbe Amable Robidoux 19

Provost, Charles 2

Provost, Constant 192

Provost, Etienne xix, xxi, Spelling of name xxii, xxv, Importance, not an Ashley man xxvi; regard of peers xxvi; Birth 2, 4; Early influence 5; Father dies, left Chambly 5; St. Louis relatives 19; Signs with Chouteau-deMun 1815 20; Member Philibert's 1814 party? 22; Member whose party? 25; Signs 1817 Deposition 30; Signs second Deposition 1841 31; Audubon comments 1843 32; Partnership with LeClerc 33, 38-39; In forefront of move to southwest in 1821 40; Member 1822 Robidoux party to Santa Fe 42; Backed by Robidoux in 1824? 44; Association with American Fur Co. 45; In New Mexico 1823 46; Chittenden interpretation 47, 48; Discoverer of Great Salt Lake 49; Shoshone (Snake) battle 1824 49, 50-51; Ends Partnership w/Leclerc? 52; Arrives Ogden's camp, 1825 53, 55-57; Meets Ashley June, 1825; recovers cached goods on Green River 58; Guides Ashley to 1825 Rendezvous 59, 60-62, 67; Builds trading posts 68; Expected in Santa Fe in 1825 69; Subject Cabanne letter 1824 70; In Uinta

Basin in 1826 71; Alleged falling-out with Ashley 72; Comments of Berthold 74; New employment 1827-28 76; Returns St. Louis 1826 78; Who backed in 1824? 80; Did not compete with Ashley 82; Osage Outfit employment 82; Tavern interest 83; Returns to fur trade 83; McKenzie sends among Crow Indians 83; 1828 Bear Lake fight 84-85; And Hawken rifle 86; Takes Crow bride 87; Starts downriver 1829 87, 88; Marries 1829 93, 96; 1829, Etienne Proveaus Advanture 97; Ft. Tecumseh credit problem 98; Not at 1830 rendezvous 99, 100; Ft. Union hunter 1830 101, 102; In St. Louis winter '31 105; Second in command 1832 caravan 106; Meets Vanderburgh & Drips 107, 108; Obtains tavern license:partnership 109, 110; AFC recruiter 111; Second in command 1833 caravan 112; Meets Wm Drummond Stewart 113; To smuggle alcohol upriver 116; Labarge's tale 117, 119; Leads 1834 AFC caravan 122-23, 125, 133; Discoverer of Great Salt Lake 134, 135; Comments by Anderson 135; Involved in court action 136-37; Sells St. Louis property; sent to Ft. Lucien (William) 1 138, 139; To Ft. William, not at '36 rendezvous 140; Trail boss of 1837 rendezvous caravan 141; Description by Alfred Jacob Miller 142-43; Sent to assess smallpox damage 146; Reports on pox damage 149-50; 1838 rendezvous, Provost's last 150-51, 155-56; Camp Conductor for Nicollet 156-58, 161; Renews tavern license 162; Guides 1840 British party 163, 165; Prairie fire, accused of neglect 166, 167-70; LaBarge story 171; Loses barge and furs on downriver trip 172; Loses second lawsuit, continues as tavernkeeper 173; Guides Audubon 1843 175; Another LaBarge story 177-79; Returns to St. Louis with Audubon, leaves him when drunk 180, 181; 1844 guide for Armand Fouche, Comte d'Otrante 183, 188; 1845 Census 188-89; Tavernkeeper 189, 190; Yet another LaBarge tale 191-92; Last river trip 193; Dies in St. Louis 1850, burial 194-95; Will and estate inventory 196

Provost, Francois 2
Provost, Gabriel 2
Provost H. N. (Etienne) 162, 188
Provost, Isabelle (Elizabeth) 2
Provost, Jean Baptiste: father and son 19, 78, 136
Provost, Joseph 2
Provost, Julien 2
Provost, Louis Antoine 19
Provost, Marianne 136
Provost, Marie Rose (wife) 83, 93, 96
Provost, Mary (daughter) 136
Provost, Michel 87
Provost, Nicolas 87
Provost, Pierre 2
Provost, Raphael 2

Provost, Toussaint 2, 6
Provost's trading posts 68
Provot, Quenon 73
Provott, Etunne (Etienne) 30
Racine, Toussaint 140
Rendezvous of 1825 60
Rendezvous of 1826 71
Rendezvous of 1828 84
Rendezvous of 1830 99
Rendezvous of 1832 106
Rendezvous of 1833 112
Rendezvous of 1834 122
Rendezvous of 1837 143
Rendezvous of 1838 150
Renville, Joseph 44
Rhodes, Caleb B. xxiv
Robidoux, Antoine 43-44, 48, 51-52, 79
Robidoux Brothers 42-43, 74
Robidoux, Joseph 19, 43, 79-80
Robidoux. Louis 43
Rocky Mountain Fur Company (RMFC) 100-01, 113, 119, 123, 131-32
Rocky Mountain Outfit 138, 152
Rockwell, Orrin Porter 88 n2, 189
Roi 23
Romero, Ana Maria 94
Ross, Alexander 51, 53
Russell, Osborne 122
Sale, Jean dit La Joie 18, 94-95, 173
Salle, Anne dit Cayolle 19
Salle, Antoine Xavier 95
Salle, Clement dit Lajoie 96, 109, 162, 170, 173, 181
Salle, Jean Baptiste 96
Salle, Lambert dit Lajoie 78, 83, 93-96, 109-10, 173
Salle, Magdeleine 78
Salle, Marie Caroline 96
Salle, Marie Gertrude 96
Salle, Marie Rose 83, 93, 96 (see also Marie Rose Provost)
Salle, Marie Rose (Vidalpane) 95
Salle, Nicholas 96
Sanford, John F. A. 111, 115
Scott, Hiram 70, 74
Shaw, Henry 38
Shrive, Benjamin 35 n26
Sire, Joseph 171, 175
Smallpox epidemic of 1837-38 146-50
Smith, Jackson & Sublette 71, 99-100
Smith, Jedediah xxv, 45-46, 53-54, 70-71, 75, 101
Smith, Thomas (Peg-leg) 47
Sprague, Isaac 173
Squires, Lewis M. 173, 179
St. Louis Fur Co. 118
St. Louis Missouri Fur Co. 13
St. Vrain, Ceran 47, 52, 69
Steamboat Amelia 193
Steamboat Antelope 157
Steamboat Omega 175
Steamboat Nimrod 181
Steamboat Yellowstone 102, 111
Stewart, William Drummond xxi-xxii, 112-13, 141, 151, 174
Stone, Bostwick & Co. 45
Strawberry River 70, 77, 85
Sublette and Campbell 108, 112, 118, 122, 130, 132
Sublette, Milton 45, 100, 123-24
Sublette, William xxv, 45, 54; partner in 1826 Ashley buyout 71; uses wagons to rendezvous 99, 101; to 1832 rendezvous, wounded Pierre's Hole fight 106; forms partnership with Campbell 108; Tavernkeeper 110, 112; cuts deal with Astor 118, 121; 1834 trade caravan 125-27; Builds Ft. William (Laramie) 1834 128; Takes RMFC trade 130;

Works for collapse of RMFC 132-33; Old Prevoe's Tale 139
Tilton, William 44
Tilton and Company 44
Timpanogos River xxiv
Townsend, John Kirk 122-23
Upper Missouri Outfit (UMO), AFC 77
Vanderburgh, William xxv, 86, 99, 101, 106-08, 115
Vasquez, Louis 70
Vernal, Sergeant Mariano 28
Vesina 23
Vidalpane, Marie Rose (see also Salle) 94
Villalpando, Pablo Francisco 94
Weber, John 54, 134
Weber River 49
Western Department, AFC 73, 121
White River 48
Wilkinson, Benjamin 13
Williams, Ezekiel 20-22, 110
Wolfskill, William 47
Wyeth, Nathaniel 119, 122-24, 127, 130
Young, Brigham xxiii
Yount, George C. xxiv, 50